The Fullness of Time

Sunday gospel meditations in preparation for the new millennium

Joseph Donders

First published in Great Britain in 1996 by
CAFOD
Romero Close
Stockwell Road
London
SW9 9TY

Reprinted 1997

ISBN 1 871549 58 2

Designed by CAFOD

Printed by The Longdunn Press Ltd
Barton Manor
St Philips
Bristol
BS2 0RL

Contents

1998: The Year of the Holy Spirit
(Year C of the liturgical cycle)

1999: The Year of God the Father
(Year A of the liturgical cycle)

Introduction

The year AD 2000 will mark the end of the second millennium and the beginning of the third. New Year's Eve 1999 will be a night of transition. For many years now, hotels and holiday resorts throughout the world have been taking bookings for this night. If you have the money to spare, you can prolong the celebrations by chasing the sun over the globe in Concorde, and celebrating the new millennium in several different countries. Governments and businesses are investing hundreds of millions in commemorating the arrival of the new millennium, and in many places great works of architecture have been commissioned to mark the occasion.

In the midst of all the millennium-fever, one might be excused for forgetting the origins of this event, which seems to have gripped the minds and emotions of the entire Western world. In Britain, we must go back to the year ad 663, and a meeting of the Synod of Whitby. At that meeting, it was decided that time in Britain would henceforth be measured in relation to the birth of Jesus Christ (although historians have since shown that it is unlikely that Jesus was actually born in the year 1). That is why we attach to our dates the prefix "AD", meaning Anno Domini, or "the year of our Lord". Therefore, what actually defines the new millennium is the birth of Jesus Christ.

From the very first paragraph of his inaugural encyclical, *Redemptor Hominis*, in 1987, Pope John Paul II has been stressing the significance of the approach of the year 2000. In that paragraph, he wrote that he was acutely aware that he was beginning his "universal service" very close to the year 2000. Since that time, he has not only mentioned the new millennium in practically all his subsequent encyclicals, but he has also been developing his ideas and hopes for what he calls "The Great Jubilee", or "The Year of God's Favour".

Every 50 years, the Jews in the Old Testament were required to celebrate a jubilee, during which the land was to be handed back and divided anew and justly; bonded servants were to be set free; debts were to be remitted, and justice was to be restored. As the culmination of the 40th 50-year period since Jesus' birth, the Pope suggests that the occasion should be used by the Church to proclaim justice throughout the world. This is what he calls the Great Jubilee.

During the Advent of 1994, John Paul II published an apostolic letter called *Tertio Millennio Adveniente*, which outlined how we might prepare ourselves for the Great Jubilee. In that letter, he suggests that we dedicate the year 1997 to Jesus Christ and his mission to bring about the Jubilee of Justice (Luke 4:19). The following year, 1998, should centre on the work of the Holy Spirit to unite the whole of creation. The year 1999 should focus on God the Father and highlight God's unconditional love for every human being, which is the ultimate foundation for universal human rights. Together, the three years leading up to the third millennium are to be a "season of expectation" – in other words, a New Advent.

The Pope asks the Church to acknowledge what went wrong in the past. The Church must repent of its consent to intolerance, the use of violence, and the silent acceptance of over-consumption in the face of devastating global poverty and suffering. Looking at the past we should, he writes, not overlook the signs of hope around us, such as the developing incarnation of justice in our world; the growing longing for reconciliation by different peoples; our increasing human solidarity (of which CAFOD's expansion over the last few years is but one expression); and the ever-greater interest in living in harmony with our environment.

In line with the old Hebrew celebration of the Jubilee year in Leviticus, the Pope even suggests that:

"Christians ... raise their voice on behalf of the poor, proposing the Jubilee as an appropriate time to give thought ... to reducing substantially, if not cancelling outright, the international debt which seriously threatens the future of many nations" (*Tertio Millennio Adveniente*, 51).

It is in the context of these preparations for the Year of God's Favour that this book was written. It offers a reflection for each of the Sundays of the three years that lead up to the year 2000, following the pattern suggested by Pope John Paul II. The book uses the Sunday readings as foreseen by the three liturgical cycles used by most of the Churches, starting with cycle B for the Advent of the year 1997. (Quotations are generally taken from the Jerusalem Bible.)

The Jubilee themes as such are not laboured in all of these reflections, as it would only serve to make them repetitive and tedious. However, the reflections do, I hope, forge links in people's minds between the year 2000, Jesus Christ, the Jubilee of Justice, our mission, and the possibility of personal meaning and public hope, as asked for in *A Chance to Start Again: Marking the Millennium* (Churches Together in England, 1996).

Joseph Donders
July 1996

1997: The Year of Jesus Christ
Year B of the Liturgical Cycle

Stay awake!
B1. First Sunday of Advent

Isaiah 63:16-17, 19; 64:2-7

1 Corinthians 1:3-9

Mark 13:33-37

This year's Advent marks not only the beginning of a new liturgical year, but also the beginning of the final phase of preparation for the coming Millennium. From his very first encyclical in 1979, Pope John Paul II suggested that the years leading up to the Great Jubilee of the year 2000 should be lived as a "new Advent". It was an invitation to reassess where we are in our Christian lives, to renew our commitment, and to start afresh.

This does not mean that we have failed up to now. Far from it, in fact: just think how Jesus has become known throughout the whole world during the last century. However, there is still much to be done, because Jesus left us with a mission that could never be worked out fully until the end of time. We are rather like characters in a story that is still unfolding, or travellers who still have some way to go before they reach their final destination. We should constantly remind ourselves of this, because there is always a danger that we might become complacent. That would be a betrayal of our Lord.

In the reading from Mark's gospel, Jesus tells the disciples to "Be on your guard, stay awake". Jesus repeats the instruction in the following chapter (14:32-42), when he is on the Mount of Olives with Peter, James, and John. Three times he commands them to stay awake, and three times they betray him by falling asleep – just as he foretold in today's parable.

At the end of this parable, Jesus makes it clear that it is not only the disciples he is warning: "And what I say to you, I say to all: stay awake!" We, too, have to stay awake and be conscious of what is happening around us. Staying awake is about being alert. It is also about patience – the patient hope and expectation that things will change. You might call it a "revolutionary" patience!

The Christians for whom Mark wrote his gospel were also waiting with this revolutionary expectancy, because they believed they were living in the "last days". Likewise, when Paul wrote to those first Christians in Corinth, he was addressing people who expected Jesus to return within their own lifetime. At any moment, Jesus might re-enter human history to gather the whole of humanity in the heavenly kingdom.

Such views may not be as widespread today, but by heeding Jesus' warning and not falling asleep in the dark night of human history, we will safeguard our hope that one day everything that oppresses, limits, and separates us will disappear; that the world and the powers that rule it will change; and that humanity, together with the whole of nature, will one day be at peace.

There is one other factor needs emphasising: when Jesus told the disciples on the Mount of Olives to stay awake, he was also at prayer. While we wait, patient and alert, we must also pray. Those who pray will always live in a world full of expectation and hope. Prayer helps us to see the world, humanity, and ourselves through the eyes of God.

In short, this prayerful, revolutionary patience is a prerequisite for being close to God. It is the only way in which we can link up with God's dynamism – the same holy dynamism that led to the birth of a new humanity, which we celebrate every Christmas.

The beginning
B2. Second Sunday of Advent

Isaiah 40:1-5, 9-11
2 Peter 3:8-14
Mark 1:1-8

If you have ever tried to tell an amazing story but wondered where to begin, you will probably have been told "begin at the beginning". Indeed, "beginning" is one of the first words in Mark's gospel: "The beginning of the Good News about Jesus Christ ..." followed by, almost as an afterthought, "... the Son of God". Biblical scholars think that this phrase was added later. For Mark, it was not necessary, because it went without saying. Scholarly opinion is that Mark never intended this sentence to be the opening line of text – it was actually the title of his book.

One thing, however, is for sure: everything that follows from this opening sentence – the whole adventure of Jesus among us – marks a new beginning, the beginning of the Good News. Jesus is that beginning; but where he leads, he expects his disciples to follow. Those of us who accompany Jesus on his journey are expected to play an active role in carrying the Good News to the rest of the world. At the end of Mark's gospel (to jump ahead of ourselves for an instant) we are all invited to meet with Jesus in Galilee, where he waits to send us out on our mission.

From the very start of Mark's gospel, when John the Baptist appears out of the wilderness, we are left in no doubt about the mission of Jesus and his disciples. With some powerful strokes, Mark paints a vivid picture of a distorted world into which a prophet – eating grasshoppers and honey, and dressed in animal skins – suddenly emerges as if from nowhere to announce a coming change. Mark summarises the charisma of this man in just a few words: "All Judea and all the people of Jerusalem made their way to him" to confess their sins and to be baptised in the river Jordan (Mark 1:5). The people flock to see John because they know that the world needs to change. There is a struggle to win and powers to be overcome – in short, a wholesale reorganisation is required.

John clearly understands this struggle, but he acknowledges that it is not one that he can win himself. That is not his task. John is the "messenger", who must announce the coming of one much greater than himself, one who is strong enough to tackle the world and its powers head on. So great is this person that John does not even consider himself worthy to untie his sandals!

This person is Jesus, and he will change the world forever. Not only is Jesus stronger than John, but he also brings a more powerful baptism. Jesus will baptise his disciples with the Holy Spirit, so that they will be equipped to bring about the peace and justice for which humanity has waited so long.

None of the traditional elements of the Christmas story have their origins in Mark's gospel. There are no angels, shepherds, or kings. There is no mention of a star in the sky, Mary and Joseph, or even the baby Jesus. If Mark knew of these things, he obviously considered them peripheral to the real issue, which was the radical breakthrough to the new world of the final Jubilee, which Jesus would later describe as the kingdom of God. Is it any wonder that people were drawn to John from far and wide to hear this momentous news? Let us concentrate on this glorious prospect in our preparations for Christmas and the coming Jubilee.

On being human

B3. Third Sunday of Advent

Isaiah 61:1-2, 10-11
1 Thessalonians 5:16-24
John 1:6-8, 19-28

The Advent readings are meant to help us prepare for the coming of Jesus. In that sense, they play a similar role to John the Baptist in today's text from the gospel of John the Evangelist. We are told that John the Baptist is not the light, but he comes to witness to the light. He is not the Messiah, and he is not Elijah – so who is he? John the Baptist makes that clear when he quotes from Isaiah's prophesy that someone would come out of the desert to prepare the way for the Messiah.

Mentioning the name of Isaiah conjures up so many wonderful prophesies: the poor will receive good news, broken hearts are going to be healed, there will be liberation for prisoners, justice will reign, and a new period of grace – the final year of God's Jubilee – will begin.

The first part of today's Old Testament text from Isaiah is the very same one that Jesus himself uses when he is asked to give account of himself in Nazareth, his place of birth (Luke 4:16 ff). It is no coincidence that this is also the text Pope John Paul II chose to introduce the first year of the final preparation for the year 2000, during which we should seek a new appreciation of Jesus Christ and his mission to bring about the Jubilee of Justice (Luke 4:19).

Isaiah's texts are also about the prophet himself as a human being. Isaiah foretells that his soul will glorify in the Lord, because he will be dressed with salvation and covered with the mantle of righteousness, like a bridegroom wearing his head-dress or a bride her jewels (61:10-11). This is what it should really mean to be human, but we are far from this ideal.

Jesus, the Messiah, will help us once again to be true human beings. We will realise why God said, at the moment of our creation, that the human being is tov, the Hebrew word for "good". In Jesus, our human glory will be restored and revealed. This theme is the core of Pope John Paul II's first encyclical *Redemptor Hominis*:

"In him has been revealed in a new and more wonderful way the fundamental truth concerning creation to which the Book of Genesis gives witness when it repeats several times: 'God saw that it was *good*'."

The English translation of that encyclical uses the non-inclusive word "man" in the title. Isaiah is more careful with the words he uses. When he explains what humanity will rediscover in the Messiah, he speaks about both women and men. He makes that clear by using the example of a bride and a groom.

A long time before Jesus said of himself "The Spirit of the Lord has been given to me, for he has anointed me" (Luke 4:18), his own mother, Mary, applied that same saying from Isaiah to herself. When she meets Elizabeth, she breaks out into song: "My soul proclaims the greatness of the Lord ... for the Almighty has done great things for me" (Luke 1:46-49). Just as Jesus does later on, she places herself in the context of the new, just, and righteous world that is dawning. Like mother, like son! Just imagine what it would be like to be rocked to sleep by a mother singing a lullaby like that!

Motherhood

B4. Fourth Sunday of Advent

2 Samuel 7:1-5, 8-11, 16
Romans 16:25-27
Luke 1:26-38

The Hebrew sacred scriptures are brimming with the expectation of the justice and peace, the Messiah, and the reign of God that will one day come to this world. The Christian sacred scriptures are full of the same expectations. Both are looking ahead to the end of time, when all these things will be fulfilled.

Like other Jewish women of her era, Mary, the mother of Jesus, would have been raised with these expectations. There are many women like her today who yearn for a brighter, more just future: just think of the Palestinian women in Israel who we see on our TV screens campaigning for liberation, or the women who continue to protest in Buenos Aires, Argentina, calling for the return of their disappeared husbands, sons, and daughters. Perhaps Mary hoped that one day she might have children who would help to make the world a better place, but she could never have imagined that her motherhood would contribute so dramatically to the realisation of the kingdom of God – and quite so soon!

When the angel Gabriel announces to her that she will give birth to the "Son of God", Mary is clearly shocked, as she has never been with a man, not even Joseph. She asks the angel: "But how can this come about, since I am a virgin?" (Luke 1:35). When the angel answers that the power of the Most High will make it possible, she responds: "I am the handmaid of the Lord, let what you have said be done to me." At that moment, not only are her own personal desires fulfilled, but the desires and hopes of all whole of humanity are also satisfied. It is Mary's willingness to take a bold step for humanity's future that we remember today.

Jesus' departure from the world was not the end of this great adventure, because when Jesus left he sent out his disciples out to complete his work of fulfilling the age-old expectations. The prospect of the end-time – the realisation of the ancient prophecies – should still lure us to the horizon of our final destiny. But, if we are honest with ourselves, is that really the case?

Do we – today's Christians – really raise and educate our families in a way that reflects that biblical expectation of a wonderful new future? Apparently not: according to a recent European survey among church members, less than 47 per cent thought that women should have children. They no longer viewed motherhood as a positive thing. Did they see the world as a too violent, corrupt place to bring up children? We do not know, because the survey did not ask why they held such views. However, the statistics revealed that more Christians feel this way now than on the last occasion the survey was conducted.

At Christmas, we celebrate how a young Jewish woman engaged herself bodily in the divine plan for the future of humanity. In our patriarchal society, we are accustomed to portraying Mary in a minor role in the Jesus story – sitting passively next to the crib at his birth, or standing sadly beside the cross at his death. This is an injustice to Mary. When the angel Gabriel comes to Mary, he finds her ready and willing to be an active participant in God's plan. She had prepared herself for this role over many years by listening to the prophets, and by praying earnestly and passionately for a new world and a new future.

Born from a woman
B5. Vigil Mass of Christmas

Isaiah 62:1-5
Acts 13:16-17, 22-25
Matthew 1:1-25

Like the rest of us, Mary, Jesus' mother, was connected to nature in thousands of different ways, not simply because of her genetic links with her ancestors, which are mentioned in Matthew's genealogy of Jesus, but also because of her dependence on water, air, sunlight, plants, and animals for her existence.

Martin Luther once said that we should never forget that Jesus was born from a woman. You might say a similar thing with regard to nature: we are all "born" from the Earth, because the elements that make up our bodies are constantly being recycled. In order to grow, our bodies have to take in essential vitamins and minerals; when we die, our bodies decompose and these substances return to the environment to be reused in other forms. Our relationship to the nature is closer than we ever care to admit.

The publication *Harper's Index* (167, 1989) once noted that our chances of inhaling a molecule of the breath of Julius Caesar are 99 in 100. It is difficult to judge how accurate this is, or even how that figure was calculated, but it is an interesting thought. Presumably, the chances of inhaling molecules breathed by Mary and her son Jesus would be equally high. This leads us to a startling conclusion, that the Earth itself is holy! It is God's creation – the same God who, when Mary gave birth to Jesus, bonded to that creation in an entirely new and revolutionary way.

The cosmos is God's holy creation and thus deserves our respect, but all too often we refuse to treat it in a proper manner. Because we perceive ourselves as being separate from the Earth, we do not hesitate to violate it. We have no compunction in doing whatever we feel is necessary to provide for our endless needs (or for what we consider to be our needs). Many of us have become addicted to the consumer mentality, and risk changing our beautiful blue-green planet into a vast, poisonous landfill site, from which nothing could ever be born.

We have forgotten (or we refuse to acknowledge) that many of the things we use are not renewable, and that we have polluted our environment, in some cases irreparably. But it is not too late to start redressing the balance. We must learn to respect the holiness of the Earth and the elements that keep us alive. God has given us stewardship over the Earth, but it is not an absolute power – it comes with responsibilities. We are not free to abuse our position of power, disposing of things as we see fit and allowing whole species to perish as we strive to sustain our wasteful lifestyle. We have a responsibility to God, and to our children, to care for the Earth and use its resources wisely.

Let us remember that Jesus was born, just like all of us, from a woman, and thus out of the Earth. Tonight we celebrate the birth of Jesus, and it is a celebration that should help us to reflecton our own, rightful place in the world.

In the dark of the night
B6. Midnight Mass (Christmas)

Isaiah 9:1-7

Titus 2:11-14

Luke 2:1-14

It is midnight, and the whole world seems to be cloaked in darkness. There is an almost total silence, and with it comes a deep sense of peace. Up above, the sky is studded with jewel-like stars, planets, and comets that silently proclaim the majesty of God. The children went to bed long ago, full of excitement and wondering what will be waiting for them under the Christmas tree when they wake up. Who knows what they will dream of during this dark night? Parents looking at their children's sleeping faces may be reminded of the words of the famous carol: "Silent night, holy night, all is calm, all is bright ...."

It is a beautiful, idyllic scene, but not one that is echoed by the liturgical texts of our Christmas celebration! There is nothing quite so cosy about the darkness of which the prophet Isaiah speaks. He is not talking about the darkness of a silent, holy, peaceful night. The horrible darkness Isaiah describes is the dark shadow cast by a fallen world. However, hope burns bright, because the darkness is going to be dispelled by the Messiah. At the end of the Midnight Mass, a special blessing will be given. In that blessing, we remember how Jesus scattered the darkness of this world with the light of his glory.

We do not set out for Midnight Mass because of the loveliness of the night. While a calm, starry night may be intensely beautiful, the darkness of a cloudy, moonless night can sometimes be ominous and frightening when we are alone. When there is no street-light to guide our way, no lantern to carry before us, no torch to flash in the dark, and no match to light, there is only darkness. And it is a darkness that can sometimes be full of threats and dangers. We frequently encounter stories on TV or in the newspaper about how people were robbed, mugged, raped, or murdered in the dark. In some places, it has got to the stage where many people feel too scared to leave their houses at night. Others will only brave the streets in their cars.

If we are really honest, we will all admit that at one time or another – even if only as a child – we have been afraid of the dark. In such a situation, the night becomes like a wall that separates us from our family, friends, and neighbours. The oppressive, isolating darkness seems to fill every corner, muffle every noise, envelope every smell, and stifle our every breath.

At Midnight Mass tonight, we celebrate the birth of Jesus in the midst of a shadowy, corrupt world. It is only when we understand the true nature of the darkness that we truly appreciate the light Jesus' birth brought into the world. At last the hope of a new beginning burns brightly in the night: "The people that walked in darkness have seen a great light; on those who live in a land of deep shadow a light has shone."

Christmas gifts
B7. Christmas (Day Mass)

Isaiah 52:7-10
Hebrews 1:1-6
John 1:1-18

At Christmas, practically everyone receives a present. It might only be something small, such as a box of chocolates, a book, or a gift voucher; alternatively, it might be something much bigger, such a mountain bike, a new suit, a car, a holiday overseas, or even a house. The important thing is the sentiment behind the gift.

When we give Christmas presents to one another, we celebrate the greatest present ever given to humankind: Jesus. Some people might disagree, saying, "No, the greatest gift God ever gave me is my own life." Yet, if you read today's gospel text carefully, you will find that even the precious gift of life was given to us through Jesus Christ.

Over the years, we accumulate so many gifts that they seem to swamp our lives – just take a quick look around your home and see how they clutter up every room. The gifts we value and cherish most are usually those we put on prominent display or hang up on the wall. But there are doubtless corners, cupboards, and boxes in your home that are like graveyards for forgotten gifts, such as the "miracle" potato peeler that never worked, the video camera you lost interest in, the coffee maker you could never be bothered with, and that old bag of marbles you kept from your childhood. These are things that never played a useful role in your life, or which you simply outgrew. That is why they now languish in the dark of cupboards, boxes, and drawers, just waiting to be thrown out.

What has all this to do with celebrating Christmas? Well, what happens to the gifts people give us at Christmas can also happen to the gifts we receive from God. Why is it that the gifts of Jesus, his Spirit, and his peace disappear from the lives of so many of us? In all probability, it is because we never allow them to play a meaningful part of our lives – to touch the core of our being.

Perhaps this failing results from a wrong perception of our true nature. Consider this for a moment: if I decide that I no longer want to see any more, I can throw my glasses, put on a blindfold, or have my eyes removed. None of these actions disguises the fact that I was born with the gift of sight, and that nature obviously intended me to see. Similarly, if I decide that I do not want to walk any more, I can throw away my shoes, tie my feet together, or even have my feet amputated, but this does not alter the fact that I was born with two fully functioning legs designed for walking.

That is how it is with God's gifts, too: if I choose not to be part of God's world, then I can easily exist without Jesus, without Christmas, and without the Holy Spirit. However, the fact remains that I was designed to live in God's world and enjoy God's gifts to the full.

In his letter to Philemon, Paul thanks him not only for having accepted the gift of Jesus, but also because Jesus plays such a pivotal role in Philemon's life. He writes: "I always mention you in my prayers and thank God for you, because I hear of the love and faith which you have for the Lord Jesus and for all the saints" (Phil. 1:4-5).

We, too, should live in such a way that others will know that we have received the gift of Jesus, and that we celebrate him in our lives.

Family values

B8. Feast of the Holy Family

Sirach 3:2-6, 12-14

Colossians 3:12-21

Luke 2:22-40

Traditionally, this first Sunday after Christmas is dedicated to the celebration of the Holy Family. At this time, we uphold Mary, Joseph, and Jesus as the ideal Christian family. However, if we think about it for an instant, it becomes clear that what we usually do is simply project the image of what the Church today officially considers to be the "perfect" model family onto that family in Nazareth 2,000 years ago.

Is it wise to mould our image of the Holy Family into something that matches established notions of what is "ideal", "normal", and "respectable"? The facts tell quite a different story. When Mary sings her Magnificat, it is obvious that she certainly does not see her family as a model of establishment ideals. Mary knows that their family is the start of something radical and revolutionary – it will change the world and overturn the established order (Luke 2:46-53).

So the essence of the Holy Family is more "radical" than "establishment". It is also a far cry from modern, suburban ideas of what is respectable. The manner in which Jesus was conceived and born – and the ensuing rumours about his parenthood – must have made of Mary a kind of social outcast. Not conforming to the "norms" of family life brought harsh disapproval, as it sometimes does today.

It seems that some considered Jesus to be an "illegitimate", or extra-marital, child. Luke mentions that Jesus was "thought" to be the son of Joseph (Luke 3:23). John, too, records how Jesus' opponents, outraged by his claims that God is his Father, pointedly draw attention to the question of his earthly parentage by asking: "Where is your father?" Then they add, "We were not born of prostitution" (John 8:41). John and Luke obviously did not agree with such gossip and rumour, but plainly considered the issue important enough to bring to their readers' attention.

The gospels paint a picture of a troubled family, with relationships often tense and fraught under the pressures they face. We find a betrothed man feeling deceived; a young woman puzzled and confused by the arrival of strangers at the birth of her son; a husband taking his family into exile because of a warning in a dream; a child who strays from his parents in a big city; a son who is misunderstood by his mother, and who rebukes her at a wedding feast; a family who doubt the sanity of this "wayward" son ... and so the list goes on.

In today's account of Jesus' "presentation" in the Temple, Simeon prophesies that Jesus' role in the world will bring great suffering upon the family of Mary and Joseph (Luke 2:34-35). Then Anna, the prophetess, speaks dramatically about the deliverance of Jerusalem (2:38). Simeon relates this to the salvation of the whole world (2:30-31), making it clear that Mary should see her son in a wider context than her own family: she will have to learn to be more than just his mother. Normal family life will have to be sacrificed for the sake of her son's mission.

The Holy Family was much larger than Mary, Joseph, and Jesus in Nazareth: it was inextricably linked to the rest of the world and to God's plan to restore justice and hope – and that should be our model for family life. Remember, it is Jesus himself who asks his mother: "Did you not know that I must be busy with my Father's affairs?" (2:49).

Mary, mother of God
B9. Octave of Christmas (January 1)

Numbers 6:22-27
Galatians 4:4-7
Luke 2:16-21

In his Jubilee document, Pope John Paul II makes several references to the role of Mary. In fact, he does that in all his documents – he hardly writes anything without emphasising her importance. And he is not alone in this: theologians around the world are constantly discussing and studying her. Witness, too, the millions of faithful who visit her shrines in Fatima, Lourdes, Knock, and Medjugorge each year. Andrew Greeley, the famous American priest, sociologist, theologian, and maverick author of many a juicy novel, once wrote that Mary plays a central role in the religious imagination of the Roman Catholic Church.

Being such a central and much-loved figure, it is any wonder that discussion of Mary's status and role in scripture, theology, and Christian life sometimes provokes impassioned debate and disagreement? For example, during the Second Vatican Council, which lasted for several years, the 1,800 church fathers present (the church mothers were obviously excluded!) had to decide whether they were going to dedicate a special document to Mary. It proved to be one of the most difficult decisions taken during the whole Council. In most of the cases where the Council had to vote on an issue, the motions were passed with majorities of 90-95 per cent. However, the issue of this Marian document was decided by a tiny majority of only 17 votes!

So what was the result? Well, in the end, Mary did not get a special document dedicated to her. As a compromise, she was mentioned at length – and honourably – in the wording of the declaration about the Church being the People of God (the Decree on the Church, *Lumen Gentium*). She was given her privileged place in the midst of us – in the midst of the people of God.

This notion of Mary's rightful place was taken up in a most unusual fashion by a parish somewhere in Australia. The church members decided to remove all the statues of Mary that adorned the walls of their church. Then they commissioned a new statue, which was made in such a way that it could take the place of greatest honour in their church – that is, right at the front, sitting on the first pew! Now, whenever the parishioners enter their church, Mary, the mother of God, is already waiting for them, sitting in the place she deserves.

This is an original and imaginative way of expressing what Elizabeth said of Mary when the two women met after the Annunciation (surely the first Christian women's support group!): "Of all women you are the most blessed, and blessed is the fruit of your womb!"

In our worship, prayer, and celebrations today, we remember that Mary is, indeed, blessed. She is the only one who can say of Jesus: "Flesh of my flesh, blood of my blood." That is because she is Mary, the mother of God.

A beckoning star

B10. Epiphany (January 6)

Isaiah 60:1-6
Ephesians 3:2-3, 5-6
Matthew 2:1-12

One of the problems with which modern Bible commentators, preachers, and Christian writers struggle is how to make the old religious imagination of the scriptures speak to us as vividly as it did to our ancestors. How do we find new insights for today's world amongst the old wisdom?

In his encyclical, *Redemptoris Missio* (1991), Pope John Paul II refers to the story of Abram and Sarai (later renamed Abraham and Sarah).

They were called to leave their old religion and start afresh with Yahweh. Abram and Sarai are not only our ancestors in a new belief, they are also our ancestors in our unbelief! They rejected the idol-worship around them and refused to accept the passive belief that everything was fated – that human history was written in the stars, and determined by the rhythms of the cosmos, which only the astrologers and soothsayers could interpret. This made them heretics and atheists in the eyes of others. Instead, Abram and Sarai embraced a new covenant and relationship with God, in which humanity would have an active, more responsible role to play. From then on, human beings would have to act on their own initiative.

Having obeyed Yahweh's call and left everything behind, they pitched their tents in the loneliness of the desert. On a starry night, Yahweh called them out of their tents and told them to look up into the sky. They must have thought; "Not again! Haven't we left all that stargazing behind?" But they did as they were told, and as they did so, Yahweh promised that their descendants would be as numerous as the stars above (Genesis 15:5). As this ageing, childless couple pondered this amazing promise, they must have seen between the stars, or maybe beyond them, the skyline of a new city – the heavenly Jerusalem on the holy mountain (see Hebrews 11:8-13).

This is the vision of which Isaiah dreams when he sees all the nations of the Earth climbing together up the holy mountain of Yahweh (Isaiah 2:2-3; 60:1-6). Mary, Jesus' mother, sings about it when she prophesies that all the nations of the Earth will praise her (Luke 1:48). It is also the vision you find described in the last book of scripture, the Book of Revelation (Rev:21).

In today's gospel text, we read how some other star-gazers discovered in their old cosmos a new star that heralded a new beginning, just as Abram and Sarai discovered new promises and a new vision of humanity's final destiny when they looked at the stars that had so dominated their old religion. The new star brought the wise astronomers and astrologers together, and together they travelled to Jerusalem, where they thought their journey would end. To their surprise, the star led them to Bethlehem – and the beginnings of a new Jerusalem!

This vision of a pilgrimage to a new city, a new society, and a new future remains a powerful spiritual metaphor. Pope John Paul II was thinking this when he began talking about the Great Jubilee at the start of his pontificate. He looks forward to making that vision a reality, although there is so much that needs to be changed in the old order to bring that about. So often, it is out of our struggles with old ideas, conventions, and attitudes the new vision arises. Do we not all suspect, deep down, that we need to relate to each other, to the cosmos, and to God in a new way? Could that twinkling star be beckoning us too?

Salvation from the underside

B11. Baptism of the Lord (Sunday after Epiphany)

Isaiah 42:1-4, 6-7

Acts 10:34-38

Mark 1:7-11

Mark's introduction to Jesus is abrupt and pared to the bone: Jesus comes from Nazareth to be baptised. If you compare it to the beginnings of the gospels by Matthew and Luke, Jesus' arrival is almost a disappointment. In Mark's version, Jesus appears on the scene without a genealogy and without the miracles that accompany his coming in Matthew and Luke. What an anti-climax! But hold on – Mark knows what he is doing. He knows that the story he is about to tell is dramatic enough, so why bother with scene-setting and peripheral details?

So where is the drama in the emergence of an unknown character from a hamlet so insignificant that it was never even mentioned in the documents of the time? To mention that Jesus came from Nazareth was like saying that he came from nowhere. Adding that it was situated in Galilee only made things worse. Every non-Galilean Israelite despised Galilee. Why? Well, regionalism obviously played its part: Galilee was right up in the north, while Jerusalem was far away in the south. Galilee was also surrounded by pagan and Hellenised (Greek-influenced) towns. It was poor and cut off from the rest of Israel by Samaria. To expect anything useful to come out of Galilee was just plain ridiculous.

Last week, we noticed that even the wise men from the east following the new star thought that their journey would end at Jerusalem. Although the experts there had sent them on to Bethlehem, the royal city of David, the traditional nationalistic belief was that deliverance and redemption (and a Saviour) could only come from the centre – that is, from Jerusalem. Mark turns that expectation on its head: salvation comes from the periphery, from the underside of society. Mark hints at this earlier, when he mentions how people actually come from Jerusalem to go into the wilderness to be baptised by John.

According to Mark, it is Jesus' apparently insignificant origins that make what happens at his baptism so dramatic. It is above Jesus – a non-entity from nowhere in particular – that heavens tear open. At that moment, it is clear to everyone that something terrific is happening here. They are witnessing a truly apocalyptic moment. Heaven and Earth are engaged in some serious business. It is a direct answer to Isaiah's prayer: "Oh, that you would tear the heavens open ... to make known your name ..." (Isaiah 64:1).

16

Mark tells us how Jesus saw the Spirit descend upon him as dove, and how he heard a voice saying: "You are my Son, the Beloved," (Mark 1:11). These are references to old titles and names for the promised renewer of the world:

"Let me proclaim Yahweh's decree, he has told me, 'You are my son, today I have become your father. Ask and I will give you the nations for your heritage, the ends of the Earth for your domain. Break their resistance ...'" (Psalm 2:7-8).

At his baptism, Jesus brings the old human world to an end. Mark could not have started more dramatically. The new world is born here in the river Jordan!

Jesus' baptism is a sign that he refuses to play according to the rules, so the conflict with the ruler of this world begins. It is a conflict in which there can be only one winner. Immediately after his baptism, Jesus goes off into the desert, where Satan tempts him for forty days. On the one side there are the worldly "beasts", and on the other side are the heavenly "angels". This is powerful symbolism, to say the least.

Touchstone

B12. Ash Wednesday

Joel 2:2-18
2 Corinthians 5:20-6.2
Matthew 6:1-6, 16-18

We begin Lent this year with a stirring reading from the prophet Joel:

"Spare your people, Yahweh! Do not make your heritage a thing of shame, a byword for the nations. Why should it be said among the nations, 'Where is their God?'" (Joel 2:17).

Joel proclaims the coming of God's judgement on all the nations, and appeals to us – God's people – to repent and return to God. We are told to ask God to be merciful and gracious to the world, to our families, and to ourselves. But Joel does not stop there: he also suggests a prayer strategy to back up this call for repentance.

Karl Barth, who left his imprint on so much of 20th-century theological thinking, once noted that praying is nothing more than reminding God of God's promises to us. Joel's prayer strategy does exactly that: he urges us to plead with God to listen to our prayers and to remain faithful to us. We have to do this to persuade God not to leave us. He advises us to warn God of the contempt, scorn, and laughter of unbelievers that will come upon the people of Yahweh if they are deserted by their God.

Jesus advocates this same "prayer tactic" when the disciples ask him: "How should we pray?" (Luke 11:1). He even gives them – and us– a model prayer that embodies this attitude: the Lord's Prayer (Matthew 6:9-13; Luke 11:2-4). We are to pray, "Abba, hallowed be thy name, thy kingdom come ...." In other words: "May things go your way, O God, our source and creator – but don't forget us and all the things we need while you prosper! Forgive us our faults, in the same way that we forgive those who fail or wrong us. Please don't tempt us, and don't put us to the test!"

So we are to remind Yahweh of the divine promises made to God's people. But there is a qualifying element to this prayer: we are to ask God to be merciful, because we are merciful. We are to ask God to help us, because we are willing to help others. What this means is that we are making our mercy the touchstone for God's mercy. A touchstone was a hard, dark stone once used to find the quality of gold or silver by the colour of the streak they left when drawn across its surface. It was a standard test. In effect, what we are saying to God is: "Let the quality of your mercy to us, Lord, be determined by the standard of our mercy towards others."

Joel's strategy asks for courageous and daring prayer. A real challenge! This strategy dares to say to God: "Recognise yourself in our attitudes!" In the final instance, this strategy does not test and challenge God but ourselves. On Ash Wednesday, we sprinkle ourselves with ashes – not just as a way of showing that we are serious in our intention to reform our attitudes, and to remind God of God's promises – but also as a symbolic forgetting, forgiving, and burning away of the wrongs done to us in the past.

Your kingdom come!

B13. First Sunday of Lent

Genesis 9:8-15

1 Peter 3:18-22

Mark 1:12-15

"The time has come, and the kingdom of God is close at hand," (Matthew 1:15). With those words, Jesus introduced into our world a tension that has not yet been resolved. It is like a riddle: God's kingdom is here, and yet it is only close at hand. We are on the point of seeing it, but we cannot yet consciously live and experience it.

How can we grasp what is meant by this paradoxical "not-yet-but-already-with-us" kingdom that Jesus announces. Perhaps the example of radio waves can help: these waves of invisible energy are all around us, but until we tune into them with a radio or TV set, we are unaware of their presence. It is when I am about to press the set's "on" button that these radio waves are "close at hand". Another example is the way we discover things: whatever we discover is already there before we find it, but to us it seems as though it only came into existence the moment we found it.

The kingdom of God existed before Jesus appeared, but in Jesus it became visible. Jesus expresses this tension in many other ways, such as when he speaks about the seed that already contains the whole tree but still has to grow, or the feast that is already underway even though the invited guests have not yet arrived.

So how should we react if the kingdom of God is close at hand? Jesus tells us straight: "Repent, and believe the Good News." But still the tension is not wholly relieved, because when you believe you accept the existence of something you have not been able to verify. Imagine, for example, that I hand my friend a parcel and say: "Can you keep these pearls safe for me? I have to travel and I don't want to take the pearls with me in case I lose them." As long as my friend has not seen the pearls, she can only believe that they are inside the parcel. If she believes me, she will take good care of the parcel.

"The time has come, and the kingdom of God is close at hand." If you believe this, then your belief will colour your life and influence everything you do. But, as in the case of the pearls, would it not help if you could just catch a glimpse or have some other concrete proof?

Looking at it another way, the kingdom is near because Jesus is with us. It is as simple as that. He gradually discloses in his life the glory given to himself and to us, as creatures moulded by the hand of God. It is in Jesus that we see revealed the original glory that is the potential of every human being.

In Mark's gospel, Jesus turns squarely against anything that hinders that human glory, which is also God's glory. This is part of the same struggle in which John the Baptist was embroiled. Before he was arrested, John said that he was not strong enough to win the fight, but that there would come another who was much stronger and who would baptise everyone with fire. This does not mean that the fire will be given to us: it is already within us – we have to tune into the Holy Spirit to become initiated into it. Jesus demonstrates the powers lying dormant within us that we have yet to realise. With this in store, we can only pray: "Your kingdom come!"

Seeing and hearing

B14. Second Sunday of Lent

Genesis 22:1-2, 9-13, 15-18

Romans 8:31-34

Mark 9:2-10

Peter, James, and John like what they see. At last! This is what they have been waiting for! Jesus is standing in front of them in clothes that are dazzlingly white – whiter than the strongest bleach could ever make them. Beside Jesus are Moses and Elijah. The three disciples are overcome: this is exactly as they always hoped it would be, and now they are seeing it with their own eyes! The Lord Jesus is finally being revealed in all his glory. They really have made the right choice in following him.

While they are still staring at this visual extravaganza, a cloud descends and a voice tells them that they should also listen to the one they see shining in his glory. The scene has a certain irony about it, because they are told to listen to someone who does not utter a single word.

It is only as they are coming down from the mountain that Jesus begins to speak. But they are still absorbed in what they have seen, and have no interest in what he has to say about the struggle he faces and about his suffering and death. He asks them not to tell anyone about it "until after the Son of Man has risen from the dead." Later, instead of asking what that death refers to, they discuss among themselves what he could mean by a resurrection.

The disciples are in a dilemma throughout Jesus' time on Earth: they are willing to follow Jesus in his glory, but they are not willing to walk the path that leads to it. It is not a question of misunderstanding, but of stubborn refusal. Peter leads them in this unwillingness, despite the instruction from the voice to heed Jesus' words. The disciples are quite prepared to call him "Messiah", and they are impressed by all he does. However, they do not know how to react to what he says, because they are simply not prepared to engage in his struggle with the world. The price is too high.

They are interested in fame, honour, and status, and they think these things will come to them by following Jesus. They think highly of themselves, and although they sometimes call Jesus "teacher", there are several occasions on which they tell him that they know better than he does about how this world operates. In one sense, they do – and that is their difficulty. Their values and judgements are "of this world" and "this generation", but not of Jesus' or God's world.

By telling us of the disciples' deafness to Jesus' call, and their blindness to the way Jesus shows them, Mark is trying to make us see the fears and false expectations that made it practically impossible for the disciples to fully understand Jesus or how they should respond to him. Mark hopes that we are not going to make the same mistake. He is challenging us to do better than those who walked with Jesus 2,000 years ago. That is quite a challenge!

God's dwelling places
B15. Third Sunday of Lent

Exodus 20:1-17
1 Corinthians 1:22-25
John 2:13-25

Translations are treacherous! Not so long ago, linguists such as the American Noam Chomsky thought that anything you said in one language could be directly translated into another, without any loss of sense or meaning. That may be true when you are expressing pure abstractions, such as in mathematics, algebra, or geometry, or in sciences such as physics or chemistry. However, it is difficult to believe when you are trying to convey concrete human realities and complex or subtle emotions. Eventually, most linguists – Chomsky included – came round to this view as well.

Putting something into words is always a battle, even in your native language. There is always the risk that the words you choose will not capture the essence of what you want to say, or that others will misunderstand or misconstrue them. In translating from one language to another, there is even more chance that meaning and nuance will either be distorted or lost, and this has been the challenge to the translators of the biblical texts over the years.

Many translations of today's gospel reading use one English term, "temple", for two very different Greek words: *hieron* (John 2:14) and *naos* (2:19-20). This is unfortunate, because there is a subtle but important difference between them. The first word, *hieron*, means "sanctuary", "sacred building", or "shrine". The second word, *naos*, means "home or dwelling place of a divinity", or "there where God is present". The first word is used when Jesus enters the Temple in Jerusalem, while the second is used by Jesus when speaking about himself. Paul also uses the second term in his letter to the Corinthians: "Didn't you realise that you were God's temple and that the Spirit of God was living among you? ... the temple of God is sacred; and you are that temple" (1 Cor. 3:16-17). He reiterates this later: "Your body ... is the temple of the Holy Spirit, who is in you since you received him from God" (6:19).

All this might seem like a lot of fuss over some simple word-play, but remember that both Jesus and Stephen, the first Christian martyr, were killed because they were accused of having said that the "temple" was going to be destroyed. For those priests, who believed that the Temple building in Jerusalem was the actual dwelling place of God, destroying the Temple would mean the end of God's presence among them.

So where is the dwelling place of God in this world? Priests in every age have grappled that question. However, since the entry of Jesus into human history, the nature of the question has changed significantly. Jesus told them that God is not in any building. He also told the priests that he was, himself, the "temple" or dwelling place of God. In the biblical accounts of the trials of Jesus and Stephen, it is clear that the priests were not happy at God changing home like this! Above all, it threatened to undermine their professional hierarchy and their privileged status.

Too often, theological debate focused exclusively on how Jesus was the dwelling place of God. But this true and marvellous fact is only part of the story, for if God's presence was restricted to the life-span of Jesus, what is left for the rest of the humanity today? Are we truly devoid of God's presence in the modern world? The answer, of course, is "No", as Paul understood. God's presence is given to all of us through the Holy Spirit – we are all God's temples.

Saved!

B16. Fourth Sunday of lent

2 Chronicles 36:14-16, 19-23
Ephesians 2:4-10
John 3:14-21

Both in Paul's letter to the Ephesians and Jesus' conversation with Nicodemus, the issue is about being "saved". In each case, this salvation is said to be possible only through Jesus.

Preachers and evangelists sometimes have to struggle hard to make others understand these ideas in our increasingly secularised society. Many people cannot see that there is anything they need to be saved from. Even when people acknowledge that there is a need for salvation – whether it be from sin, divine wrath, their own self-centredness, or ultimate separation from God – the question still arises as to whether

Jesus is the only one who can save us.

It is a question that will definitely be asked at the celebration of the 2,000th birthday of Jesus. However, some would say that as we look back at the historical legacy of Western "Christian" society in this tumultuous century, the nature of the question changes dramatically. Daniel Leochty, an American Quaker theologian, puts it in a radical way in his book *Theology in Post-liberal Perspective* (1991):

"The question of the uniqueness of Christ has traditionally been expressed in the question: 'Is there salvation outside of Christ?' In our time, as we stand in solidarity with the victims of Christian anti-Semitism, with our Native American brothers and sisters, with the victims of economic and cultural imperialism, with people marginalised by sexism and homophobia, the question is reversed: 'Can one still find salvation in Christ?'"

Through sermons and Sunday school classes, we have grown accustomed to the idea that Jesus saved us by dying on the cross for our sake. His death is acknowledged as a sacrifice to God to atone for our sin and guilt. Although this is true – and something for which we should continually praise God – many people still perceive this as a salvation from something negative, rather than as a life-transforming liberation into something uniquely positive. It is almost as if all our salvation does is return us from a minus figure to a zero on the divine score chart. Even the knowledge that our salvation has healed us and made us whole can be viewed in the same way – in being redeemed, we simply become "normal" again. Perhaps that is why we so often stand as passive onlookers to injustice and oppression.

Paul and John were both witnesses to the way the first Christian communities discovered how God shows – in Jesus Christ – the full potential and range of possibilities that our human life offers. They had seen the very real changes this brought in people's lives. Through Jesus, God shows that we were not born to perish and end in misery and negativism. God shows us that we do not need to be "victims", whether it be of wrong decisions, hatred, envy, greed, materialism, or whatever else. God shows us that each Christian has a core that became Christ when we believed in Jesus, and that this core will enable us to grow towards our full human potential and to start attaining some of those possibilities. It is by this new positivism in their lives that Paul and John knew that they were saved.

With this new-found positivism, we can amend, correct, heal, and even restructure our lives. We can find the strength to confidently challenge injustice and evil. We can help each other by offering solidarity through groups such as CAFOD and Amnesty International. We can help comfort and support one another when disaster or depression strikes.

But surely there is still one final enemy that renders all this pointless and futile: death? That is where Jesus' crucifixion comes in. Jesus meets and beats death, turning it into something positive. Jesus has shown us that we need no longer fear death, and that is the sure foundation of our salvation.

The hour has come

B17. Fifth Sunday in Lent

Jeremiah 31:31-34

Hebrews 5:7-9

John 12:20-33

If you read today's gospel text carefully, it will become obvious that it marked a turning point in Jesus' life. Jesus acknowledges this himself with the words, "Now the hour has come" (John 12:23). It is as if everything in his life has been building up to this moment: "Now sentence is being passed on this world; now the prince of this world is to be overthrown" (12:31).

What had provoked this? Some Greeks had come to Jesus' disciple Philip (the only one with a Greek-sounding name), asking to be introduced to Jesus. It was a simple and innocent request. Hundreds, maybe thousands, of others must have come to the disciples seeking an audience with Jesus. Yet Raymond Brown, the respected American commentator on John's gospel, reckons that the visit of the Greeks was a watershed in the gospel story. Why should this be?

We might find it easier to understand this episode if we bear in mind the troubles in the Middle East. In the days of Jesus, the Greeks were considered a real danger to the Jewish nation. Although they no longer posed a military, political, or economic danger, they were seen as a genuine cultural threat. They were looked upon in the same way that Western people, especially Americans, are viewed by Muslims in the Middle East. The presence of US military personnel in the region is, by and large, deeply resented, because these people introduce customs and attitudes that are felt to undermine the Muslim civilisation, religion, and culture.

So it was quite a breakthrough when those Greeks at last came to see Jesus. It was something unexpected and – from the first reaction of the disciples – quite unwanted. The disciples by then must have been accustomed to being with people they normally would have avoided, such as Samaritans and Syro-Phoenicians, but here, of all people, were Greeks! Philip is at a loss to know what to do and goes to consult

Andrew. Finally, they decide to tell Jesus. When Jesus hears of this, he realises that everything at last is falling into place, and that he and his Father will at last be glorified.

He adds, amid the enthusiasm, that this new development will bring pain and suffering. The seed that up to now has kept its genes safely protected, will have to break open and risk a new existence in order to bring forth its fruit. The lives they have lived and loved up to now will have to be left behind to begin the new life ahead.

At the end of this text, Jesus says: "And when I am lifted up from the Earth, I shall draw all people to myself." With these words, Jesus reveals a great truth: we belong together, and the basis of our together-ness is that we are all equally loved by the one Jesus calls "Abba".

To believe and live out that truth is simultaneously our greatest joy and our greatest difficulty. There are times when all of us have prob-lems relating to people of different ethnic, racial, or religious groups, if only because we feel separated by the cultural differences between us. At such times, we should resist the temptation to withdraw into our shells and ignore or rebuff them. Jesus tells us that the hour has come to bridge the gulf between ourselves and our fellow human beings. After all, we are all loved in the same measure by God. We should throw open our arms and welcome anyone who comes asking to be introduced to Jesus.

Faithful to the end

B18. Palm/Passion Sunday

Isaiah 50:4-7
Philippians 2:6-11
Mark 14:1-15:47

Do you know the saying "Where there's life, there's hope"? It is a say-ing that makes life, and not hope, the foundation or bedrock of our exis-tence. However, it usually seems that the reverse is more accurate: where there is no longer hope, life gives up. Hope, it seems, keeps us going.

For this reason, the Passion story told by Mark appears to be a real tragedy, because it seems as though Jesus is abandoning hope. It begins with Jesus telling his disciples that they will all desert him. Mark describes a very different scene in Gethsemane from the other gospel authors. No angel comes to give him strength, as happens in Luke's account. Neither does Mark's Jesus have the foreknowledge he has in John's gospel, knowing that everything is unfolding according to God's fixed plan, as foretold by the prophets. When Jesus is on the cross, Mark hardly mentions any comfort or consolation: Jesus is alone, surrounded by a murderous crowd. Even the person who eventually reaches out with a wet sponge on a stick to moisten his lips derides him. And the women who have so faithfully followed him are now kept at a distance.

Just before he dies, Jesus shouts: "My God, my God, why have you deserted me?" Where was God at that moment? It is a question that has often been asked in times of suffering and tragedy. In his book *Night*, Elie Wiesel tells how two Jewish adults and a boy were executed in his concentration camp during World War II. The victims were hanged. The older men quickly died because of their weight, but the boy, who was much lighter, had an agonisingly slow death. As the boy vainly struggled, a voice among the watching inmates was heard to ask: "Where is God?" Wiesel notes that he felt a voice in his heart responding: "Where is God? He is hanging from the gallows."

The Roman centurion under the cross gives the same answer of Jesus. Having stood by the cross watching Jesus die, he comments: "In truth this man was a son of God." So God was present, even though the rest of humanity seem to have deserted Jesus. Practically everyone betrayed Jesus, but Jesus did not betray our humanity. This is what the Roman officer realised.

Jesus' humanity survived his death. In Jesus, it is manifest that a human being can overcome his or her personal interest – and all consequences of such an act – to remain faithful to a greater, more human, more divine cause. That Jesus could do this is the foundation of our ultimate hope – not only in God, but also in that divine creation, the human being.

The gospels tell us that before he was arrested, numerous people begged Jesus not to go to Jerusalem, to be "reasonable" and think of his own interests. Even his own family did the same, bringing his mother with them to try and dissuade him. If he had given in to that temptation, he would have sacrificed his vision and ideal to save himself. He would not be the bedrock of our hope as he is today. If he had not been faithful right to the end – to death on the cross – we would, indeed, feel forsaken by God!

Washing feet
B19. Maundy Thursday

Exodus 12:1-8, 11-14

1 Corinthians 11:23-26

John 13:1-15

Jesus and the disciples are about to eat the Passover meal on the occasion we now call the Last Supper. Suddenly, Jesus stands up, removes his garments and wraps a towel around his waist. Then he pours water into a basin and goes down on his hands and knees to wash their feet – all 24 of them – one by one, carefully and lovingly. Some time before, an unnamed woman had washed Jesus' feet and anointed them with ointment (Luke 7:38-50). Jesus praised her for the tremendous love that she had shown him.

Why is the washing of other people's feet considered such a wonderful gesture? Well, if you wash someone's feet out of love, you are no longer concentrating on yourself. Your focus is upon the person whose feet you are washing. When Peter objects to Jesus' actions, concerned that such an act is too lowly for his Lord and Master, Jesus responds: "If I do not wash you, you can have nothing in common with me." So washing another's feet is also a way of bonding or identifying with that person.

Jesus washed the feet of each of his disciples, and it was his intention never to stop doing it. He said to them:

"Do you understand what I have done to you? You call me Master and Lord, and rightly; so I am. If I, then, the Lord and Master, have washed your feet, you should wash each other's feet."

John ends his account in the same way that Luke ends his account of the breaking of the bread and the sharing of the wine – that is, with an instruction from Jesus to repeat the gesture among themselves. He says: "I have given you an example so that you may copy what I have done to you."

So we should also be washing one another's feet. We should not only wash the feet of those we know or to whom we are related, but also the feet of others, such as the poor farmers who grow and pick the coffee we drink without paying them a fair price; the feet of those who stitch our shirts, skirts, trousers and coats together in Third World sweatshops; the feet of the homeless people in our own streets and squares; and – it may surprise you – the feet of the rich who hide behind the gates and fences of their luxurious villas and mansions.

Just think what could happen if we took this command of Jesus as seriously as we take his instruction to share the bread and the wine.

Imagine the scene if world leaders and multi-millionaire entrepreneurs got down on all-fours to wash one another's feet before they began their meetings and negotiations, after having already washed the feet of the orphans and widows, and the poor and marginalised in their own societies! Then we would truly know that the kingdom of God was being realised among us.

The folly of the cross

B20. Good Friday

Isaiah 52:13-53:12
Hebrews 4:14-16; 5:7-9
John 18:1-19:42

They executed Jesus. Killing him was the last and worst thing they could do to him. They never even considered that they needed to do anything else: after all, they had killed him – what could be more final than that? Death was their ultimate weapon, just as it is for all those who are willing to use violence against others.

It may sound contentious, but I firmly believe that our willingness to sanction or legitimise violence of any sort – even if it is simply agreeing to the maintenance of potentially devastating "deterrents" such as nuclear weapons – ultimately explains the violence in our parks and streets, and on our public transport systems. Even when people buy guns purely for self-protection, they still unwittingly succeed in convincing their children that using violence is the only way to survive in the world.

Some might suggest that this is just the product of "soft", wishy-washy thinking. Far from it: it is the result of a hard-nosed analysis of Jesus' attitude to violence. When Jesus stands before Pilate, he says that he could have resorted to violence: he could have called in the heavenly army and the divine weaponry of his heavenly Father. He told Pilate that he had chosen not to. He chose life, not death, even in his bitterest hour, when he knew that his end was near. That is the only way to end violence. You simply have to refuse to sanction it in any form. You must refuse to turn in that vicious circle, or walk in the way of violence. Following Jesus, there is no other option.

The curtain in the Temple was torn from top to bottom. The Earth shook. The Sun darkened, making it pitch black in the middle of the day. When Jesus' friends were allowed to take his dead body down from the cross, his opponents must have thought that he had lived a sad life of self-deception. Certainly, God had forsaken him. His efforts and life had been a complete failure, a pitiful mistake, just as they had always suspected.

Just three days later, after Jesus had risen from the dead, his opponents must then have realised that it was they who had been deceiving themselves! They were the ones who had made the mistake, and everything had turned out exactly as Jesus has thought it would! He was killed, but he rose again from the dead. The vicious circle of violence had finally been broken. Folly? Perhaps, in the eyes of the world. But in reality, the folly of the cross is the salvation of the human race.

Easter rising
B21. Easter Vigil

Mark 16:1-8

The gospel of Mark tells how very early in the morning – as soon as the Sabbath regulations allow them to leave their homes – Mary Magdalene, Mary the mother of James, and Salome go to the tomb of Jesus. They take with them oil, herbs, and spices, to wash, anoint, and properly bury the body of Jesus, which the men had put in the tomb rather hastily because the Sabbath was imminent.

They know it is a rather risky undertaking, because they have heard that there are soldiers guarding the tomb. In their anxiety, they have not really thought things through: it is only on their way to the tomb that they wonder whether they will be able to roll away the heavy stone from the entrance. As it turns out, this is an unnecessary worry, because when they arrive at the tomb they find that the stone has already been moved. The tomb is open!

Inside the tomb, they find a young man dressed in white, just as all the baptismal candidates are tonight. The white clothes are a sign of the new life that was given to us at Easter.

The young man tells them that the Jesus they have come to bury is no longer there. "He has risen, he is not here," he says almost nonchalantly, and he even points out the place where Joseph of Arimathaea had laid the body. Then he gives them a message: "Go and tell his disciples and Peter, 'He is going before you to Galilee; it is there you will see him, just as he told you.'" It is all too much: the women flee from the tomb, shocked and frightened out of their wits – so afraid, in fact, that they do not even pass on the message to Peter and the disciples.

It is only later, when they understood what has happened to Jesus, that their faith and hope are revived. What has happened in the tomb renews their lives. The risen life of Jesus opens a whole new world to them. No wonder that their first reaction was raw panic! Who would not be afraid of such a radical change? But, with understanding, that fear turned into joy – a joy that altered their lives for good. Everything changed: their payers, their relationships, their lives.

End and beginning

B22. Easter Sunday

Acts 10:34, 37-43

Colossians 3:1-4

Mark 16:1-8

The liturgical calendar today gives us a choice of two gospel texts, one by John and one by Mark. Both tell the same resurrection story, but they do it in very different ways. John's story ends well: Peter and "the other disciple" (probably John himself) believe in Jesus' resurrection. It is a beautiful text with a happy ending. Mark's text is much more difficult. It ends with the flight of the women from Jesus' tomb, who run away because they are afraid. It is such an unwelcome ending that someone (maybe even Mark himself) later added a more upbeat finale to round it off.

Mark's original ending is as abrupt as the beginning of his gospel, in which John the Baptist suddenly emerges out of the desert. Almost immediately, John is joined at the River Jordan by Jesus, who arrives from Nazareth in Galilee. As we have already seen (B11: Salvation from the underside), Jesus' origins are hardly auspicious: Nazareth was a place of little significance, while Galilee was known as a robber's den and scorned by many. And yet, at the end of Mark's gospel, those details are pointedly reiterated. The women at the tomb are told: "Jesus of Nazareth ... is going before you to Galilee." It is a strange end to a strange story.

But why does the angel tell the women and the rest of the disciples to leave Jerusalem and join Jesus in the despised Galilee? We noted before that Mark gave his gospel the title: "The beginning of the Good News about Jesus Christ, the Son of God". Jesus' life is just the beginning – the rest has to follow on at a later date. We belong to that "rest", and we are invited to follow Jesus, leaving behind our comfortable "Jerusalem" to start all over again with him in our own "Galilee". In other words, following Jesus will inevitably lead us to into places and situations that perhaps we would ordinarily prefer to avoid: places where there is need and suffering, places in which there are issues of justice and peace to be settled, places to which Jesus has already gone before us.

In some translations, the last verse of Mark's original ending is followed by three dots (...), which signify that something has been left out, or that it is not complete. Mark's gospel is supposed to be continued ... by us!

The Spirit of Jesus

B23. Second Sunday of Easter

Acts 4:32-35

1 John 5:1-6

John 20:19-31

Pentecost means "50th day", and 50 days separate Easter from Pentecost. During this time – both on Sundays and on weekdays – one of the daily readings in the liturgy is from the Acts of the Apostles, so that the whole book is covered from beginning to end. The book was written by Luke, and it tells how the first-century followers of Jesus reorganised their lives under the influence and inspiration of his Spirit, offering one another love and support as they faced their problems together.

In today's text, we read that no one in the early Christian community was poor, because all those who owned land or houses sold them and presented the money to the apostles, who distributed it equally among those who needed help. Everything else that these early Christians possessed was held in common ownership. There is a similar description in Acts 2:44-45, which also tells how they shared their food gladly and generously. Luke is not trying to advocate a specific programme to achieve a perfect, selfless community of believers. The point Luke wants to make is that these followers of Jesus actually succeeded in making that kind of solidarity and mutual support a reality.

Of course, problems and difficulties arose. For example, the kind of "soup-kitchen" they set up in Jerusalem was a wonderful idea, yet in no time at all it was in difficulties. In the distribution of food, the Hebrew widows got preferential treatment, and the pagan widows began to be overlooked. It was as if at the backdoor of the kitchen one group was getting the best bits of the soup – the meatballs and the pasta – while the other group was waiting at the front door for the dregs! Peter appointed Stephen to remedy this discrimination (Acts 6:1-6)

They had to heal ethnic, racial, and nationalistic divisions such as this, because they were following the model of the life of Jesus. Remember how Jesus disregarded social convention and asked the Samaritan woman at the well for water? How he willingly received the Greek visitors who wanted to see him? How he praised a Roman officer for his faith? And how he told the story of the good Samaritan who stepped out of his ethnic circle to help a mugged Jewish traveller? This is the lifestyle those first Christians took up. It is a lifestyle that sets out to demolish the age-old barriers that separate people from each other. It intrigued Luke so much that he wrote two books about it!

Like an oasis in the desert, a radically different type of society was slowly emerging, bringing freshness and new life into a barren world. But where did this newness come from? Luke weighs up the evidence and comes to the conclusion that it all had to do with the Spirit of Jesus that was alive in those communities. In the whole of the New testament, Luke is the only one who states that Christians – he is the first one to use that name too – have the Spirit of Jesus (Acts 16:7).

His directness still troubles many of us. It troubled the ecclesial authorities from the very beginning. It is not for nothing that Luke's book is called the Acts of the Apostles. It is as if, from the outset, some people tried to keep the Spirit of Jesus a secret, and to make it the exclusive preserve of an elite few. Some chance! We know that the Spirit of Jesus is given to all, not just to the apostles. Influenced by the Spirit, we, too, can carry on building that new society.

Wounds

B24. Third Sunday of Easter

Acts 3:13-15, 17-19
1 John 2:1-5
Luke 24:35-48

A student from one of the better theological schools in the United States decided after his training to live with some impoverished people in the Andes of Peru. He became their pastor and remained there for some years. When he returned home for a well-deserved holiday, his former school invited him to speak to staff and students about his experiences. After much thought and deliberation, he agreed. When he was asked why he had taken so long to make up his mind, he began by emphasising his gratitude for the training he had received. His listeners knew that, somewhere along the line, there was a "but" waiting to happen.

He told them that he had learned a "resurrection" theology at the school, and that he had been very enthusiastic about it as a student. It was the kind of "alleluia" theology that fitted in so well in North America. And then the "but" came: "But", he said, "it is a theology that was no great help to me in the Andes, where people had difficulty in identifying themselves with the risen Lord."

The young man explained that he had especially become aware of this while celebrating Holy Week with them. On the days before Good Friday, the liturgical rules require the crucifix to be covered or taken away, but the people prevented him from doing that, because their devotion was directed almost exclusively at the cross. People came from far and wide to celebrate Good Friday, but at Easter hardly anyone turned up. He had been amazed the first time he saw the veneration of the cross on Good Friday. Many of those present had brought cotton wool and a carafe of oil with them. When it was their turn to venerate the cross, they dipped the cotton wool into the oil and used it to anoint the body of Jesus of the cross. Some took the cotton wool home afterwards, but others swallowed the greasy cotton wool immediately. To understand this more fully, the young priest kindly suggested, theologians would find it helpful to pay more attention to the suffering of the world's poor.

His story reminded me of a speech by a Polish woman at the World Council of Churches in Nairobi in 1975. She presented a series of slides of her country. One of them showed a picture of Jesus after his scourging, deeply exhausted and sitting on a rock. She explained that this picture can be found in the houses of poor Polish farmers who, after having worked on their land or the land of others, come home dead-beat and sit in front of that image to find the courage to go on.

In Luke's story, resurrection and suffering are interwoven. The risen Lord shows his wounded hands and feet to the disciples. Jesus' resurrection gives meaning not just to his own suffering and death, but also to our own. Following Jesus means facing up to the suffering of the world. We know that our hands and feet will be wounded, as his were. Those wounds will be unavoidable, because the life of Jesus goes against the grain of the life the world is living. It is a life that struggles to create a new, better, alternative world. This is the world Pope John Paul II champions with his call to celebrate the Great Jubilee. Out of the sufferings of this world, a new world will be resurrected.

Theologians who only think about Jesus' resurrection promulgate a very unbalanced view of Jesus, as do those who remember only his suffering. True hope comes from an appreciation of both, because each gives the other meaning.

The miracle
B25. Fourth Sunday of Easter

Acts 4:8-12
1 John 3:1-2
John 10:11-18

On their way to the Temple, Peter and John had healed a paralysed beggar at about three o'clock in the afternoon (Acts 3:1-10). The incident had caused a disturbance, and towards the evening the Temple guard and the priests decided to restore order. They arrested Peter and John and locked them up for the night. The next day we find them standing in front of the same judges who had condemned Jesus. In today's reading, Peter has just started his defence:

"If you are questioning us today about an act of kindness to a cripple, and asking us how he was healed, then I am glad to tell you all ... that it was by the name of Jesus Christ ... that this man is able to stand up perfectly healthy ..." (4:9-10).

In other translations, Peter speaks about the kindness that made him heal the beggar, and then explains that this kindness is due to Jesus. Peter seems to gloss over the physical healing of the paralysed man, but emphasises the new kindness that he has experienced and been able to share with the man – that is, the kindness and the love of Jesus Christ. Of course, the miracle is still central to the story, but there is another wonder that made that miracle possible. You see, Peter and John have been changed. The judges are amazed that these two educated, simple men could be so kind, courageous, and assured. They come to the conclusion that something must have happened to the two men in the presence of Jesus (4:13).

So there are two miracles: the physical miracle of the man who had never walked before in his whole life but who is suddenly leaping around, and the moral miracle of the change in Peter and John. Which of the two miracles is the most important?

Let us turn to another of Jesus' miracles: the feeding of the hungry crowd with the loaves and the fishes (John 6:1-15). That miracle, too, can be viewed as a physical miracle. Every time a piece of bread was broken off, a new piece replaced it; every time a fish was handed out, a new fish appeared in the basket.

But there is another possible explanation: Jesus asks whether anyone has any food with them, but only a small boy comes forward. It seems strange that only a young child would have been carrying food on such an occasion. Is it possible that the others were simply not answering, because they were afraid they would have to give up the food they had with them? They are so humbled and ashamed when Jesus presents them with boy's bread and fish that they open their hearts and are willing to share what they have so that all can be fed.

The second explanation presents the episode as a moral miracle. It is not the bread and fishes that change, but people's hearts. When you ask a normal group of Christians which explanation they prefer, the majority opt for the physical one. Is this because the second version makes us feel uncomfortable, particularly when we know that the cause of world hunger is not that there is insufficient food in the world, but that people are not willing to share the food they have with others?

To witness a physical miracle would, indeed, be astounding, but perhaps what the world needs most is the type of moral miracle about which Peter spoke. This is the moral miracle that occurs when we are in the presence of the Jesus.

Witness

B26. Fifth Sunday of Easter

Acts 9:26-31
1 John 3:18-24
John 15:1-8

In his famous book *The Brothers Karamazov* Fyodor Dostoyevsky lists the arguments against the Christian belief in a loving God. In a chapter called "Revolt", Ivan, one of the brothers, puts forward the most serious objection: how can a loving God allow people to inflict suffering and cruelty on innocent children? Ivan backs up his objection with some horrific stories. One of the most cruel is about a landowner whose dog has been crippled by a small child who accidentally hit it with a stone. While the boy's family looks on, the landowner has the boy stripped and then sets his dogs upon the frightened child, who is quickly devoured.

Ivan tells the stories to Aljosja, his pious and religious brother. Aljosja does not answer Ivan's arguments point by point. How can he, when he knows that the stories Ivan has told him are true. We, too, can recognise the type of story Ivan tells, because the newspapers are full of such horrific stories, whether they come out of conflict zones such as Rwanda or the former Yugoslavia, or from a few streets away in our own towns and cities. It is a genuinely difficult objection to argue against.

Perhaps that is why Aljosja does not bother. Instead, he takes another approach. He explains that the cruelties of this world are not the only stories we know about. There are also countless stories of compassion, sincere love, solidarity, fidelity, and forgiveness. Aljosja's response is simply to highlight that whole dimension of human life.

Indeed, Luke's descriptions of the first Christian communities are perfect examples from this "positive dimension". In today's reading from Acts, he tells us that the early churches were building themselves up "encouraged by the Holy Spirit". Wherever there is mutual love, support, and solidarity, there we will find something of God, of Jesus Christ, and of the kingdom of heaven. Luke does not say that those glimpses of the divine are exclusively present in Christian communities. He is only describing what he found there himself.

It is obvious that those experiences were something completely new to Luke, something he had never encountered before. It made quite an impression on him. As far as we know, Luke never met Jesus in person. He knew Jesus through those first Christian communities, and he experienced Jesus' love through the fellowship of those believers.

Surely that is still the best way of getting to know Jesus? We can meet with God in our prayers and in our sacramental life, and draw spiritual comfort and consolation from such activities. But if we are not in the right frame of mind or are feeling out of sorts, we are just as likely to be filled with feelings of our own emptiness as we are with the living presence of Jesus Christ. Neither is the experience of Jesus to be found in our endless discussions on theology or ecclesial discipline. The easiest way to meet Jesus Christ and his Spirit, and to experience the out-working of God's love, is through the fellowship of Christian communities like the ones Luke so enthusiastically describes in Acts.

Such Christian communities still flourish throughout the world today. The essence of Jesus is no more likely to be found in official meetings, discussion groups, and conventions than in the Christian networks and small communities that endeavour to heal the world, humanity, and themselves through living the risen life of Christ. Luke considers such groups and communities to be the artisans of the kingdom of God. They are the beginning of what Pierre Teilhard de Chardin called: "The wild hope that our world will be reshaped."

Powerful presence

B27. Sixth Sunday of Easter

Acts 10:25-26, 34-35, 44-48
1 John 4:7-10
John 15:9-17

It may well not have been Luke who gave his second book the title "Acts of the Apostles". In the world of books, it is actually quite common for the title of a work to be decided by someone other than the author – perhaps the publisher or maybe the marketing director. They will want to be sure that the title appeals to the people they want to buy the book.

Whatever the marketing view on it, "Acts of the Apostles" is not a very appropriate title, because it does not accurately describe the content. In the first place, Luke mentions many more women and men than just the twelve apostles. Scores of others are mentioned by name, and thousands more anonymous believers make up the Christian communities of which Luke speaks so highly.

In addition, the word "Acts" is too restrictive: the book is far more than a catalogue of what Jesus' disciples got up to. It also outlines a whole new dimension: life in the presence of the Holy Spirit. Again and again in Acts, people become aware of the power of the Holy Spirit within them – witness the dramatic experience of Cornelius and his family in today's reading. The Holy Spirit lives within each of us, but if we are not willing to be attentive to it, we will never truly be filled with its power, and it will have little influence on our lives.

As Christians, we tend to place much more emphasis on "acting" and "doing" than "being". We may well act in a morally commendable way, but unless we also concern ourselves with our inner being, we will not penetrate to the place where the Spirit lives within us.

In his book *In the Name of Jesus*, Henri Nouwen says that it is important to rediscover the mystical aspect of our theology, so that every word spoken, every piece of advice given, and every strategy developed really comes out of hearts that intimately know God. He adds that he thinks that so many of our discussions on the ordination of women, the marriage of priests, homosexuality, birth control, abortion, euthanasia, and so on, are restricted to the moral level. The different parties argue about what is good and what bad, but too often get embroiled in a struggle that is far removed from God's primary, unlimited, and unconditional love, which should be the basis of all human relations. We end up resorting to labels such as "right" and "left", or "reactionary", "conservative", and "liberal", which make our discussions seem more like political campaigns. What is needed is a spiritual investigation into which courses of action are in the true Spirit of Jesus.

Luke links the activities of the early Christian communities to their attentiveness to the presence of God. This is not to say that these communities are conflict-free. In fact, they argue about everything, from how to divide the food they give to the poor, to whether a pagan such as Cornelius should be circumcised before being baptised. Sometimes, the arguments become personal, such as when Paul refuses to travel any further with Mark.

According to Luke, they always solve their problems in the same way. They come together, they discuss, and they pray. Even after the most painful difference of opinions, they are still able to state: "It has been decided by the Holy Spirit and by ourselves ..." (Acts 15:28).

Together with the Spirit, they looked after one another and the community as a whole. Living in the presence of the Spirit made others decide that it was good to know them – something that could not be said of every church or Christian community today. If we do not discover God's Spirit within ourselves, rest assured that others will certainly not be able to!

Leaving things to us

B28. Ascension Day

Acts 1:1-11
Ephesians 1:17-23
Mark 16:15-20

Jesus stayed with the disciples for 40 days. They were glad to see him again, but something had obviously changed. In Mark's gospel, there is no mention of Jesus performing a single miracle during that time. So what did he do? Well, he talked with them, saying that he would give them the power to forgive one another and to chase away evil. He told them that they would be able to pick up snakes with their bare hands (snakes had always been a symbol of sin), and drink the deadly poison of an evil world without being harmed. He told them that he would send them the Holy Spirit. Apart from that, there was nothing new or spectacular until the 40th day, when they met with him on a hilltop just outside Bethany (Luke 24:50).

Once there, they asked the question that had been burning in their hearts for so long: "Lord, has the time come?" (Acts 1:6). Was Jesus going to restore the world now? I imagine that, even as they asked this, Jesus' feet were already beginning to leave the ground – just a tiny fraction. Perhaps they pressed him further: "When are you going to bring the salvation and redemption," – his feet were a bit higher by now – "the wholeness and the life, " – higher still – "the development and the kingdom that you promised, and for which we are still waiting?" By now, he was way above their heads.

The more insistent they became, the higher he rose. Eventually, he spoke: "Let us not speak about the time and date when all this will be fulfilled. Let us talk about how you – yes, you! – will become aware of the power of the Spirit within you; how you will proclaim the Good News, baptising all those who believe, chasing away evil and the devil, picking up snakes, laying on hands, and speaking in unknown languages. Go! It is now up to you – I am placing everything in your hands!" And he rose higher and higher until he disappeared from view.

How many of us self-proclaimed followers of Jesus are really willing and prepared to take up the task he left us? We live in a world that is full of "snakes", corruption, hunger, neglect, and deceit. Sometimes we even dare to use Jesus as an excuse for our inaction. "We are not of this world, alleluia! We are washed in his blood and redeemed!" we say, and we praise God, distribute our Bibles, and contribute to church collections. Blessing the world in our prayers, we close our eyes, ears, hands, and mouths to the problems of the world. Comfortable in our salvation, we focus resolutely on the one sitting at the right hand of God the Father, and we refuse to be distracted by secular troubles.

On the day we celebrate Jesus' ascension, we should take time to consider what Christ is actually doing at the right of the Father. In Hebrews 10:13, we read:

"He ... has offered one single sacrifice for sins, and then taken his place for ever at the right hand of God, where he is now waiting until his enemies are made into a footstool for him."

Jesus is waiting – waiting for us to fulfil his mission in the world. We cannot be passive and inactive when confronted by the suffering and corruption around us. We are the salt, the yeast, and the light that Jesus left in the world. So often we wait for Jesus to do something about the world, while in reality he is waiting for us to take the initiative!

Apostolic succession

B29. Seventh Sunday of Easter

Acts 1:15-17, 20-26
1 John 4:11-16
John 17:11-19

The text from the Acts of the Apostles we are reading today is an important one, because it deals with the apostolic succession. There is an apocryphal story of how the prime minister of a European country visited by Pope John Paul II asks the Pope why women cannot be ordained as priests. The Pope allegedly answers, "There were no women at the Last Supper, were there?" to which his host responds: "But there were no Poles at the Last Supper either"! In a frivolous way, this anecdote raises a serious issue. What are the norms, standards, and criteria that we should apply when we consider such serious theological issues? What is the proper "Christian" way of making decisions?

Our text makes it clear how the apostles went about deciding who should replace Judas Iscariot as one of the Twelve. It was really very simple: after having considered the personal attributes of the possible candidates, they nominated two, then they prayed, and finally they drew lots. Luke presents norms and criteria that remain timeless and permanently valid. Christians in every age are asked to consult holy scripture when trying to discern God's will. We are also asked to take the personal qualities of different candidates into account when trying to choose between them. Above all, we are told to pray. Ultimately, we should leave the final decision to God.

Obviously, nowadays it would not be considered acceptable to draw lots to decide such an issue. It is a procedure we no longer use to elect a pope, bishop, or priest. There are also other criteria that were used in those early days that would not be relevant any more. It is not surprising, because none of us knew Jesus during his lifetime or witnessed his resurrection. The details of the methods of decision-making are bound to have changed, but the principles remain the same: consulting scripture; prayer; genuine, unbiased consideration; and trying to discern God's will.

Certainly, we have to be careful when we apply the norms, standards, and criteria from those days to the Church today, because they will undoubtedly raise questions that are difficult to answer. For example, take the question of mandatory celibacy for priests. How are we to respond to the fact that Peter was married? And how do we respond to Paul's text of 1 Corinthians 9:4-5: "Have we not every right ... to be accompanied by a Christian wife, like the other apostles and the brothers of the Lord and Cephas?"

Too often in the past, biblical texts were simply manipulated in order to justify a particular theological position. In the translation used in the liturgy, the two candidates Joseph (known as Barsabas) and Matthias are nominated by the eleven. The verb to choose or nominate is in its plural form: estesan. In another version of the same text (a newer version than the one we use) the verb occurs in the singular, estesen, showing that the two were selected by one person – that is, by Peter. This minor, but significant change suggests a development in ecclesial thinking. It indicates a "monarchistic" trend in the thinking of the church leadership and in their understanding of the apostolic succession. One wonders whether it was a trend embarked upon after following the timeless criteria laid down by Luke?

Fullness

B30. Pentecost

Acts 2:1-11

1 Corinthians 12: 3-7, 12-13

John 20:19-23

Time is a strange thing. We do not need a philosopher like Immanuel Kant to tell us that – we know it intuitively. The riddle of time puzzled Saint Augustine just as much as it did the great physicist and mathematician Albert Einstein. The world's different languages show us that time is something perceived differently from age to age and from culture to culture. For example, European languages distinguish between a present, a past, and a future, but some native North American languages do not make that distinction. John Mbiti, a theologian from Kamba country in Kenya, once explained to me that his traditional language presents the future very differently from Western languages. In his linguistic tradition, the future is seen as a return to the past.

As we approach the year 2000, film and television screens are awash with science fiction tales that play on the mysterious nature of time, and the fascinating prospect of time travel. The "time warp" is a popular scenario, in which there is a temporary interruption or distortion of the normal flow of time. Past, present, and future become balanced in such a way that you cannot distinguish between them. Scientists even tell us that such a criss-crossing of the barriers of time may be possible through "worm holes" in space-time.

In today's reading from Acts, we find the disciples in a kind of time warp. They are sitting in the upper room in Jerusalem waiting for something that had already happened. The Holy Spirit – the Spirit of God and the Spirit of Jesus – is already present in their lives, and yet at the same time they seem to lack that presence. It is a curious situation: they are waiting to be made actively aware of something they have already experienced. The Spirit of Jesus is with them, although that Spirit is not yet being expressed in their lives.

In the gospel text for today, Jesus blows his Spirit into them 50 days before Pentecost. Even though the Spirit had been blown into them, 50 days later the book of Acts shows them sitting there at Pentecost waiting to receive that same Spirit. This tension between "already" and "not yet" is a tension we should acknowledge and celebrate in our own lives. The Spirit of Jesus is in us, and at the same time we still have to grow into the fullness of the Spirit. It is the same with the kingdom of God, which is with us and yet has not yet been fully realised (see B13: Your kingdom come!).

This tension is the answer to the question of whether our belief in the salvation of humanity is not horrendously naive. If the kingdom of God has already been accomplished, how can we possibly explain Holocaust, the war in the Middle East, the horrors of the ethnic conflict in Rwanda, the atrocities committed in the former Yugoslavia, two world wars and the atomic bombs dropped on Nagasaki and Hiroshima. The list is endless – we can all think of things to add to it.

Jesus explained the dilemma using parables and metaphors. The reign of God – the Spirit in us – is like a seed that has to grow; like yeast that has still to enliven the dough; like a treasure that has been discovered, but still has to be dug out of the ground. The Holy Spirit and the kingdom of God have been given to us, but they have to grow to maturity within us. We should welcome the prospect, and celebrate that process.

Everyone
B31. Trinity Sunday

Deuteronomy 4:32-34, 39-40
Romans 8:14-17
Matthew 28:16-20

Matthew's gospel ends with the baptismal formula of the Father, Son, and Holy Spirit. Jesus names the three persons of God intentionally. He wants to say something not only about God, but also about all those who are going to be baptised. He is making the point that anyone who is baptised is entitled to call God "Father".

To this stirring truth, Jesus attaches the command that we must announce to all nations the Good News that everyone is of divine origin, that everyone is defined as a child of God, and that everyone finds in that truth the foundation of his or her human rights.

This is not a widely accepted truth in the world, as racial hatred, political and religious persecution, and ethnic rivalry testify. We often lapse into the mentality that certain groups or types of people – especially those we consider to be different from ourselves – do not "count" in the same way that we do. In the realm of news reporting, this is true in a literal sense. During and after the US invasion of Panama some years ago, the American news services knew exactly how many Americans died in the brief conflict. However, the number of Panamanians who lost their lives is still unreported, and therefore unknown. From the perspective of the American reporters, the Panamanians simply did not count. They did not matter to the reporters' audience.

All of us are formed in the same way from the heart, hands, and Spirit of God. That is what the word "Father" indicates. It is because people have overlooked this truth that we have done so much evil to each other during this century. It is the lack of belief in our fundamental nature that is the killer.

Returning to the baptismal formula, the term "Son" refers to Jesus. John writes in his gospel that everything that exists was created through the Son (John 1:3). It is a second way in which the whole of humanity (and in fact the whole of creation) finds its unity and common origin in the persons of God. We are created together, and together we form God's offspring. Only when we truly understand and accept what this means will we be able to understand our obligations and responsibilities towards each other, towards the animal kingdom, and towards the environment.

Finally, there is the Holy Spirit, who gives life to all. The Holy Spirit is the dynamic breath of God that lives and works in everyone and everything. It is the same Spirit that has been blown by God into human beings from the very beginning (Genesis 2:7), and that is manifested in Jesus. We pray repeatedly during our Eucharistic celebrations to be filled with the Holy Spirit so that we may become one in body and spirit. The Holy Spirit connects us all to each other, and to the created world around us.

It is no wonder that Jesus, in mentioning those names – Father, Son and Holy Spirit – adds an assignment for his followers. He asks us not only to proclaim this truth to the peoples of the world, but also to live it out in our day-to-day lives.

Celebrating the Blessed Trinity is about celebrating God. It is also about celebrating our common divine origin, as one collective offspring of God with one shared life in the Holy Spirit.

Flowers
B32. Corpus Christi

Exodus 24:3-8

Hebrews 9:11-15

Mark 14:12-16, 22-26

Today we celebrate Corpus Christi, the body and blood of Jesus Christ. In many churches the tabernacle will be surrounded by flowers, lovingly arranged by devout believers. Some people, however, do not think flowers are appropriate for such an occasion. They have nothing against flowers, as such; it is just that we traditionally give flowers as objects of comfort when people go through bad times. Even those of us who have never received flowers before will get them when we are seriously sick, and we are certain to get many more when we die. People who never bothered to look at a flower during their whole existence are suddenly buried under them – almost literally! – when they are dead.

Mark may well have disapproved of those flowers around the altar. As is often the case, Mark's description and interpretation of the Last Supper differs from the ones to which we are accustomed. We do not find Jesus instituting the Eucharist as a personal memorial – there is no mention of Jesus saying, "Do this as a memorial of me", as we find in Luke (Luke 22:19). Neither does Mark's last Supper ask us to look back to the past when we share in the Eucharist. Rather, it compels us to look forward. Jesus tells us that this will be his last cup of wine until the kingdom of God is realised (Mark 14:25). It is a remark that expresses

Jesus' expectation and sure knowledge that the kingdom of God will be realised in the future.

The whole evening starts off as a normal Passover meal. The two disciples go to the upper room, as instructed by Jesus, and make all the usual preparations, as they must have done so many times before. They think they know what to expect from this familiar occasion. However, as the evening unfolds, it turns out to be anything but a normal Passover meal. When Jesus breaks the bread during the meal and passes the wine round the table, he does not recite the usual words that would remind those present of their people's past – the misery of forced labour in Egypt, the sacrifice of the lambs to escape Yahweh's wrath, and the drama of the Exodus. Instead, Jesus uses words that give the occasion a new meaning and point the way to the future.

During the Passover meal, Jesus calls the bread "my body", and explains that the wine symbolises his blood, which he is willing to shed to establish a new covenant between God and humanity. At this point, Jesus is not really concerned with celebrating the Passover meal. Mark does not even tell us whether they eat the slaughtered lamb. It is irrelevant, because here something new is beginning: a new covenant and a new ritual – the ritual of someone who gives his life "for many" (14:24).

Jesus changes the memorial of a past event into the initiation of a programme for the future. At the Passover meal, he asks his disciples to eat bread and drink wine with him. Everyone at the table does just that (14:23). Although they later desert him, they all – with the exception of Judas – commit themselves to working for the realisation of God's kingdom. It is the same commitment we make when we partake in his body and blood in today's celebration of Corpus Christi.

By all means surround the altar with beautiful flowers, but do so in celebration, rather than in memoriam. And make sure that those flowers do not obscure the real issue – the body and blood of Jesus Christ.

Christology

B33. Second Sunday of the year

1 Samuel 3:3-10, 19
1 Corinthians 6:13-15, 17-20
John 1:35-42

In this year of the B-cycle, the first year of the final preparations for the Great Jubilee dedicated to Jesus Christ in the year 2000, the gospel readings are generally taken from Mark. There are some exceptions to this. The Mark cycle is interrupted by two sets of readings from John's gospel. It is interesting that John's gospel was not given its own liturgical cycle like the other gospels. Why did church leaders decide to have three liturgical cycles, and not four so they could include John's gospel as well?

The reason may well have been the special nature of John's gospel. If we only had John's account to follow throughout the year, we would miss out on many important elements of Jesus' life. For example, we would not only miss the Sermon on the Mount, but also almost all the parables. We would not know Jesus as the travelling teacher described by Mark, Luke, and Matthew. We would have no idea of the contacts Jesus had on those "safaris" with the ordinary people he came across. We would have a Jesus who mainly gives long talks and discusses difficult issues in a rather abstract way. John attributes to Jesus characteristics the other gospels hardly seem to recognise.

Even the synoptic gospels have their own difficulties. Mark, Matthew, and Luke all try to show that there is more to Jesus than meets the eye. All three want to show that there is something in Jesus that transcends our normal, everyday existence. Yet that "extra" element they discover in Jesus is never defined in concrete terms, and seems to be left hanging in the air, as if the true nature of Jesus will only be revealed in the future.

John solves the issues in another way. His approach is to begin the prologue to his gospel by speaking about the pre-existence of Jesus: "In the beginning was the Word; the Word was with God, and the Word was God. He was with God in the beginning" (1:1-2). John starts his narrative in virtually the same way, with John the Baptist saying of Jesus: "Look, there is the lamb of God ... This is the one I spoke of when I said: a man is coming after me who ranks before me because he existed before me" (1:29-30).

But John's approach also has its disadvantages. When you stress Jesus' divine origin to such an extent, you risk underestimating his humanity. John McKenzie (*The New Testament Without Illusion*, 1980) thinks that this is the reason John stresses more than other gospel writers that Jesus really did die on the cross. John is the only one who offers proof, telling how the Roman soldier pierced the heart of Jesus.

All gospel authors face the same problem: how do you describe Jesus in our inadequate human language in a way that expresses the whole truth about him. John tries to do it in a slightly different way from Matthew, Mark, and Luke, but none of them fully succeeds. That is why it is good to let the different stories interrupt each other now again, so that we get a fuller flavour and a more rounded picture of the character of Jesus.

Fishers of men

B34. Third Sunday of the year

Jonah 3:1-5, 10

1 Corinthians 7:29-31

Mark 1:14-20

If we look at the context of today's gospel reading, we might be surprised that Jesus – having dramatically and urgently proclaimed, "The time has come ... and the kingdom of God is close at hand. Repent, and believe the Good News" – then went for a walk on the shore of the Sea of Galilee, where he talked to some fishermen casting a net. It is all a bit of an anti-climax, and rather strange that Jesus, seemingly on the spur of the moment, turned those fishermen into evangelists.

In that time, with Israel under Roman occupation, there were any number of "disciples" waiting for a new master to follow who would give them hope of change. Jesus, however, "hand picked" his followers for a specific task. He told them that he would make them "fishers of men". It is a phrase we often associate with missionaries trained in the art of sharing the Gospel.

Some Bible commentators, such as Ched Myers (*Binding the Strong Man: A Political Reading of Mark's Story of Jesus*, 1988), prefer another reading. To Myers, Jesus is picking up on the imagery of fish and fishing used by the Old Testament prophets. Jeremiah, for example, writes how the fishermen of Yahweh will sift out of those who are unjust and godless (Jeremiah 16:16). Then there is Ezekiel, who foretells how the rich and powerful will be caught with hooks through their jaws (Ezekiel 29:4), while Amos strengthens that metaphor when he adds that those exploiting the poor will be caught and dragged away by fish-hooks (Amos 4:2).

The fishermen Jesus met – Simon, Andrew, James, and John – were hardly impoverished. Admittedly, they were not powerful traders or merchants, but the business of Zebedee (the father of James and John) was large enough to employ not only his family, but also some additional labourers. Jesus called these two pairs of brothers to leave behind the security of their income and family and follow him.

Jesus asked the four to give up their past lives because something new and marvellous was about to begin. An end had come to the old world, and a new world – the kingdom of God – was beginning to take root. All the negative elements of the old world had to be dragged out on fish-hooks, hauled up in nets, and left behind. That was the task Jesus gave to those fishermen.

In the new world of the kingdom of God, even familiar terms like and "fisherman" gained a new significance – although perhaps it was not so new after all, as the prophets had foreseen this long before. That is, after all, what prophets are for!

Authority

B35. Fourth Sunday of the year

Deuteronomy 18:15-20
1 Corinthians 7:32-35
Mark 1:21-28

Mark's stories are concise and well constructed. It is as though he builds a stage on which his characters can perform, and then carefully dismantles it. Unfortunately, the liturgists who chose our Sunday readings from Mark's gospel obviously did not fully appreciate his talent, because they often cut pieces off his stories.

Mark begins his account of Jesus' appearance in the synagogue of Capernaum by using the Greek word eiselthon (Mark 1:21), which tells us not only that he entered the synagogue, but also that he did so in a solemn manner. When Mark ends his story, he uses the Greek word exelthontes to explain that Jesus also left the synagogue solemnly (1:29). It is this solemn departure that has been cut from today's reading, and yet it is a vital part of the story, because it is a sign that something very important has happened. Jesus entered a holy place, the synagogue, on a holy day, the Sabbath, and he left it changed once and for all by a gesture and a few words. He ended the domination of holy places by priests and scribes.

Mark uses the technique of repetition to emphasise the importance of key issues. The word "teach", for example, occurs three times in the space of a couple of lines: "he began to teach" (1:21), "his teaching made a deep impression" and "he taught them with authority (both 1:22). Jesus entered the synagogue very solemnly and determinedly, and – to the consternation and surprise of those present – he began to teach.

To understand what is happening here, think of some of the overseas visits Pope John Paul II has made in recent years. Think, especially, of the occasions when the status of the Pope as our sacred teacher was undermined by people who did not keep to the official, agreed text of their speeches, but instead used the opportunity to make their own, uncensored statements.

I witnessed a similar event at a meeting in Kenya's Maasai region.

Some government officials, including a minister, had been addressing a crowd of people for some time. Suddenly, a Maasai warrior in full dress stood up and interrupted, telling the crowd that he was tired of listening and that it was now his turn to speak. Everyone turned to him, but the minister gave a sign and, quick as a flash, the security police grabbed the man and removed him from the scene before he had reached the end of his first sentence. The minister understood only too well that his authority was at stake.

The people in the synagogue were surprised by the fact that Jesus began to teach, but even more so by the way in which he taught. He was so different from the scribes, their usual teachers. You always knew that they would come out with the same old compromised party line. Jesus, however, spoke differently and with a new authority. Again, Mark gives emphasis to the word "authority" by repeating it.

Jesus was then confronted with a man possessed by an evil spirit. The spirit challenged Jesus: "What do you want with us, Jesus of Nazareth?" as if taunting him about his lowly origins and trying to put Jesus in his place. But the challenge turned to fear, and he asked, "Have you come to destroy us?" Jesus cast out the spirit, astonishing his onlookers.

By demonstrating his own authority, Jesus undermined the authority of the scribes, and by casting out the evil spirit, he threw down the gauntlet to the spiritual ruler of this world. Conflict was inevitable.

Healing

B36. Fifth Sunday of the year

Job 7:1-4, 6-7
1 Corinthians 9: 6-19, 22-23
Mark 1:29-39

When Jesus, James, and John arrive at Simon's house, they hear that Simon's mother-in-law is sick with fever. Jesus goes to her, takes her by the hand, and helps her up. Her fever leaves her immediately. It is such a dramatic recovery that she at once begins to prepare something for them to eat!

The news of that healing spreads like wildfire through Capernaum. As it is still the Sabbath, the people have to wait until sunset before they can come to see Jesus, but by early evening it seems as if the whole town is gathering at the house, bringing with them the sick, diseased, and mentally disturbed members of their families. Jesus heals them as many as he can, but clearly some will have to return tomorrow. In the early hours of the next morning, a new crowd assembles in front of Simon's house, but Jesus is no longer there. Without telling anyone, he left the house in the middle of the night to find a quiet place to pray.

Confronted by the crowd, and with no sign of Jesus, Simon and his companions set out find him. When they eventually catch up with Jesus, he explains that he is not going back to heal the people at Simon's door. He must move on elsewhere, because he is being distracted from his real task. Jesus' healing powers are causing him a crisis of conscience: the sick need to be healed, but should he let himself be diverted from his real mission of preaching the kingdom of God?

I once heard of a congregation of sisters who set up a hospital in an East African country. Every morning there were long lines of sick people waiting at the hospital doors. The staff treated as many as they could each day, but they could never treat them all. No matter how many they treated, more seemed to return the next day.

The doctors and nurses in the hospital began to feel they were fighting a losing battle. They knew that they were successfully healing people and that their medicines worked well, especially because their patients never had any antibiotics before. However, it slowly dawned upon them that they would never make any progress until they tackled the real reason so many people were falling ill. It turned out that most of their patients were sick because, in their poverty, they lacked a balanced diet and had to drink polluted water.

Some of the staff wondered whether it might not be better to close the hospital temporarily and put all their efforts into trying to do something about the root cause of their patients' illnesses. Others proposed that the hospital should devote some of its resources to setting up programmes of health education and preventive medicine, so that people could begin to help themselves. The decision to move resources away from the immediate treatment of the sick into education and preventive health-care caused much heart-searching. Throughout the world, health-care resources are under increasing pressure, and the issue of how to allocate these resources is always a difficult one.

It is impossible to know what exactly went on in Jesus' heart that night but, in not returning the next morning to carry on healing, Jesus made it clear that the healing he had come to bring to the world was ultimately to be found elsewhere – that is, in the kingdom of God, which Jesus had come to preach, and which would change our world forever.

Keep it a secret

B37. Sixth Sunday of the year

Leviticus 13:1-2, 44-46

1 Corinthians 10:31-11:1

Mark 1:40-45

A leper approaches Jesus and falls on his knees. With his right hand over his mouth, he pleads, "If you want to, you can cure me!" Jesus looks at him as a brother would. As the tears well up in his eyes, Jesus replies, "Of course, I want to! Be cured!" Having learned from earlier miracles that such a dramatic healing might lead to misunderstandings, crowds, and possibly even riots (see B36: Healing and B25: The miracle) Jesus asks the man not to tell anyone except the priests, from whom he needs to get a certificate of good health.

Unfortunately, the healed man does exactly the opposite of what Jesus asks: he tells not only told the priests, but also every single person he comes across! Suddenly, Jesus is surrounded by a great throng of people, all looking for a quick cure. If we could see that crowd today, I am sure that many doctors and nurses would recognise some of their patients among them, especially those who readily come to the surgery for treatment and medicines, and yet refuse to change their harmful lifestyles or moderate the eating, drinking, and smoking habits that cause their sicknesses.

We tend to react to the world's problems in a similar fashion. We are only too ready to engage in heated debates about how we can redistribute the world's resources, assist the poor, rehabilitate alcoholics and drug addicts, provide shelter for the homeless and a new start for refugees, and how we can resolve age-old conflicts. One meeting leads to another, churning out endless papers and reports. Yet nothing concrete is ever achieved. It all remains very superficial and barely scratches the surface of the problem, because we are fundamentally unwilling to make changes to our own lives in order to change the world.

In effect, Jesus says to the leper: "Of course I am willing to heal you, but make sure you don't tell anyone about it. Keep it a secret, because it is not the main focus of my mission – I have far more important work to do. If you go round telling everyone about your miracle, people will get a wrong impression of why I am here." But the man could not keep his mouth shut. He had not really been changed inside by his physical healing. Just as Jesus had feared, the crowd emerged as if from nowhere, clamouring to be cured of their illnesses and diseases.

Even today, we still approach Jesus in that way. We go to him for the easy solution or the quick fix, craving his healing hand. But, inside, we are unwilling to listen to what he tells us about the changes and conversions we have to make to our own lives in order to heal the world and realise the kingdom of God.

The Jesus threat

B38. Seventh Sunday of the year

Isaiah 43:18-19, 21-22, 24-25
2 Corinthians 1:18-22
Mark 2:1-12

Jesus was back in Capernaum. He was home. Once again, the people came from all around to see him. This time he was teaching rather than healing them. He explained to them what he thought about the world, God, the Temple, and humanity. However, some scribes and other listeners in his audience did not agree with him. They saw him as a threat – a danger to the status quo. Each time he seemed to contradict their traditions they tried to interrupt him.

It was as if he were using a completely new language to talk about God and speaking with a new kind of authority. Where did he get this authority from? How could the priests and scribes tolerate this from a common lay person? They could not possibly allow him to continue.

When he was not attacking them and the Temple policies directly, he was outlining new, radical ideas that might start people questioning their authority. So they tried to ridicule him and catch him out, hoping to undo his influence and kill the hope of change he engendered in his followers.

While Jesus was teaching, he was not healing. Some people in the crowd became impatient with all the theological talk, because they had come to get their sick companions healed. The four men who had carried their paralysed friend to the house finally decided they had to act. They climbed onto the roof and opened it. Without any hesitation, they lowered their friend through the roof, right in front of Jesus. The conversation stopped abruptly. There was nothing to be heard except for the sound of jaws dropping. Everyone gazed intently at the man lying on the stretcher dressed in rags. His two penetrating eyes implored Jesus to help him, to lift him out of his old world and into a new one.

Jesus looked at the man and granted him his wish: "My child, your sins are forgiven!" Suddenly there was a commotion among the priests and scribes surrounding Jesus. They were furious and outraged! If Jesus could forgive sins, what would remain of their status and their power, not to mention the atonement sacrifices in the Temple, which proved so lucrative a sideline? Surely, this was all just vain, empty words – an unforgivable, arrogant, and blasphemous hoax to increase his own standing?

Jesus looked at the religious figures gathered there. I imagine that he smiled at them. He knew their thoughts and how they would react, so he said: "Why do you have these thoughts in your hearts? Which of these is easier: to say to the paralytic, 'Your sins are forgiven,' or to say, 'Get up, pick up your stretcher and walk'? But to prove to you that the Son of man has authority on Earth to forgive sins ..." he paused, turning to the paralytic, "I order you: get up, pick up your stretcher, and go off home."

To the anger of the scribes and the wild joy of the crowd, the man got up from his stretcher and walked away. The scribes were stunned. They had made the mistake of underestimating Jesus, and now everything had changed. The established order – the order that they represented – suddenly collapsed there before their very eyes. Something would have to be done about this man ....

We are the bride

B39. Eighth Sunday of the year

Hosea 2:16-17, 21-22
2 Corinthians 3:1-6
Mark 2:18-22

It was a simple question: "Why is it that John's disciples and the disciples of the Pharisees fast, but your disciples do not?" However, Jesus' answer was far from simple. He compared himself to a bridegroom preparing for his marriage, adding that the disciples were like the guests at the wedding. He was effectively saying, "I, Jesus, will marry you, the whole of humanity. My friends, the disciples, will be my witnesses, so they can't fast until after the wedding feast."

This probably would not have sounded quite so bizarre to the ears of Jesus' contemporaries, who would have remembered the words of Yahweh spoken by the prophet Hosea: "I am going to lure her [humanity] and lead her out into the wilderness and speak to her heart ... I will betroth you [humanity] to myself for ever, betroth you with integrity and justice, with tenderness and love; I will betroth you to myself with faithfulness, and you will come to know Yahweh." It is difficult to get our modern minds around such a mystical, romantic, poetic, daring passage.

Jesus' concept of the human family was obviously very different from our own. For most of us, the day-to-day world in which we live is the only one that exists. Our blinkered eyes cannot see that there might be more to life. Although we think we are self-sufficient, we have merely become one-dimensional. We believe only in what our senses tell us – what our eyes, ears, noses, fingers, and tongues can detect in the world around us.

Even in prayer we are one-dimensional: we ask for our material wants to be provided for, we ask to be healed here in this world rather than in the next, and we pray that we may spin out our days on Earth for as long as possible. In fact, we differ very little from the people who petitioned Jesus: "Please, stop my bleeding," pleaded one woman; "Heal my son," begged another; "Take my sickness away," asked a leper; and "Please, return Lazarus to us," asked Martha and Mary.

Our preoccupation with this world leads many Christians to think that the resurrection simply means that we will continue to live as we do now for all eternity. They forget that Jesus did not arise, like Lazarus, to return to his old life. Jesus rose to a new, glorified life. Surely that is good news? Who could honestly say, with their hand on their heart, that they would really like to live the way they do now for ever more?

There is a nice old story about a monastery where the monks were unable to die, but simply grew older and older. Tired of their endless existence, the monks began to pray for their own deaths. One night, the abbot had a dream in which it was revealed to him that the gate used by the angels to come to and from heaven was right above their monastery. In effect, the monastery, which the angels used as a sort of entrance lobby, had become part of heaven. He realised that this was why the monks never died. The abbot related the dream to monks. They decided to demolish the monastery and rebuild it several miles away. As soon as they had done so, the ancient monks began to die – and they were very, very happy.

Like those monks, we should look forward to a life beyond this world. We should not restrict ourselves to the here and now, because of the new life to come, here and later.

Unhealthy rites
B40. Ninth Sunday of the year

Deuteronomy 5:12-15
2 Corinthians 4:6-11
Mark 2:23-3:6

The presbytery telephone rings late in the evening. An anxious voice asks: "Father, do you have a Mass intention for this Sunday?" "Yes, I have one already. I'm sorry," replies the priest. "But Father," the voice implores, "can't you change it? It's the anniversary of my dad's death and we always have a Mass said for him on that day – for the last 20 years in fact. This year we forgot to arrange it, but it would be terrible if we couldn't have one ...." The fear and panic in the voice on the other end of the line are almost tangible. She seems convinced that if a Mass is not said for her father something awful will happen. It is as if she is worried that he might return from the grave to take revenge.

It sounds laughable that people can become obsessively superstitious like that. However, most of us would probably admit that we, too, sometimes lapse into little customs, rites, gestures, and "magic" words to keep the world around us under control. We say little prayers, touch wood, throw salt over our shoulder, or light a candle to ward off ill fortune. We all feel the urge to keep the world, other people, and even God in check.

The Pharisees were the same. They were religious purists who insisted that the Law and traditions should be adhered to in every exact detail. They faithfully obeyed hundreds of rules, customs, and restrictions, such as ritual washing, combing their hair in a special way, saying their prayers aloud, forbidding the picking of grain on the Sabbath, and so on. All this, they felt, helped them to keep a firm hold on their religion, their culture, their people, and their history – and, ultimately, on God, too. They believed God could only be known and pleased by observing to the letter their religious practices.

Jesus did not dispute the importance of observing the Law, scripture, or religious duties, but he did react against the way the Pharisees put ritual observance before mercy and love. He contested the way their legalistic attitudes restricted God's grace and goodness.

Even today we try to get God on our side through our self-assumed piety, usually to justify our wrongful actions. When we say, "God is with us," we often mean it divisively, implying that God is not with our opponents. When the "pious" say "God is with us," they infer that God is not with "sinners", an attitude that through the ages has resulted in the burning of witches and heretics, the hatred of prostitutes, the torture of political opponents, and the execution of criminals. For decades, the God-is-with-us-but-not-with-you mentality was used to rationalise apartheid policy in South Africa, while the German Nazis quoted the Bible to justify their persecution of the Jews.

In today's gospel, Jesus turns against all the religious practices and attitudes that limit God's love and goodness by dividing people or encouraging them to be fearful and worried. There is no need to worry or fear, because God's grace and mercy overrule every law and rite.

Never let such things restrict your own love and mercy towards others, or make you overlook Jesus' only command to us: to love one another and to break bread with each other.

Slander of the Spirit

B41. Tenth Sunday of the year

Genesis 3:9-15

2 Corinthians 4:13-5:1

Mark 3:20-35

Jesus goes home to get some privacy, but does not succeed. The crowd that gathers is so great that he cannot even get to the table to eat! Then his family, having heard a rumour that he is out of his mind, try to drag him away from all this before it is too late. Their fear is understandable, because he is being watched closely by the scribes – the agents of the religious authorities in Jerusalem who are out to put an end to his activities, and are even plotting to liquidate him (Mark 3:6).

They accuse him of being possessed by the devil. Such an accusation may seem old fashioned, but it is not. Faced with a threat to its power-base, a ruling class – whether it is religious, economic, or political in nature – usually responds by demonising its opponents. The ruling class identifies itself with God; consequently everyone who opposes it must be of the devil. In the recent past, US presidents have been willing to describe communist and some Muslim leaders as "demons". Saddam Hussein spoke in the same terms about the Americans and their allies. It is the simplest way of dividing the world: people are labelled as being either for or against God – there is no middle ground.

The scribes from Jerusalem considered that they were the proper representatives of God, and that Jesus must therefore be from the devil. Jesus takes up their argument and says (to paraphrase): "Do you not see how I cast out evil spirits, liberate people, and heal the sick? If I am from the devil, how is it that I fight against the devil? If Satan were fighting against himself in this way, then his kingdom would already be at an end."

Describing his role as one who is fighting against the devil, Jesus adds: "No one steals the property from a strong man's house without first tying up the strong man." That is what Jesus came to do. He enters like a thief in the night to bind Satan and steal us back from the ruler of this world (Matthew 24:43).

From defending himself, Jesus then goes on the attack. He claims that, from now on, all sins will be forgiven – even blasphemies. With this, he pulls the rug from under the scribes' feet, because if forgiveness of sins no longer comes through religious obligations, services, and offerings, then the priests and scribes will no longer be able to profit from people's weakness and guilt. Such a move would shake the foundations of their religious structures (see B38: The Jesus threat).

But there is more to come. Jesus is obviously offended by the accusation that, as Mark puts it, "He has Beelzebul in him." Jesus will not allow them to slander him, so he turns on them and adds: "But anyone who blasphemes the Holy Spirit will never be forgiven, because this is an eternal sin."

It is obvious from the dynamics of the quarrel that this last remark is aimed directly at his at his opponents. They are the ones who blaspheme against the Holy Spirit, because they refuse to welcome the human liberation and emancipation Jesus seeks to bring about. They see such things as direct threats to their position and income. It is a familiar scenario: the old order trying to snuff out the first flickering flames of positive change as soon as it gets the chance.

After this incident, Jesus' family makes another attempt to reclaim him. It does not work, because God's will still has to be done.

Earthly power
B42. Eleventh Sunday of the year

Ezekiel 17:22-24
2 Corinthians 5: 6-10
Mark 4: 26-34

Today's gospel reading concerns sowing seeds, seeds germinating, plants reaching maturity and being harvested, and fully grown trees offering shelter and shade to wildlife. There is also another seed story at the beginning of this fourth chapter of Mark's gospel (verses 1-9). It is the story about the farmer who goes out to sow, and how the seed he sows gets scattered over the road, rocky ground, among thorns, and into the good earth. Jesus is certainly following a theme here, but what it is all about? Even the apostles asked him for an explanation.

Thus, we have three parables about sowing seed. Bible translations, understandably, usually give them titles that include either one or both words, for example: "Parable of the sower", "Parable of the seed growing by itself", and "Parable of the mustard seed". Most commentators assume that the seed is the key element in these parables.

That may be true of the seed parables that appear in the gospels by Matthew and Luke, but it is not so in Mark's gospel. Mark makes the earth his focus. Mary Ann Tolbert (*Sowing the Gospel*, 1989), points out that the three stories in Mark are not "seed" but "earth" parables. The seed obviously remains significant, because it represents the word of Jesus that is sown among us. But in Mark, it is not the sowing that is stressed, but the receiving of the seed by the earth, and the earth represents us – that is, humanity.

The earth has to receive the seed, meaning that we have to listen to the word of Jesus. If we listen, then the word will bring forth fruit in our lives. Something that has until now been hidden will then be revealed. The word of Jesus Christ working within us will show us who we really are.

Without the earth, the seed would remain powerless; without the seed, the earth would never be aware of its own potency. That latent power may still be thwarted or blocked in a number of ways once the seed has been sown. The seed is just a catalyst that unlocks the potency of the earth, helping the earth to bring forth fruit. When we begin to listen to the word, the full God-given potential hidden within us begins to be fulfilled.

Jesus' parables about the seed and the earth deal with the interaction between ourselves and his word. The process Jesus describes is one of revelation and disclosure, rather than of complete change. You reach the same conclusion when you study another of the metaphors used in the gospels: light. It is in the light of Jesus that we discover our true selves. It is a point Pope John Paul II often makes in his encyclicals leading up to the Great Jubilee. Looking at Jesus, we see ourselves as in a mirror. Light does not fundamentally change a darkened room, it merely shows what is already there, hidden in the shadows.

The earth-seed and light metaphors show us that we can only become the human beings God intended us to be when our true potential is illuminated by the light of Christ, and when the word of Jesus sown in the earth of our hearts enables that potential to grow.

The other side
B43. Twelfth Sunday of the year

Job 3:1, 8-11
2 Corinthians 5:14-17
Mark 4:35-41

Slicing Mark's gospel into little pieces so that it fits neatly into our liturgy does not aid our understanding of his text. We see just a fragment plucked from a carefully constructed, well-integrated sequence of events and meanings. Mark's gospel is a complicated tale, in which one thing explains the next, and in which all are ingeniously woven together to form a coherent tapestry. Looking at a single, short extract is like examining one particular detail from a large painting without reference to the whole.

Today, the liturgy presents us with a text we know well – the story of the storm at sea. Well, it is actually one of two stories about storms in Mark's gospel. And these are just two of six boat trips Mark mentions. In four of them, Mark records how Jesus and his disciples use the boats to go to "the other side" of the sea. Even that word "sea" is interesting: why does Mark not speak of a "lake", because that, after all, is what it is. Why does he turn it into a sea? Perhaps it is because the lake separates two worlds that are so different from each other that the stretch of water between them may as well be as wide as an ocean. On one side of the lake is the Jewish world, and at the other side is the pagan world. An ocean of difference lay between the eastern and western shores of the same lake!

Jesus says to his disciples, "Let us cross over to the other side," and, against all their instincts and intuitions, they do as Jesus requests. They know Jesus only too well by now, and are fully aware of what is in store. Jesus will put them, once again, in that awkward position where they will find themselves mixing with people whom they would normally shun. The disciples are afraid to lose themselves in the process of integration, just as they are afraid that they will drown during the storm.

We all know how a short distance, a few cultural differences, or even just an unusual accent can seem to put a whole ocean between us and our fellow human beings. But Jesus asks us to cross over to the other side and meet with those whom our in-built prejudices would naturally make us avoid. Like the disciples, we have nothing to lose – in fact, we have something to gain, because in reaching out to all our brothers and sisters without reservation or bias we will find something of our true selves.

Jesus takes a cushion and falls asleep in the rear end of the boat – so sure is he that there will be no problems in crossing over to the other side. But a storm gets up, and the water crashes down on them. The boat is almost swamped, and yet still he sleeps! They finally wake him, shouting: "Master, do you not care? We are going down!" Jesus rebukes not only the wind, but also his companions. "Why are you so frightened?" he asks, "How is is that you have no faith?" Still wrapped in fear, they say to one another: "Who can this be? Even the wind and the sea obey him."

And that is how the story ends. Those two questions are left hanging in the air, unanswered, and they still ring in our ears today: "Just who is he to think that we can cross over to 'the other side' without losing ourselves?" He knows, because he did just that.

Her own initiative

B44. Thirteenth Sunday of the year

Wisdom 1:13-15; 2:23-24
2 Corinthians 8:7, 9, 13-15
Mark 5:21-43

Although the disciples readily receive the word of Jesus, the problem is how to make it grow within them. It is belief in Jesus that provides the growing power, but that is where the disciples always fall short. When Jesus gives Simon the name Peter (*petra*), meaning "rock", it may well be for a different reason than what we sometimes assume – Simon's stubbornness! Did Jesus choose the disciples because they were all so stubborn? Did he want to show that, in the end, he could sway even the most resolutely immovable?

The Twelve's lack of faith is often in sharp contrast to the behaviour of the people around them, and it is surely intentional on Mark's part that the two miracles today have something to do with the number 12. In the first, a 12-year-old girl is raised from the dead. In the second, a woman who has been bleeding for 12 years is healed. In both cases, faith precedes their healing, and in neither case does Jesus take the initiative.

So what happens? A leader of the synagogue – who is from the upper crust of society and so important that his name, Jairus, is even mentioned – falls on his knees in front of Jesus. An anonymous woman with an illness that has probably made her an outcast follows the crowd to the house of Jairus. She is not that brave, and when she later shows herself it is "in fear and trembling". Yet she is full of faith, and it is a faith that is derived simply from what she has heard about Jesus. She pushes herself through the crowd towards Jesus, reaches out, and touches him without permission or apology. At that very moment her bleeding stops and she is healed.

It is interesting that all this happens without the direct involvement of Jesus. The woman believes that she will be healed by touching Jesus, and so she lets her faith overcome her fear – maybe that is an even greater miracle!

When the woman touches him, Jesus turns round, asking: "Who touched me?" The disciples answer him sarcastically: "You see how the crowd is pressing around you and yet you say, 'Who touched me?'" Admittedly, it does seem a silly question. However, of all the scores of people who touched Jesus that day, nothing happened to them. Simply touching Jesus does not make any power flow out from him. That only

59

happens when you have faith. It is at that moment that you share in Jesus' vision, and consequently in his power.

In Mark's gospel, faith in Jesus is not the result of a miracle, it is a prerequisite. You do not start to believe because you are healed, you start to heal because you believe. It sounds almost heretical, yet Jesus says it himself: "Your faith has healed you."

Dishonoured

B45. Fourteenth Sunday of the year

Ezekiel 2:2-5
2 Corinthians 12:7-10
Mark 6:1-6

In today's gospel reading, we see how Jesus makes a less than happy return to his family's village of Nazareth. Jesus is hurt by the dismissive and scornful way the villagers react to him. His reputation must have travelled before him; yet, knowing all that he has done and said elsewhere, they still only refer to him as "the carpenter", as if to say, "Who does he think he is?" More pointedly, they call him "the son of Mary".

While experts debate the exact meaning of this last expression (as they do almost every word in the Bible!), some do not exclude the possibility that the words "son of Mary" may have been intended to remind Jesus that there were still doubts the circumstances of his birth, and that some considered him to have been an "illegitimate" child, to use an unfortunate phrase. Perhaps they wanted to make him aware that they disapproved of him, because his questionable parentage upset the norms of their society.

There is probably also another reason for their animosity – something that would have carried even more weight in their traditional society, and for which they felt they could not forgive him. It was this: Jesus had left his mother Mary (who by that time was probably a widow) to take care of herself. He had set a bad example and a poor precedent. To the villagers, it seems that Jesus shows not even the slightest respect for traditional values and obligations. His shoddy behaviour gives them all a bad name.

Even the way the villagers express their "admiration" for him sounds pretty sarcastic: "Where did the man get all this? What is this wisdom that has been granted him, and these miracles that that are worked through him?" They have a deep distrust of his fame. In short, he is too much for them. Instead of being glad that he has come back to be with them, they are scandalised. They cannot bring themselves to believe in him.

Jesus is surprised by their reaction and feels dishonoured. He leaves them and goes to the neighbouring villages, where he knows he will be more welcome. As far as we know, Jesus never returns to Nazareth. He has left behind for good his family home and his roots.

There is another indication of the tragic sadness of the situation: Jesus is unable to perform any mighty works among his acquaintances and family, except to lay hands on a few people and heal them. What prevents Jesus from using his power to the full is the people's lack of faith in him. Their unbelief not only excludes them from his vision, but also from his power. The Jesus we find here is the same person who works mighty miracles elsewhere; the difference is in the people.

Jesus cannot persuade the people of Nazareth to be like him. They do not believe that they can follow Jesus' example and break the bonds that bind them to their old ways. It is easy to condemn their unbelief, but do we ourselves always believe that everything is possible through Jesus?

Not to believe in Jesus means not to believe in yourself. That is why Jesus insists, again and again, "Your faith has saved you!" The problem is not that Jesus is not honoured in Nazareth, but that the people there do not honour themselves by believing in him. That is what surprises and amazes Jesus.

Hospitality

B46. Fifteenth Sunday of the year

Amos 7:12-15

Ephesians 1:3-14

Mark 6:7-13

According to Mark, Jesus wants two things when he appoints his apostles (Mark 3:14). First, he simply wants companions for the times ahead. Second, Jesus is looking from the very beginning for people who can "be sent out to preach, with power to cast out devils."

In today's reading, we find the Twelve fully initiated into what Jesus stands for. They have been with Jesus for some time and, after much tuition from Jesus, they are now ready to be sent out. Jesus gives them a series of guidelines to follow, which are also intended as directives for all missionary work in the ages to come.

The rules Jesus gives them are simple and brief. They are to use the normal means of transport of their time and class. For the apostles this means they will have to walk, for which they will be equipped with a staff and some sandals. They are to take no food with them, no knapsack, no extra clothing, and no money. They are to rely solely on the hospitality of others. Once they have been received by a family, they have to stay with them for as long as they remain in the district.

The story does not tell us whether Jesus' disciples were faithful to those rules, but history tells us that there have been many occasions since then when missionaries and evangelists did not adhere to them. Such people have always had to rely on the hospitality of others. But in our more colonial past, they often insisted that their hosts and hostesses learned their language, wore their kind of clothes, and adopted their customs. Instead of learning something of the cultures they encountered, they sometimes showed not the slightest interest, and even ridiculed them.

Thankfully, those days are – by and large – over, but even today some missionaries stick to their own lifestyles and diets when working in foreign countries. Considering that we have stayed at home and left them to get on with the work of spreading the Good News, we should be the last ones to complain. Indeed, the missionaries' attitudes usually arise from the flawed attitude of the Church as a whole. Too often, we are only prepared to be received on our own terms. Church leaders are sometimes of the opinion that the only way to follow Jesus is by following their way – by which is usually meant, the Western way. The Church itself seems to forget the guidelines Jesus' laid down 2,000 years ago!

Not listening to Jesus' directives has its consequences. If others do not feel at ease in our church culture, then – excuse me if I use a rather academic phrase here – the "inculturation" of Jesus' person, his doctrine, and his life becomes practically impossible.

Only by entrusting ourselves to the hospitality and culture of other people will the real essence of Jesus ever become part of world culture.

Shepherds in sheep's clothing
B47. Sixteenth Sunday of the year

Jeremiah 23:1-6
Ephesians 2:13-18
Mark 6:30-34

Today's short gospel text is about Jesus' compassion. First, he has pity on the apostles, who, just back from their mission, do not even get the time to eat. He invites them to come with him to a quiet place, far away from the crowd. He has pity on the apostles again when his attempt to get them away from the crowd fails, so he sends the apostles away and keeps the crowd occupied. Then he has pity on the crowd, because they are like sheep without a shepherd, so he begins to teach them.

We often spontaneously identify with a particular character in a story. Perhaps we do this because it makes listening to the story so much more interesting, and we feel personally involved. Children, for example, love to listen to the fairy tale Cinderella, because they can see something of themselves in her. Similarly, adults enjoy seeing a tragedy such as Antigone, because they like to identify with the central character, who resists everyone and everything because she wants to remain to faithful to her ideal.

The same thing applies to the gospels. Whether we are reading alone at home or listening in church, we frequently associate with characters in the gospel stories. So who are we in Mark's story? Most of us would probably say that we identify with members of crowd rather than with the apostles – with the sheep Jesus pities because they have no shepherd to care for them.

In one sense, it is perfectly fine to identify with whomever we want to in a story, but we might ask ourselves whether that is actually the character the author intended us to relate to. In the case of today's gospel story, I would think it highly unlikely that Mark wants us to see ourselves as dumb, bleating, rather smelly sheep, painfully wandering aimlessly through life. We may feel like that sometimes, but that is not the self-image we are expected to embrace.

It might be more positive to identify with the apostles, whose recent mission testifies that they have been transformed from sheep into shepherds. But the author really wants us to identify with Jesus, and to see in him the qualities that lie dormant in us all.

Too often, preachers and church leaders make it difficult for us to identify with Jesus, because they emphasise how different we are from him. Cowed by this idea, we say to ourselves: "We ought to keep our mouths shut in his presence and fall upon our knees before him." However, if we start to think like that, how can we possibly conceive of Jesus as our emancipator? It is not hard to guess why some church leaders try to present Jesus like that – after all, it keeps people "in their place".

It was never Jesus' (or Mark's) intention that we should be wandering sheep. Jesus begins to teach the crowd because he wants to get them out of that situation – to change them from sheep into shepherds, who then, in their turn, can help others to liberate and emancipate themselves.

We should have the same compassion as Jesus when we look at the world around us. So many people are just pale shadows of the people they could really be. We have to be shepherds to them, just as Jesus is to us, and help them to realise their full potential.

Politics

B48. Seventeenth Sunday of the year

2 Kings 4:42-44
Ephesians 4:1-6
John 6:1-15

Albert Nolan, a South African Dominican priest, pointed out that when we read the story of the barley loaves and the fish, we usually concentrate on the miraculous way the crowd is fed, rather than the political undertones of the story. He came to that conclusion some years ago, when "apartheid" was still the ruling ideology in South Africa, and at a time when groups of people were coming together throughout the country to organise themselves against the ruling regime.

The event is recorded in all four gospels (Matthew 14:13-21; Mark 6:30-44; Luke 9:10-17). Each gospel writer specifies that there were about 5,000 men present. (Matthew is the only one to mention that there were women and children present.) But why would so many men have come together in those days in Palestine? And why had they gathered in such an isolated place? Was it a secret meeting? Nolan thinks that there is only one possible explanation: it was a political meeting – perhaps the first stirrings of a rebellion or a liberation movement. And it seems as though they had targeted Jesus as the person who was going to lead them! John says that they are even willing to use force in order to compel Jesus to become their king. Somehow, Jesus manages to wangle his way out of this predicament and then goes into the hills on his own to pray.

Nolan believes that the crowd was far from peaceful. They were not only hungry, they also were rowdy – so rowdy in fact, that Jesus had to ask them to sit down in order to restore some calm. It is far easier to control a group of seated people than a standing, rowdy crowd. Jesus told them to sit down in groups. Anyone who has ever had to control a large crowd knows that dividing the people into smaller groups is a tremendous help. It was probably the only way in which Jesus could handle the situation.

It was not just the crowd putting pressure on Jesus: the disciples would also have liked him to become a king, and had already started fighting over their positions in that new kingdom. Jesus had to force the disciples to get into their boat and out of the way. He told them to go on ahead to Bethsaida (Mark 6:45). Once they had gone, he sent the crowd home and then left for the solitude of the mountains.

Right from the beginning of his ministry, Jesus had to resist the temptation to take on political power. Later on, he told Pilate that he could easily have opted for it, but refused to give in. Jesus would never have done that, because it would have meant siding with one group (in this case the Jews) against another (the Romans and their allies). That type of choice is not divine and has no place in the kingdom of God. Jesus chose to champion not individuals and groups, but the whole of humanity.

Definitive answer

B49. Eighteenth Sunday of the year

Exodus 16: 2-4, 12-15

Ephesians 4:17, 20-24

John 6: 24-35

In our last reading, we saw how Jesus surprised the hungry crowd by feeding them. Now they have come back for more. Jesus rebukes them for not understanding that the bread they were given was, primarily, a symbol of something else. They have not given a thought to that possibility – they simply want another free meal, and they are not afraid to admit it! They ask Jesus to do for them what Moses did for their ancestors: that is, provide daily bread from heaven.

Jesus responds by telling them that they should ask for a different kind of food. Even the bread Moses gave their ancestors was not "the" bread of heaven. It may have helped them physically from day to day, but it was not lasting, sustaining food. It was not the definitive answer to their problems. His audience probably recalls that the manna from heaven could only be eaten on the day it fell. Whatever was left over became spoilt by the next day.

Jesus then begins to speak about another bread: himself. When he says, "I am the bread of life," he is describing a remedy that will definitely take away all hunger, just as our thirst will definitely be quenched once we listen to him. Or, to express it another way, the definitive solution for all the hunger in the world is to take Jesus as our bread for life – to "eat and drink" Jesus himself.

Let us briefly change tack. Many reasons were given to justify the Gulf War of 1990, but most were merely smoke-screens to disguise the fact that the West was fighting to preserve its oil supplies. Even the generals and politicians, who had at first solemnly stated that the war was necessary to protect the universal rights of nations and peoples, later admitted added that it had also been fought over oil. In effect, they were saying: "If Kuwait had just been a producer of bananas, avocados, or kiwis, we would never have gone to war to protect it."

Oil is the "food" that keeps our Western lifestyle going. However, it is not a lasting or sustaining food, because we all know that eventually the oil reserves will run out. Oil is not the definitive answer. The scramble for diminishing oil reserves will also guarantee us further international strife in the future. The only real solution is to change our lifestyles and liberate ourselves from that oil-dependency. The crucial thing is not what we have, but how we live.

Jesus tells the crowd that he could, if he chose, give them enough bread to keep them all fed every day of their lives. Yet those bread supplies, even in they were limitless, would not solve the problems of hunger and poverty conclusively. To do that, we need the "bread from heaven" that gives life to the world. If we eat from that bread, our hunger will be satisfied and our thirst quenched, because we will be fundamentally changed.

When the phrase, "I am the bread of life," resounds at the celebration of the Eucharist, we should try to relate Jesus' words to the concrete reality of our world, because he intended that they should have a practical application. If we were to live life in the way Jesus showed us, no child would ever die of hunger and no elderly person of loneliness. We would be washing each others' feet and serving each other at the table of this world. We would pass away but we would never die, because we had shared in the bread of heaven.

Divine magnetism

B50. Nineteenth Sunday of the year

1 Kings 19:4-8
Ephesians 4:30-5:2
John 6:41-51

According to Jesus' words, noted here by John, a mysterious power is at work in our world. It is so mysterious that you cannot see, smell, touch, hear, or taste it. Nevertheless, it is still there.

Why should we believe this? If we cannot detect this power with our senses, why should we give it credence? Well, there are plenty of examples of the way we accept things we cannot see. Look out of your window just before dawn, and you will hear the silence of a sleeping world. Unseen and undetected by your senses, the atmosphere is awash with radio waves and microwaves. If you need proof of this, you only need to turn on your radio or TV set to shatter the silence of the morning. Think also of the awesome power of nature that makes seeds germinate, flowers bloom, and clouds scud across the sky. We cannot see the energies and forces that make these things happen, but we can see and feel their effects, and so we accept their existence.

Jesus is speaking about another type of power: a mighty and terrific power that attracts us to God like an enormous magnet. It is a power that also makes us come alive to one another. I believe that we can see this power at work in our world today. Protestants and Catholics, Muslims and Jews, Americans and Russians, and so many other groups once seemingly poles apart, now seem to be talking to each other more than ever before. Conflicts that have been rumbling on for generations are moving slowly towards resolution. It is as if the whole of humanity is in dialogue with itself. The power of God is changing the face of the Earth.

It is the same power that makes us feel that there is more to the world in which we live, that the colours we see are not all the colours to be seen; that the music we hear is not all the music to hear; that the languages we speak are not all languages that can be spoken; that our relationships do not satisfy all our hopes and desires; and that the love we experience – however deep that love might be – is only the first stirrings of a much greater and ultimate love.

Jesus not only speaks about the origin of that power, but also predicts what its outcome will be. This divine magnetism, which has been with us from the very beginning, will draw us all towards our point of common origin – the Lord's table. We will be enveloped by that power and carried along inexorably by it. This power will carry us towards the fulfilment of the vision that Abram and Sarai saw in the stars, that the prophets proclaimed, and that John described in Revelation – that is, the New Jerusalem, the heavenly city of God (see B10: A beckoning star).

The famous Jesuit philosopher Pierre Teilhard de Chardin named the point to which this divine power attracts us "Point Omega". Like a space rocket travelling through space towards a distant star, humanity is moving through the ages towards Point Omega. And when we reach Point Omega, we will find God.

The language of love
B51. Twentieth Sunday of the year

Proverbs 9:1-6
Ephesians 5:15-20
John 6:51-58

The gospel texts we are reading at this time of the year are all from John.

Again and again they repeat the same topics: Jesus is the bread; he is the life; he comes from the Father; he has seen the Father; if we eat his flesh and drink this blood, we will live; if we do not, we will die. It is a long series of repetitions that, in the end, can be too much and a little tedious if we do not understand the mystery underlying these statements. Jesus repeats himself over and over again because he is not being listened to. It is the kind of discussion with which we are all familiar.

Your son is standing in front of you. You are worried sick, because he is into something much worse than cigarettes – something much more dangerous. You talk to him about it. You talk and talk and talk, but whatever you say does not seem to register: he just stands there looking at you without saying a word. And you think: "If I could only creep into your head and heart I could convince you, I could persuade you to look at the world through my eyes."

Or it could be your daughter, who is always out partying and never comes home until morning. And what about her friends – they all seem a bit strange, and you do not really trust them. You talk, you weep, and you plead. You practically fall on your knees in front of her saying: "If you only knew what I know! If you would only learn from the disappointments I experienced!"

You are lying in bed next to the one you love, but you have a serious difference of opinion. Your feel very strongly about something, but your partner does not see things your way. Holding your loved one in your arms, you say: "If only you could feel the way I do, then you would understand. If only you could share my emotions, then everything would be all right."

Jesus is speaking in a similar way in today's gospel reading. He knows that only his way of living – that is, a loving, simple, forgiving, God-fearing, and life-respecting way – can save the world and humanity. He knows what will happen if the human family does not listen to him, so he pleads: "Listen to what say! I know what is happening to you. Try to see things as I do. Try to feel them as I feel them. I am coming from God. Eat the bread I eat. Drink the wine I drink. Eat my body, drink my blood. Then you will live!" Jesus asks us for our understanding. He asks us to see the world through his eyes. He also asks us to change our lives. In fact, he is imploring us to do so.

We know how Jesus went about his mission 2,000 years ago, but we have to find out how he would go about it now, in a world in which millions are starving while a privileged few live in plentiful luxury. We know that he has bequeathed his mission to us, his followers. Jesus pleads with us to feed his hunger for justice and to quench his thirst for righteousness.

Science and technology

B52. Twenty-first Sunday of the year

Joshua 24:1-2, 15-18
Ephesians 5:21-32
John 6:60-69

The last extract from John's gospel during this liturgical year (the remaining gospel texts are from Mark) presents Jesus speaking about the spirit and the flesh. He speaks about "flesh that has nothing to offer" and "spirit that gives life". This text can lead to serious misunderstandings.

In the past, such misunderstandings led to an asceticism in which the flesh – that is, the body – was not only despised but even loathed. They led to spiritualities in which the body was viewed as a prison from which the soul should try to escape. The body was the cause of sin, so it had to be disciplined, starved, and even flagellated. The body was not to be enjoyed, and preferably used as little as possible. From the stories about Jesus in the gospels, it is clear that Jesus did not follow this line of thinking. In fact, he was accused of not fasting, and he obviously liked to be invited to meals and to organise large picnics in the middle of nowhere. He not only went to a wedding feast, but he also produced a load of first class wine!

When Jesus said that "the flesh has nothing to offer, it is the spirit that gives life," he did not want to say that we have to separate the spirit from the body, and only cultivate the spirit. He wanted to say the opposite: we have to keep spirit and flesh together. Without the spirit giving life, the flesh would be useless. Without that spirit, the "flesh" would be dead, like a body in a coffin. As long as we live, spirit and flesh belong together. They belong together in our lives.

Academies of science were established in France in 1633, in England in 1646, and in Italy in 1660. They wanted to study empirical science and use the results of their research to develop new inventions. In all three cases, they stipulated in their statutes that they did want to be influenced by what they called religion, metaphysics, or ethics. This was understandable, considering the clerical oppression in their time.

From such academies grew the technologies that dominate our modern world today. But the development of science – which has largely been the development of the "flesh" without the moderating influence of the spirit – has left us some questionable legacies. Scientific research is likely to be unbeneficial and even dangerous to humanity if it does not examine at the same time the moral, ethical, and religious implications of the progress it purports to bring.

In every field of life, when flesh and spirit are uncoupled, malignant growth takes place. We know that such wild growth is happening when we hear people justifying their actions by saying things like "business is business", or "research is research", "administration is administration", and especially "war is war".

Do you remember the proud descriptions of the "smart" bombs and the "clinical efficiency" of modern military hardware that the Press came out with during the Gulf War? Such purely technical reporting without reference to the human cost – without reference to the spirit – sends shivers down the spine.

It is the spirit that gives life. The flesh has nothing to offer on its own. The flesh on its own is just a corpse.

Breakthrough

B53. Twenty-second Sunday of the year

Deuteronomy 4:1-2, 6-8
James 1:17-18, 21-22, 27
Mark 7:1-8, 14-15, 21-23

Today we read how the Pharisees tried to catch Jesus out with questions about the rites they called the "tradition of the elders". They criticised Jesus' disciples for not obeying ritual customs such as washing their hands before eating, purifying food bought in a market, cleaning kitchen utensils in a certain matter, and so on. Jesus' answer would, they presumed, provide evidence they could use to bring an end to his ministry.

The rituals Mark mentions all sound very hygienic, but they were also there to make things pure in the eyes of the Jewish Law. The sprinkling of holy water on food bought in the market was done because the farmer might have harvested it on a day when it was forbidden, or because he had not paid any Temple tax for it. The ritual washing of hands was not done because your hands were dirty, but because you might have been in contact with a pagan. The washing of dishes, receptacles, and crockery was – besides being hygienic– a question of legal purity.

This was the purity Jesus discussed with his opponents. The Pharisees upheld this notion of religious purity to guarantee the identity of the Jewish people. By emphasising the importance of these rituals and customs, they aimed to make their culture distinct from others. The Pharisees also introduced all kinds of discriminatory customs and regulations to reinforce the hierarchy in their own society.

Jesus opposed all this. It was something that went against the grain of his inclusive love, which welcomed all with open arms. They had seen how Jesus put this principle of inclusivity into action in his dealings with people normally ostracised by society. Remember how he declared the leper legally pure (Mark 1:44)?

In Jesus' defence of his disciples, he gave the term "purity" a different meaning to the one used by the Pharisees. First, he explained that it was wrong to think that someone was "pure" because of their adherence to the Pharisees' purification rites and rituals. What people touch or put into their bodies cannot make them impure, he said, because purity is judged by what comes out of a person in the form of their words, deeds, and lives.

Jesus told them that purity is about what goes on inside a person's heart; in other words, it was about what happens in their inner selves. And because everyone has a heart and an inner self, purity is something given to all, not simply to one ethnic or social group. He then added a list of things that make a person impure: fornication, theft, murder, adultery, avarice, malice, deceit, indecency, envy, slander, pride, and folly. "All these evil things," he said, "come from within and make a person unclean."

In evading the trap set by the Pharisees, Jesus also took the opportunity to break through the religious code they used to put divisions between people. He did that by deconstructing the old fundamentalist ritual laws ascribed to their ancestors, and by saying that "purity" had to be defined in a new, inclusive way.

Jesus' moral and ethical principles apply to everyone.

Strictly personal
B54. Twenty-third Sunday of the year

Isaiah 35:4-7

James 2:2-5

Mark 7:31-37

Mark is the only one who tells us the story about the deaf and dumb man in the Decapolis region. It is Jesus' second miracle in this pagan region: the first is the healing of the Syro-Phoenician woman's daughter. Mark would have deliberately chosen to include these stories in order to challenge some of his prejudiced readers who were unwilling to open their communities to strangers, aliens, and immigrants.

In the story, a deaf man with a speech impediment is brought to Jesus. We all know how people like that are often bullied by others – not just in school playgrounds, but all through their lives. We sometimes call people like that "handicapped", and in doing so we indicate just how little we expect from them, and how little they can expect from us. They are supposed to have their caps in their hands and beg for our help. Only too often they are ignored as though they were not full members of society

Some commentaries explain that, in all probability, the man's family had such pity on him that they decide to bring him to Jesus and beseech (parakalousin) Jesus to help him. That may be so, but it seems rather strange that the man has to be brought to Jesus by other people – surely he would have been capable of making his own way? Perhaps the man initially did not want to come at all, because he felt that he would – once again – be used as an object for people's curiosity, scrutiny, and ridicule. He would be a good case for Jesus to heal, thereby satisfying their lust for sensation. He may have doubted their genuine concern for his well-being.

Jesus' actions would tend to reinforce this view. He takes the man to one side and tells the crowd that they are not to follow. It is only when the two are alone that he puts his fingers in the man's ears, puts some spittle on his tongue, looks up to heaven with a sigh, and says: *ephphatha*, which means "open up". The man is healed, and the two go back to the crowd.

There is also another angle to all this. It concerns something known as "inculturation". Jesus adapts his ways to the culture of the people around him. He performs his miracle in the way people of that region thought miracles should be performed, and his actions are what the deaf man might have expected of him: he touches his ears and his tongue, and says an Aramaic word that must have sounded like a magic spell. In other words, the man and the crowd get what they expect.

The man not only regains his ability to hear and speak, but he is also addressed and listened to as a person in his own right for the first time. He comes back transformed. Nobody will ridicule him any more! And he can speak! He does that so well that he tells his story everywhere, even though Jesus has asked him not to. Does Jesus really expect him to be so restrained with his new-found gift?

Just like him

B55. Twenty-fourth Sunday of the year

Isaiah 50:5-9
James 2:14-18

When you ask people what they think of you, you are really asking them to tell you something about themselves – about how they experience and perceive you, and how they relate to you. Jesus asks this question to his disciples, in order to examine their relationship with him. His opening gambit of, "Who do people say I am?" is not a particularly probing one, as there are all sorts of answers. The disciples reply: "John the Baptist, others Elijah; others again, one of the prophets" (Mark 8:28). Then his real question follows: "But you, who do you say I am?" Peter, who so often answers first and thinks later, says boldly: "You are the Christ."

This time, Peter is right. With that one word, *christos*, he says it all. The Greek word christos is the translation of the Hebrew word masjiach, meaning the "anointed" one. Ever since Daniel's prophecies, the term had been used to indicate the king anointed by God who would deliver God's people and introduce God's kingdom.

It is interesting that, while Jesus does not disagree with Peter's assertion that he is the Christ, he does seem to want to qualify that statement. When he then begins to teach them, he conspicuously avoids the use of this term, instead preferring to describe himself as the "Son of Man". The title Son of Man is the one Jesus uses for himself most often – in fact, he uses it a total of 81 times in the gospels. Nobody else – neither friend nor foe – ever refers to him as Son of Man. In Hebrew scripture, such as in the Psalms, the term Son of Man often simply means "human being".

All this reminds me of a contemporary American "saint", Dorothy Day. She was a co-founder of a community called "The Catholic Worker", which runs homes and hostels for homeless people in New York and other American cities and towns. Dorothy was a very special human being who did extraordinary things in her life, but whenever she heard anyone saying so, she became indignant. "You only say that," she would say, "because you are not prepared to do what I do. You could do these things, too, if you really wanted, but by making me out to be 'extraordinary', you are simply wriggling out of your own responsibilities. You like to tell yourself that you are not like me, but in fact we are just the same – we are both human beings!"

When Jesus changes the title Christ to Son of Man, he seems to be making the same point. He deliberately tries to change both his disciples' expectations and our own expectations. Peter is right, Jesus is the Christ, but Peter is wrong if he consequently assumes that he is not like Jesus. Indeed, as the Christ, Jesus sets an example to us all of what it means to be fully human.

Jesus explains that when you engage yourself in the kingdom of God, which is a kingdom of peace and justice, it will cost you your life. Peter disagrees. He is thinking along other lines: as far as he is concerned, the Messiah is a conqueror in the mould of other human rulers and power-brokers. Jesus rebukes him by calling him "Satan". The old ways and models will never solve anything, and will simply result in the same old song – a song that has oppressed billions throughout history.

To be a human being is different; to be a human being is to be like just like him; to be just like Jesus, whose spirit is with us (Acts 16:7).

Servant
B56. Twenty-fifth Sunday of the year

Wisdom 2:12, 17-20
James 3:16-4:3
Mark 9:30-37

They are on their way south. The decision to go Jerusalem has been taken. They will visit Jesus' home in Capernaum for the last time. On the way there, the disciples quarrel about which one of them is the greatest and the most powerful. They seem to have understood nothing of Jesus' idea of power, even though he has already told them that he is going to hand himself over to people who are going to kill him. They cannot come to terms with his non-violent attitude.

Gandhi once said: "If you do not practice non-violence in your daily personal relations with others, and yet think that you will be able to do that at more extra-ordinary occasions, you will end up being deceived." The reason the disciples cannot grasp Jesus' philosophy of non-violence is that they are still competing and conflicting with one another in their personal lives. They are constantly trying to score points off each other.

Later, Jesus is at the table in his home, with the disciples sitting round him in a circle. They have been eating and drinking and are fairly relaxed, but they become embarrassed when Jesus asks them what they were arguing about on the road. Jesus can guess only too well what it was. He tells them that if they want to be first in his eyes, they must consider themselves last and put themselves at the service of others.

Jesus wants to show them that the powerful should always use their power to help the powerless. He always looks to reinforce his words with a concrete example from his surroundings. This time, he calls a child from the street. This is often depicted as a sweet little scene, with Jesus and a small, snotty child in the midst of a group of rough-looking disciples. However, Jesus is trying to put something profound across to his disciples. They have seen his mighty power at work and they believe that he is the Christ, and yet here he is emphasising his concern for little children, who are on the lowest rank of the social ladder, totally devoid of status, power, and rights.

Jesus embraces the child and puts it in the centre of their circle, saying: "Anyone who welcomes one of these little children in my name, welcomes me; and anyone who welcomes me, welcomes not me but the one who sent me" (Mark 9:37). It is not the only time in the gospel of Mark that Jesus insists that a loving, protective concern for children is a key pillar in his social program (9:42; 10:13-16). The disciples are taken aback, because this implies that children are as important to God and God's Son as the divine persons themselves. It also demands a reversal of the received notions of what is most important in life. The first becomes the last. What had no status at all is suddenly given top priority.

But the most important thing Jesus wants to tell them on that occasion is about themselves. They have to review their notions of themselves, each other, and other people, and revise their relationships accordingly. They must stop quibbling about who is the most important among them, because those old hierarchical ideas are no longer relevant – in fact, they are now of the lowest priority. The main priority is to put themselves at the service of others.

Perhaps there would be less in-fighting in the Church if a child were present at every ecclesiastical debate!

Christian arrogance

B57. Twenty-sixth Sunday of the year

Numbers 11:25-29

James 5:1-6

Mark 9:38-43, 45, 47-48

Simon is not the only disciple who has difficulties in receiving the seed of the word of Jesus. (In Mark's gospel, Simon's hardness seems to be the reason that Jesus gives him the nickname Peter, which means "rock", implying that he is like the rocky ground in the parable of the sower!) John, too, had his problems in tuning in to Jesus.

John's problem, however, is one of arrogance. He has noticed that someone who does not belong to their group is chasing out evil spirits in Jesus' name. He says to Jesus: "Master, we saw a man who is not one of us casting out devils in your name; and because he was not one of us we tried to stop him." John is upset because this man's actions undermine his conviction of his own importance.

When you read a story, it is always good to pay attention to the author's repetitions. Mark mentions twice how John indignantly says that the man casting out devils is "not one of us". John is trying to restrict Jesus' influence to the small circle that has formed around Jesus. He wants to appropriate the healing work of Jesus because he sees a chance to climb the social ladder, to improve his status, to be honoured, and to exercise power over others. He wants to have something that others do not. He would like to safeguard his monopoly on Jesus, but in doing so he is thinking in a way that is anathema to the kingdom Jesus proclaims.

As well as being possessive and arrogant, John is also jealous. Just before this incident, the apostles themselves had been unsuccessful in trying to exorcise an unclean spirit (Mark 9:14-29). They had to wait for Jesus to help the young victim. John wants that power for himself.

Jesus does not respond directly to John. Without getting personal, he gives two reasons why they should let that "stranger" go on his way. First, when someone heals in Jesus' name he is, of course, on Jesus' side: "Anyone who is not against us is for us." The second reason is more important. (You can tell that by the way Jesus uses the term "Christ".) John must understand that the disciples themselves will often be the ones who need to be helped and healed, but if John and his fellow disciples have a monopoly on Jesus, who will be there to help them?

In other words, the mission of healing and saving humanity and the world is not the sole responsibility of the disciples. It is a mission that is entrusted to everyone. It is the fulfilment of what Moses hoped in our first reading from the book of Numbers: "If only the whole people of the Lord were prophets, and the Lord gave his spirit to them all!"

It does not matter in whose name that healing or liberation is worked out. The important thing is not the name, but what is happening. Jesus does not want to close the circle around him. He refuses to give his disciples a kind of kingdom-of-God monopoly, or an exclusive franchise on his Spirit and power. As long as the healing and saving is taking place, Jesus does not draw any lines or borders. His followers are supposed to cooperate with all those in the world who are healing and redeeming it.

Marriage

B58. Twenty-seventh Sunday of the year

Genesis 2:18-24

Hebrews 2:9-11
Mark 10:2-16

After serving for a number of years in East Africa, I had become quite sensitive to cultural differences. You learn to accept that you cannot apply all your Western ideas in an African context. When I was then assigned to Washington DC, USA, the whole cultural scene changed once again. I asked a local parish priest for some tips on the sort of things I should be aware of when preaching to an American congregation. After some reflection, the 70-year-old priest told me that I should bear in mind that 40-50 per cent of his congregation were divorced or had their marriages annulled, and that a fair proportion of them had remarried.

Divorce is a delicate topic, so one has to be very careful when preaching about today's text from Mark's gospel, in which Jesus speaks about divorce and remarriage. The Pharisees ask Jesus whether it is lawful for a man to divorce his wife. Jesus counters with a different question: "What did Moses command you?" They reply: "Moses allowed us to draw up a writ of dismissal and so to divorce." Jesus responds by quoting a text that is even older than the instructions from Moses. It is a text from Genesis, in which we are told that man and woman are equal, and that they are married in that equality.

Jesus then explains that Moses ceased to uphold that equality because of the hardness of their hearts. The writ of dismissal permitted by Moses was not to condone their actions, but was more of an acknowledgement of how far they had strayed from God's ideal. Between the creation of the world and the time of Moses, something had happened: the original equality between man and woman had been suppressed by the introduction of a patriarchal structure in which, by definition, the male ruled. That was certainly not God's intention.

Jesus strengthens his argument by adding: "This is why a man must leave his father and mother, and the two become one body. They are no longer two, therefore, but one body." This text implies that in marriage a woman is not to be owned by a man and used by him so that he may continue his family's line. The man and woman must break through that patriarchal structure to be truly one with each other. It is that God-willed equality and unity that Jesus says no one may tear apart. In his answer, Jesus is reacting more to the implied inequality between men and women than to the direct thrust of the question.

Later on, when they are back at home, the disciples raise the issue again. As they talk, it seems that Jesus does accept the reality of separation. However, he makes it clear that both parties should be in an equal position to initiate the divorce, that both parties have to accept responsibility for the consequences of their failed marriage, and that they should not marry again.

Jesus, like Paul (1 Cor. 7:10), excludes the possibility of remarriage if the two really had become one in body and in spirit (something that frequently does not happen). Anyone who has witnessed or experienced the tragic death of a marriage in which this oneness did occur cannot but agree with Jesus. Whatever God unites should not be torn apart. It is often only in the death of a marriage that the two realise just how much a part of one another they once had been. The ashes of an old fire can be very bitter indeed.

Property
B59. Twenty-eighth Sunday of the year

Wisdom 7:7-11
Hebrews 4:2-13
Mark 10:17-30

Mark's Jesus sets out to tackle head-on the structural problems of his time. For example, in today's story about the man who comes to Jesus asking how he can inherit eternal life, Jesus challenges our attitudes to money, property, and privilege. We hear that the man would like to join Jesus, but we do not know at this stage that he is a wealthy member of a privileged class.

The story begins with the man falling on his knees before Jesus, just as the leper did in the first chapter of Mark's gospel (1:40). He uses the unusually courteous term "Good master" to greet Jesus – a term rarely used in Hebrew literature. When you use such a flattering term in a Middle Eastern context, you would expect to be answered in the same complimentary way. Jesus refuses to be flattered, and refuses to flatter the man in return. In fact, Jesus starts by correcting the man, saying that only God is good, thus reminding him that all the titles, ranks, and plaudits we attribute to each other are meaningless in God's eyes.

It is a very cool beginning, and it does not get any better, because Jesus then reminds the man of the commandments. The young man responds rather naively by saying that he has kept all the commandments. I say naively because Jesus has already stated that no one can call himself or herself "good", and good is the very least you would want to call yourself if you had never broken a commandment!

If you look carefully at Jesus' list of commandments, you will find an extra one there: "You must not defraud"! According to some Bible commentators (Chet Myers, *Binding the Strong Man: A Political Reading of Mark's Story of Jesus*, 1988) the Greek word Jesus uses means "not to return deposited goods or capital" or, more appropriate in this context, "not to pay the wage of a hired hand". This phrase focuses the spotlight on the class of people to which the man belongs: that is, the wealthy landowners who become rich because they withhold what they owe to their workers.

Surely this near-perfect man, who claims never to have broken a commandment in his life, is made of the right material to be one of Jesus' followers? However, "There is one thing you lack," says Jesus. "Go and sell everything you own and give the money to the poor, and you will have treasure in heaven; then come, follow me." The man stands up and leaves, deeply distraught by Jesus' words. Only at this point does Mark tell us about his wealth.

Mark adds Jesus' remarks about the rich man and the eye of a needle, and about the difficulty the rich will have entering the kingdom of God. It is the same thing we learned in the parable about the sower and the seed: the rich were the seeds that became overgrown by thistles so that the Good News got suffocated within them (Mark 4:19).

The disciples despondently exclaim, "Who can be saved?" Meanwhile, Peter, perhaps conscious that he is not from the poorest of backgrounds, reminds Jesus that he and the disciples have left everything behind to follow him. Jesus reassures them, saying that for God, all things are possible, and that the sacrifices they make for his sake will not go unrewarded.

Jesus promises that our journey with him – though not without problems or persecution – will be a fruitful one, both "in the present time" and "in the world to come".

Ransom

B60. Twenty-ninth Sunday of the year

Isaiah 53:10-11
Hebrews 4:14-16
Mark 10:35-45

The final sentence of this Sunday's gospel text reads: "For the Son of Man himself did not come to be served but to serve, and to give his life as a ransom for many." A ransom is the price you pay to free someone. The ransom paid here is Jesus' blood, the receiver is God the Father, and we are the ones freed.

Some believers and theologians question Mark's theology here. They do not deny or dispute that it might have been helpful in another time, but they wonder whether Mark's explanation of what happened to Jesus is appropriate to our day and age. According to many theologians, it is no longer comprehensible to many contemporary Christians that God could have willed the suffering and death of his Son in that way. It seems to presuppose an angry and vengeful God, who can only be bought off by the blood of his Son. This problem strikes right at the very heart of Christianity.

Fortunately, one of the four gospels does not speak in such contentious terms. In Luke's gospel, Jesus is murdered simply because he lived the kingdom of God among us. He lived a good, healing, and liberating life that so contradicted the prevailing religious, political, and economic credos of the time that a conflict was unavoidable.

This is also the opinion of Mark, although Mark dares to use that difficult term "ransom". In the gospel of Mark, Jesus is the servant sent into the world by God the Father to ask the tenants to give account of their behaviour, and to introduce by word and deed the kingdom of God (Mark 12:1-8). The tenants do not accept Jesus and kill him.

Jesus is not the innocent victim of a resentful Father who demands that a sacrifice must be paid for the sins of humanity. Rather, Jesus' suffering and death are the unavoidable consequences of the words he spoke and the life he lived among us. By calling himself a "ransom", Jesus shows that he is conscious of what is going to happen to him, and that he is willing to pay that price for our salvation.

Robert Coles, a psychiatrist at Harvard University, asked children why they thought Jesus died on the cross (*The Spiritual Life of Children*, 1990). One girl, a nine-year-old of Irish descent, replied: "You mean why Jesus came and why he died? Now, he was expected, that is in the Bible. So he came, he tried to be a good teacher, and he was also a doctor. He healed people. But then he was murdered. He was too good for this world ... and we should not forget that. He did not mind dying. He was sad about it, but he knew that he would continue to live, and that is why we do too ... that is what he did for us."

The ideal
B61. Thirtieth Sunday of the year

Jeremiah 31:7-9
Hebrews 5:1-6
Mark 10:46-52

The healing of Bartimaeus, the blind man of Jericho, is the last miracle Mark describes in his gospel, and it is also his masterpiece. Like a good author, Mark saves the best miracle till last. In it, Mark uses many of the techniques and themes that occur elsewhere in his gospel. The first thing to note is that the blind man is given a name. Apart from the Twelve and a few key people, Mark tells us the names of very few other characters in his story. This immediately alerts us to the fact that a special event is about to unfold.

As usual in Mark's healing stories, the person who wants to be healed takes the initiative. When Bartimaeus hears that Jesus is passing close by, he calls out. (It is a recurring theme in Mark's gospel that things only start to happen when people "hear" or "listen".) He shouts to Jesus using a messianic title: "Jesus, Son of David!" When Peter used this title for Jesus, he was told to keep his mouth shut. Here in the street, the people around Bartimaeus tell him to do the same; but the blind man only shouts louder, because he has faith in Jesus. When Jesus asks what Bartimaeus wants, the blind man replies that he would like to be healed. Jesus heals him and, as he always does, adds: "Go, your faith has saved you."

The story of Bartimaeus is like a blueprint for the ideal disciple: Bartimaeus believes that Jesus is the Messiah, he is called by Jesus, he has faith in Jesus, and he experiences Jesus' healing power. No wonder he decides to follow Jesus! Likewise, this last miracle is the ideal miracle, because it creates a new disciple. It is something that should happen to all of us.

The story describes two energies are coming together: the energy of Jesus and the energy of the believer. We mentioned Robert Coles, the psychiatrist at Harvard University, in our last reflection. When he asked teenagers about the role of Jesus in their lives, he sometimes got unexpected answers. After one particular session, the kids were packing up to go home. A 15-year-old girl was walking out the door when she turned and made a final remark to him, saying: "You know, I guess the Lord and us, we're all in this together: us hoping to be saved, and him wanting to save us."

That is also true of Mark's story of Bartimaeus. In that story about how a blind humanity is searching for God, we see that God is also looking for us. As so often happens in Mark's gospel, the two vital energies meet, like the earth that gives growing power to the seed, and the seed that makes the earth bring forth its fruits.

By giving the non-apostle Bartimaeus the rare honour of being named in his gospel, Mark may also be trying to tell us something else: we, too, can get an apostolic name! All of us are called to follow Jesus as his apostles.

To listen is to love

B62. Thirty-first Sunday of the year

Deuteronomy 6:2-6
Hebrews 7:23-28
Mark 12:28-34

It is Jesus' last confrontation with the religious authorities before his arrest and condemnation. The question he is asked – "Which is the first of all the commandments?" – is, indeed, an important one, but it is deliberately asked in a legalistic way in order to catch him out. The question could easily have been phrased in a less confrontational way, such as: "What is the secret of living a good life?"

Jesus' answer is well known. He tells the scribe that the first commandment is to love God with your entire being, and that the second is that you should love your neighbour as you love yourself. However, we have omitted a very small part of Jesus' answer. The first thing Jesus actually says is "Listen, Israel!" The most important thing is to listen and pay attention. That very act of listening speaks volumes for our love of God.

On Sundays, *The New York Times* includes a literary supplement, *The Review of Books*. Each week the supplement lists the best-selling books over the preceding week. There are lists for hardback fiction and non-fiction books, and lists for paperback fiction and non-fiction. It is very rare that those lists contain any religious titles. The Bible itself is excluded from the list on the grounds that it would top the non-fiction lists for ever.

Now and then a "spiritual" book does make it into the lists. One such book was *The Road Less Travelled*, by the psychiatrist M. Scott Peck. Its subtitle describes it as a book about the psychology of love, traditional values, and spiritual growth. This volume has been in the best-seller lists for more than 650 consecutive weeks, which is quite an achievement for a book about the psychology of love!

In the book, the author explains that he believes the most active form of love is to listen to another person. When we genuinely love someone, we have no trouble paying attention to them. Parents know to their financial regret how their love-struck offspring will spend hours on the telephone listening intently to the sugary words of their sweethearts. We are also familiar with the opposite extreme, when someone's eyes look away from us in boredom in the middle of a conversation, and we know that they have no feelings for us because they cannot be bothered to listen. Many a relationship ends with the bitter words: "You never listen to me any more."

You know that someone loves you when that person listens to you attentively with genuine interest, and shows an active concern for your

82

growth and your well-being. When the scribe comes up to Jesus and asks "Which is the first of all the commandments?" Jesus answers, "Listen". Living a good life – a life that is pleasing to God – involves listening to God, to your neighbour, and to yourself. No commandment is more important that this one. To listen is to love life.

Mark tells us that the scribe agrees with Jesus' full answer to the question, saying "Well spoken, Master." He understands, but understanding is not enough. Jesus tells his interrogator that he is not far from the kingdom of God. If only he would listen as well as understand! It is in listening that we enter the kingdom of God.

Givers and takers
B63. Thirty-second Sunday of the year

1 Kings 17:10-16
Hebrews 9:24-28
Mark 12:38-44

Juan Luis Segundo in his book *The Hidden Motives of Pastoral Action* (1978) describes how the Church often allows its word and worship to be manipulated in order to maintain the status quo and the existing (dis-)order. It happens when people of wealth and influence feel threatened by the message of the Good News. The knowledge that through Jesus we all form part of the one family of God, that we are all equal in God's eyes, and that we all share in the same gift of the Holy Spirit is a potent force for change. People in positions of power are often not prepared to sanction that change, so they exert pressure on the ecclesial authorities.

According to some Bible commentators (Derrett, Wright, Fledderman, and Myers, for example), the usual explanation of today's gospel text is a prime example of such a biased, manipulative interpretation. It is the story about the widow who offers her last two coins to the Temple. Her behaviour contrasts sharply with that of the scribes. Jesus compares their hypocrisy with her piety. He praises her and admires her intentions and her devotion. She gives all she has. How often have we heard preachers using her example to persuade the congregation to contribute to all kinds of ecclesial causes?

But this approach overlooks an important point. Jesus' admiration for the widow is coupled with strong reservations about what is happening. Remember that just before this event, Jesus had been speaking about the relationship between widows and the scribes. He condemns the scribes for "swallowing the property of widows". On an earlier occasion, he criticised the Pharisees for persuading people to neglect their parents' welfare to the benefit of the Temple, while cashing in on their false piety (Mark 7:9-13).

Jesus sits down opposite the offering block in the Temple. He studies (that is the word the Greek text uses) what is happening around him. He sees the widow with her two coins, which were the smallest in use. Once he has seen her offering those two coins, he calls his disciples to him. We can guess that they were admiring the Temple with gaping mouths. He tells them what he saw the widow do: "She from the little she had has put in everything she possessed, all she had to live on." He praises her behaviour, but at the same time it sounds like a bitter protest that the scribes and their Temple do not protect a poor widow like that, but only seek to exploit her piety.

Jesus then leaves the Temple. You can almost see him throwing his coat around himself, calling his disciples together, and storming off in protest. In Mark's gospel he never returns. Outside, the disciples exclaim: "Master! Look at the size of those buildings!" He turns to them and says: "You see these great buildings? Not a single stone will be left on another: everything will be destroyed."

It is a strong warning that should make the Church seriously examine its relationships with the poor and needy of this world.

Appointment

B64. Thirty-third Sunday of the year

Daniel 12:1-3
Hebrews 10:11-14, 18
Mark 13:24-32

In our last reflection, we saw how Jesus forecasts the destruction of the Temple. Jesus and the disciples then go to the Mount of Olives, where the disciples ask him when this will come about (Mark 13:3-4).

Jesus' reply (of which today's gospel text is an extract) goes beyond the disciple's original question to consider the events leading up to the end of time. Jesus warns that his followers will be persecuted, and that false prophets will come after him. He tells of the terrible events – the "tribulation" – that will precede his return in glory, and tells his followers to be watchful and on their guard.

That, at least, it the traditional interpretation, but is it possible that Jesus' is also referring to what will happen at his own death? Jesus says that "the sun will be darkened" (13:24) and Mark tells us how, when Jesus is hanging on the cross, there is darkness over the whole land

(15:33). Could it be that "the powers in the heavens" that will be shaken (13:25) are the evil spirits that have been on the run ever since Jesus first cast out an unclean Spirit in the synagogue at Capernaum (1:21-28; see B35: Authority)?

If this is true, it gives verse 30 even more significance: "I tell you solemnly, before this generation has passed away all these things will have taken place." Jesus' generation will, indeed, witness the destruction of the Temple and Jerusalem (in AD 70); we, the readers of Mark's gospel, may well witness the end-time, although only the Father knows when it will happen; and the disciples will witness Jesus' death in a few days' time.

Like all endings, these calamitous events also herald a new beginning. Mark tells us that the Son of Man will send out his angels to gather all his chosen ones from the four corners of the Earth (13:27). The text does, of course, refer to Jesus gathering the faithful into the New Jerusalem, but it may also refer to the fact that Jesus is going to send his disciples out to baptise all the nations in the name of the Father, the Son, and the Holy Spirit.

What this multi-layered text tells us is that when Jesus' life ends on the cross, it marks the beginning of the new humanity, and that this new humanity will reach its fulfilment at the end of time.

After Jesus' burial, the women go to his tomb, only to find a young man dressed in white (Mark 16:5). Is he is an angel? Could he also be an apocalyptic, symbolic figure who represents the reborn humanity made possible by Jesus' resurrection? Whatever the nature of that apparition, the women are given a message that Jesus' followers are to meet him in Galilee.

At the beginning of the Great Jubilee, we have two appointments to keep with Jesus. The second is at the end of time, and who knows when that may be – all we can do is to prepare ourselves and be watchful. The first appointment is now, in "Galilee", where Jesus waits to send us out into the world. This appointment is the event around which the whole of Mark's gospel turns. Mark gave his gospel the title: "The beginning of the Good News of Jesus Christ, the son of God"; Jesus began it, and we are to help him finish the job.

Kingship
B65. Thirty-fourth Sunday of the year

Daniel 7:13-14
Apocalypse 1:5-8
John 18:33-37

On this last Sunday of the year, Pilate asks Jesus: "Are you the king of the Jews?" What a question! How could the Son of God be so partisan as to be king of only one group of people? Jesus' kingdom is not a secular domain full of petty, divisive nationalism and xenophobia.

In some churches, you will find a national flag hanging on the wall or from the ceiling, sometimes over the altar. With such a sad symbol of humanity's division above your head, how could you celebrate the universal love-meal of the Eucharist in a true spirit?

Seeing flags in churches reminds me of my youth in the Netherlands during World War II, when the country was occupied by the Nazis. We boys would never have accept anything from a German soldier, and we stole from them whenever we could. We certainly would never have considered sitting with them at the same table to eat. However, there was one occasion when we broke that rule. It was at Christmas. Some German soldiers had come to our church for Midnight Mass, and we sat with them at the communion table. The Lord's table bridged our enmity. Jesus is not the king of any one group, he is the king of all.

Jesus tells Pilate that he is a king, and that he came into this world to "bear witness to the truth". Then he speaks about all those who listen to him, who hear his voice, and who believe what he tells them. Does that mean all those who listen to him are kings and queens in the way he is? Is that the message he brings? Is that the Good News?

Our traditional Christology does not often discuss such issues, because it is more interested in how Jesus relates to God than how Jesus relates to humanity. As a result, new Christologies are being developed to address these questions. The German theologian Jurgen Moltmann wrote that he is not interested in an eternal Christology for heaven, but in a Christology for men and women who are on their journey through life, and are looking for beacons to show them the way. While the traditional Christologies study Jesus as a divine person, he would like to pay more attention to Jesus as a "social" person.

The texts chosen for our liturgies tend to reinforce the ideas of traditional Christology and stress how different Jesus is from us. The new Christologies take their inspiration from texts that emphasise Jesus' humanity and, indeed, how similar we are to him. Take the text of John 10:34, which says: "Is it not written in your law, you are gods?" Or John 16:7, in which Jesus explains that it is to our own advantage that he is going to the Father, as we would otherwise never receive his Spirit, through which we will do even greater things than Jesus (see John 14:12). The message that we are not so very different from Jesus has been underplayed by the Church for too long.

Throughout this cycle of reflections we have seen how Jesus points the way for each of us to become fully human like him, in the way that God had always intended. As we grow more and more like him, we will share in his kingship, and become kings and queens in the eyes of God. Amen!

1998: The Year of the Holy Spirit

Year C of the Liturgical Cycle

Lord-our-integrity

C1. First Sunday of Advent

Jeremiah 33:14-16

1 Thessalonians 3:13 – 4:2

Luke 21:25-28, 34-36

Sometimes it seems as though the world really is flat, because there is so little depth and perspective to our society! Humanity, it seems, has become one-dimensional, obsessed to the exclusion of all else with the material things of life. We amuse ourselves, we consume, we work, and we drink and eat, while we ourselves are eaten alive by the worries and cares of daily life. There is so little in our politics and national life that has anything to do with new hopes and expectations, or that positively looks forward to the future and promises a better world.

In this information age, the mass media keeps us up to date with everything that is happening in the world. What it shows us is often enough to make us weep or quake in our boots. Without doubt, we need a lot of courage to allow ourselves to be confronted with the state of the world day-in, day-out. Many people do not want that confrontation any more, and avoid watching or listening to the news because it only ever seems to announce more calamities and disasters. They cannot stand what is happening.

It is not selfishness that makes people react in this way: it is a simply a survival technique. Faced with the misery and suffering around us, we retreat into our shells – into our inner fortresses – because the less we expose ourselves to the outside world, the less we can be hurt by it. It is the only way we can cope psychologically and spiritually. We tell one another that it can only get worse. We feel powerless.

Thinking like this, we make our way through life on a day-to-day basis, afraid to look back and only looking forward so that we are not surprised by the calamities that our hearts tell us lie ahead. Consequently, there are no positive plans for the future any more, as if the word "future" refers to nothing more than the duration of our own life. It is this hopeless lack of perspective that Jesus seems to be describing in today's gospel text. Jesus must have met many men and women like this in his own time – people reduced to shrivelled husks by the fear hanging over them.

Jesus and Luke do not deny the seriousness of our human condition. In fact, they dramatise our situation in apocalyptic terms: there is the roar of the ocean and the shaking of the Earth; people will die (or, translating it literally, they will "lose their breath") of fear and terror. These events will be followed by a terrible tension. For those who understand what is happening, it will not lead to a spiritual powerlessness, but to an active alertness, because they know that their "liberation is at hand" (Luke 21:28).

During this time of Advent, when we also look forward to the Great Jubilee, we are invited to face the coming events with our heads held high. We can do this because God is going to establish the heavenly city, which Jeremiah calls "Lord-our-integrity". That is God's promise to us. However, we are no mere passive observers in all this: we are to be God's labourers, laying the foundations for the holy city. We are to help realise God's promise through our lives and work. There is no other way.

With this promise in mind, we can enter Advent with a new, deeper, broader perspective on life.

On the threshold
C2. Second Sunday of Advent

Baruch 5:1-9

Philippians 1:3-6, 8-11

Luke 3:1-6

Israel is in a sorry state: the country is occupied by Roman troops and ruled from afar by the Emperor Tiberius, a corrupt dictator. The occupying army is commanded by a frustrated governor named Pontius Pilate. The local collaborating puppet is Herod. The treacherous and untrustworthy religious leaders are called Annas and Caiphas. The oppressed population pays high taxes to keep Temple and state running.

This is the world John leaves behind when he withdraws into the desert. Like many of us today (see previous reflection), John wants to escape from the misery and corruption of the world around him. He wants to be on his own, to "take off the dress of sorrow and distress" as we read in today's extract from the prophet Baruch. In the loneliness of the desert, the Word of God comes upon John, bringing him a realisation of his true identity and his mission in life.

When John emerges from the wilderness he is calling for repentance, because retribution is imminent. The Belgian theologian Edward Schillebeeckx sees John the Baptist as a prophet of doom, who would have preferred to announce the end of the world than the new beginning Jesus was bringing. Many people today share John's doom-laden outlook on life.

I once met an elderly nun who told me that she could not understand why God did not finish this world once and for all. She confessed that if she were God, her patience and tolerance would have run out by now. I asked her why she felt like that, and in reply she described a world similar to the one from which John was trying to escape: a world full of violence, oppression, misgovernment, and the abuse of power.

During the 1930s, when the Great Depression was at its worst, a play called *Green Pastures* was performed 1,635 times on Broadway. What made the play such a great success was the hope and inspiration it gave its audience during those bleak times. In the play, every time the archangel Gabriel sees the abject misery of the world, he asks God: "May I take my bassoon and give the final signal?" God refuses each time. The audience was reassured that, no matter how bad things were, there had to be better times ahead, because God had not forgotten them.

The doom-laden John would, no doubt, like to play that final note! He uses words rather than music to announce the coming end, speaking of the axe that is poised at the roots of the tree of life, a fire that will burn away everything, and a winnowing-fan that will sift the wheat from the chaff (Matthew 3:10-12). However, this is only half the story: God's judgement may be upon the old world, but salvation is at hand.

John sees himself as standing on the threshold between the old world and the new. In calling for repentance and baptism, he helps others to step over that threshold. He even helps Jesus over it, putting him on the right path from his quiet life in Nazareth to his public ministry in the world, with all its associated political and religious tensions.

In "preparing the way for the Lord", John also crosses the threshold. He will never be able to get back to the quiet of the desert, and neither will Jesus be able to retreat to the privacy of his old life in Nazareth. The same applies to us: once we begin to tread the path that leads of God, there is no turning back.

Conversion is not enough
C3. Third Sunday of Advent

Zephaniah 3:14-18

Philippians 4:4-7

Luke 3:10-18

The people in the crowd understand that John the Baptist's preaching alone will not spare them from the coming retribution. John says that they need to convert, and he asks them to be baptised. They are quite willing to do that – to dispense with the old world and with their old selves – but are conversion and baptism enough? What happens next? Three times they ask John, "What must we do?"

In the southern states of the USA today there are many Christian churches in which those questions are rarely asked and never answered. You could call these churches "conversion communities". Week after week they come together to hear that they are on the wrong road, that they are sinners, and that they should convert and profess that Jesus is their personal saviour. You can find such churches, with their marquee revival-meetings, in Asia, Eastern Europe, and Africa, as well as in the USA. The exclusive emphasis on conversion often prevents their members from developing a spiritual life of any real depth. They are liberated and saved – and that is all. Just as the marquee is taken down and folded up before you know it, the baptismal water quickly washes away the past, leaving the new converts to wonder: "What next?" The American author Mark Twain once wrote: "Revival-mission. Everyone was converted except myself. Within a week they were all sinners again."

John knows that conversion is essential. However, he knows that his converts need to progress beyond this, so he gives advice to the people who ask "What must we do?" He does not advise them to go into the desert like he did or to make sacrifices and wear sackcloth and ashes, or tell them that they should become his disciples. Instead, John tells them to go back into the world and make good their conversion by the way they treat their neighbours.

This all sounds a bit of a let-off, because he even says that tax collectors and soldiers can maintain their status and profession on condition that they are honest. However, the fundamental piece of advice John gives to everyone applies equally to the tax collectors and soldiers: "Anyone who has two tunics must share with the one who has none, and anyone with something to eat must do the same."

This is a is radical command, because it proclaims that the goods of this world are to be shared with everyone, without exception. This beautiful principle is so obvious, so logical, so humane, and at the same time so divine that it is hardly ever put into practice!

No gospel author took the difference between rich and poor as seriously as Luke. It is Luke who disapprovingly writes about those who "live in luxury" (Luke 6:24-26), and he is the only one who puts that remark about tunics and food into the mouth of John.

The crowd around John must have reacted to the advice just as we would do, saying; "You must be joking! You can't really expect us to do that!" That is why John adds that the baptism he brings is not powerful enough to give them the strength to do this. Someone else is going to come who is more powerful than he is; someone who is not only going to wash away the sins of the past, but who will baptise with Spirit and fire. It is the baptism of Jesus that will give them the strength to live out their conversion in their day-to-day lives.

Blessed among women
C4. Fourth Sunday of Advent

Micah 5:1-4

Hebrews 10:5-10

Luke 1:39-45

In the gospel text of today, Mary's "kinswoman" Elizabeth says to her: "Of all women you are the most blessed, and blessed is the fruit of your womb" (Luke 1:42). Notice how Elisabeth uses the word "blessed" twice: once to refer to a woman, and once to refer to a man. Mary is blessed because she is the only woman whom each of us can address as "the mother of my Lord". Jesus is blessed because he is God's Son in this world. Even today, the Church still struggles to understand the full ramifications of this.

Mariology is currently one of the most rapidly developing themes in theology, especially in liberation theology. This is hardly surprising, considering the failure of the Church's hierarchy through the ages to recognise the role and place of women in the Church. When you read the words of Mary's Magnificat – with its promise that the hungry will get their fill while the rich will be sent away empty – it is easy to see why Mariology has found many enthusiasts among liberation theologians. This much-loved hymn contains several echoes of older freedom songs sung by women throughout the Bible. It is a liberation song that often still sounds from the mouths of women throughout the world.

In 1979, the Brazilian liberation theologian Leonardo Boff suggested that Mary's femininity is so intimately related to the character of the Holy Spirit that one might speak of a hypostatical union between the two. According to Boff, the continuing development of feminist theology and the trend towards deeper reflection on the assumption of Mary into heaven will inevitably lead to this conclusion. All this sounds very abstract, especially when compared with the concrete hope expressed by the two women in Luke's text.

Karl Rahner was once asked why he thought that devotion to Mary had diminished. In reply, he said that since the Second Vatican Council, theologians had gained too much influence in the Church. This had diverted attention away from Mary and onto all kinds of theological abstractions. He added: "Abstractions are in no need of a mother."

Hopes, however, are more concrete than theological abstractions, and they do need a mother – they need Mary, the mother of God. That is why Mary's Magnificat is still sung wherever there is injustice in our world. It was sung by the women who protested in front of the palace of President Marcos in the Philippines, and by Polish trade union leaders when the Pope visited the Black Madonna, as a protest against the oppression of their country. By singing that song, they held up the figure of Mary as an emblem of human hope, pregnant with the new life of God.

"Yes, blessed is she who believed that the promise made her by the Lord would be fulfilled." This is Luke's first beatitude!

Christmas story
C5. Midnight Mass (Christmas)

Isaiah 9:1-7

Titus 2:11-14

Luke 2:1-14

Christmas is a special time of story-telling, when parents enthral their children with tales of Father Christmas, the Nativity, classics such as *A Christmas Carol*, and all kinds of fables and fairy tales. Children love stories. In fact, stories are indispensable to children, because it is through stories that they learn so many of the norms, values, and standards that underpin our society. Child psychologists know this is true because it is proven by research, but children know it instinctively. Children are always asking you to read or tell them stories, and they will often ask you to repeat the same story over and over again until they have squeezed the last drops of meaning and enjoyment out of it.

Television will never completely replace story-telling. Most younger children prefer a well-told story to a television programme, because television translates everything into pictures and leaves nothing to the imagination. In the freedom of your own imagination, you can compose whatever images you want as the words leap out at you from the page. Perhaps that is why a film adaptation can be so disappointing if you have already read the book.

Children often feel confused and threatened by things they do not understand. They may feel trapped in certain situations, and at a loss to know how to behave. This is nothing new – people have always known that about children. One on the functions of fairy tales was to help children overcome these difficulties. Fears, anxieties, and the unknown were personified as strange beats and monsters that were always tamed or slain at the end of the story. Interwoven with the plot would be coded moral instructions, role models, and societal values. Of course, the stories were also meant to entertain.

In Africa, there are many stories about the Spider Anansi, a trickster who uses his cunning and guile to outwit others. In one story, Anansi tells himself: "If only we knew the stories God tells about us, then we would be as wise as the Almighty." Anansi spins the longest-ever thread and climbs all the way up to heaven. After many days of climbing, Anansi arrives at the throne of Nyame, the god of the sky, who keeps all God's stories locked up in golden safe next to his throne. When Anansi asks for those stories, Nyame says that he can only have them if he can first perform three feats – of course, these feats are well-nigh impossible. However, using his cunning and deceit, Anansi accomplishes all three and makes off with the stories.

I could flesh this tale out with more details, but the reason I mention it is to illustrate the point that stories are highly valued and cherished in every culture and in every continent and country. We all know that we need those stories – especially stories about our creation and origins, which tell us where we come from, where we are now, and how we should behave in life.

On Christmas Eve we get to hear one of God's stories: the story of how God sent us a new beginning in the form of the Prince of Peace, who was born in a stable in Bethlehem. God's own offspring, Emmanuel (meaning "God-with-us"), came to live among us and unite us in God's love. It is a moving story, full of stars and angels; sheep and shepherds; a mother, father and a new-born baby, a death-threat from a tyrant, an escape, and a happy ending. It is a story that cannot be matched.

Many children (and more than a few adults!) will ask you whether the story is true and whether those events really happened. That is a difficult question to answer: it was a long time ago, and not all the facts can be verified from historical records. Perhaps we should look at the question from a different angle: is the true story not the tale which helps us most in life? If that is so, then the truth of the Christmas story will be attested by the hordes of people – both believers and unbelievers – who come together tonight to hear it told once again.

Even people who never come during the rest of the year will be in church tonight to listen to God's story. After 2,000 years, the stars on the horizon of our human destiny many seem very faint to the poor, the oppressed, the lonely, the sick, the marginalised, and those paralysed by fear and worry. We need that story, with its bright, guiding star!

First and foremost
C6. Feast of the Holy Family

Sirach 3:2-6, 12-14

Colossians 3:12-21

Luke 2:41-52

How can we celebrate the feast of the Holy Family when our gospel reading shows that family group in conflict and turmoil? Jesus is 12 years old, which means that society no longer considers him a child; by the same token, neither is he yet a man. It is a difficult period for an adolescent child, and also for the parents.

When the family leaves Jerusalem after their Passover pilgrimage, Mary notices that Jesus is not returning with her and the other women. She probably thinks: "Only 12, but he considers himself a man! He must be walking ahead with Joseph and the other men." However, in front of her Joseph has noticed that Jesus is not with his group, and muses: "Even though he's 12 years old, he still walks with his mother like a child!"

Amazingly, it is the evening before Mary and Joseph realise that Jesus is missing. The next day, they hurry back to Jerusalem, but it is another three days before they find him – in the Temple, of all places, and asking questions of the doctors of the Law! The text says that Mary and Joseph are "overcome" when they see him. Do they weep, laugh, or get angry? The answer is probably that they do all three!

Mary scolds him, protesting: "My child, why have you done this to us? See how worried your father and I have been looking for you." Had Jesus not spared a thought for them? Jesus looks at her and says, "Why were you looking for me? ... Did you not know that I must be with my Father's affairs?" It was as if he wanted to tell them: "I am quite willing to listen to you, but my priority is to listen to my Father ... God is the Father I am thinking of, whom I love first and foremost."

Luke adds that neither Mary nor Joseph understands what he means. Mary stores it all up in her heart, along with a host of other strange events that have happened since his birth. It is only later, when she is standing at the foot of the cross, that she fully understands all these things. But, at this moment in time, there is clearly something about her son that remains a riddle to her. In due course, she learns to respect this, and in the end it becomes the foundation of her own existence.

Our own families and communities experience all kinds of problems, from quarrels, infidelity, and betrayal, to financial difficulties, breakdowns of communication, and so on. Do we ever find among those conflicts the problem the Holy Family experienced in Nazareth? Are we, as families and communities, seriously committed to realising God's plans in our world and genuinely interested in issues such as justice, unity, and peace? If we were, it would help us to see our own problems in perspective, and thus make them easier to solve.

Jesus obeys his parents and goes home with them, but something will be different from now on. Mary and Joseph now know what his first priority will be, and it will be theirs, too. Their life as a family will be determined by their relationship to God. That is why they formed a "holy" family.

Mary, mother of God
C7. Octave of Christmas

Numbers 6:22-27

Galatians 4:4-7

Luke 2:16-21

In his book *The Anthills of the Savannah*, the Nigerian author Chinua Achebe remarks that both the African and biblical traditions blame the woman for everything that goes wrong in the world.

In African stories, God originally lived so close to people that women often hit God when they were crushing grain with their pestles. God repeatedly asked them to be more careful, but each time the women got back to their chatting and started swinging their pestles carelessly, hitting God again. Eventually, God gave up and disappeared up into the sky, leaving humanity to face the consequences. After that, things just got worse and worse.

In Genesis, we see how God visits paradise to talk with Adam and Eve, and discovers that the woman has been beguiled by the serpent into eating the forbidden fruit (Genesis 2:8-13). God returns only once more to paradise, and that is to chase them out.

Achebe comments that in both traditions the men knew that their stories did not add up, which is why they devised other stories to rid themselves of their guilty feelings. In Africa, it is said that women will save society when it becomes totally corrupted. This is not dissimilar to the Judeo-Christian tradition, which tell that, in the final instance, a woman will squash the devil's head (Genesis 2:15).

You have to be suspicious when a patriarchal society enthrones a woman, as ours does. The Church has sometimes glorified Mary to such an extent that the Church's portrayal of her hardly resembles a real woman – her feet do not even touch the ground! Is there more to this than centuries of male clergy assuaging their guilt? Could it be that emphasising Mary's extra-ordinariness is a way of keeping "ordinary" women in the background, playing second fiddle in the Church to men?

The gospels give a more realistic, meaningful picture of Mary, without many of the "glorious" trimmings. When we first meet her, Mary is covered by the shadow of God's power (Luke 1:35). Yet, even at that moment, she is ready with a question: "But how can this come about, since I am a virgin?"

The gospel descriptions of Mary that follow are rather reserved. Today's text tells us that Mary does not understand the events surrounding Jesus' birth, just as she does not comprehend what it means when Jesus gets lost in the Temple at Jerusalem (Luke 2:41-50). She is puzzled by her son's life and actions, and sometimes even has disagreements with him (John 2:1-12). She is not so far removed from reality after all.

In a list of heresies of the year AD 374, the writer Epiphanius mentions a group of women who separated from the Church because they were disappointed by the Church's attitude to Mary. Part of their heresy was to hold that Mary never died. Was this a way of protesting about male domination of the early Church?

Those who have difficulties in recognising the role of women in the Church still have to admit that Mary was the mother of Jesus, and that it was through her – a woman – that he came into the world. The lay-preacher Sojourner Truth, an African-American woman, once pointed at a clergyman in her audience and said: "Then that little man in black there, he says women can't have as much rights as men, because Christ wasn't a woman! Where did your Christ come from? From God and woman! Man had nothing to do with him!"

We should promote a real appreciation of the Mary of the gospels, and strive tirelessly for the equality of women in the structures and theology of the Church.

True wisdom

C8. Epiphany

Isaiah 60:1-6

Ephesians 3:2-3, 5-6

Matthew 2:1-12

According to Matthew's story, at least three people came from afar to visit Jesus. They are sometimes described as kings, but the preferred term these days seems to be "magi", or wise men. This is certainly more appropriate, because although the world has virtually dispensed with kings and queens, we definitely need as many wise people as possible!

We do not know how the wise men would have described themselves, but the fact that they made the journey to Bethlehem shows that they were, indeed, seekers after the truth. Asking questions always has been considered as the beginning of wisdom, and I am sure that the magi were continually asking questions about the world, about the workings of the Universe, and about human destiny. They sought the truth, they asked questions, and they must also have been watchful and alert, because they saw the star in the sky. The magi recognised this star as a sign.

To these wise men, there were more dimensions to life than the physical one in which they ate, drank, and slept. While they accepted the physical world, they also looked beyond it to a different world. That is the secret of true wisdom. They knew that there is more to reality than what we can see, touch, taste, hear, and smell. They were "religious people". Religion indicates that you feel "ligated" or bonded to something beyond yourself, that your life is connected to the spiritual dimension of reality.

To the magi, the star was like a big question mark in the sky. What did it mean? According to the legend, the star beckoned them to follow it, with its long tail indicating the direction in which they should travel, and where the answer to the question lay. To be so adventurous as to follow the star, they must have felt that something new and significant was going to happen – that it heralded a great change in the world.

Their wisdom is indicated by the fact that they already knew half the answer to their question. They knew that they were not looking for a learned book or document, or for a new political system or a novel sociological, economic, or psychological theory. When they arrived in Jerusalem, they said that they are looking for an "infant" (Matthew 2:2).

In our heart of hearts, we all know that in times of difficulty only another person can help us – not books, ideology, or wealth. A hospital or clinic may have the most advanced scanners, drugs, therapy techniques, and so on, but if we do not find someone who is personally interested in us and willing to help us, that impressive inventory is of no use at all. Similarly, the best textbooks and learning tools are no substitute for a good teacher.

The three magi knew that. They were looking for an answer or a solution – salvation, even. They also knew that it would come in the form of a person from another dimension – that is, from the dimension of the divine and the heavenly. They were looking for the way God's answer to the world's problems was going to break through into human history and change our destiny.

Activating the Spirit
C9. Baptism of the Lord (Sunday after Epiphany)

Isaiah 42:1-4, 6-7

Acts 10:34-38

Luke 3:15-16, 21-22

In Luke's gospel, Jesus' baptism takes up just two pithy sentences. Jesus is baptised and then begins to pray. Until this moment, Jesus has been completely inconspicuous. Jesus is simply one among hundreds, maybe even thousands. However, while Jesus is at prayer, all that changes. From our other reflections on this event, we know what happens next off by heart: the Holy Spirit descends on Jesus and a voice rings out, saying: "You are my Son, the Beloved; my favour rests in you."

Immediately after heaven has opened for this dramatic revelation, Luke gives us the genealogy of Jesus. It is as if Luke is worried that we might be so overwhelmed by Jesus's divine origin that we will forget that he is a human being, just like us.

Does Jesus' baptism give him something that he did not have before? This question brings one of those "yes-no" answers. Jesus does not suddenly become the "Beloved" at the moment heaven opens – he already is that, and he always will be. Nevertheless, Jesus seems to react as though he has been unexpectedly struck by the Holy Spirit. The transformation is dramatic: he does not return to Nazareth but disappears into the desert, re-emerging to start his public ministry. The most likely explanation is that Jesus' baptism marks a milestone in his understanding of himself – a realisation of exactly who he is.

Our own baptism is often described as an initiation rite, and it may be useful to think about Jesus' baptism in those terms. An initiation rite does not give you anything new, but simply formalises something that is already in you or that has already occurred. Take the young Africans who are introduced into adult society through an initiation rite. These adolescents already possess the potency to become fathers and mothers, but the initiation rite publicises that potency and makes it "official" in the eyes in the community.

Pope John Paul II constantly repeats in his encyclicals how every human being is equipped with the Spirit of God, which is breathed into us at the moment of our creation. When we encounter Jesus Christ, we see ourselves as in a mirror. That discovery invites us to activate the Holy Spirit within us, and formally accept its guiding and empowering role in our lives. For the unbaptised adult, baptism means entering a new understanding of our true nature and relating to God in a new way.

The principle of the indwelling of the Holy Spirit pervades all the encyclicals of Pope John Paul II. This wonderful truth is at the heart of all the concrete things he has written on the role of the Trinity and of

100

Jesus Christ in the life of a human being; on human rights and the rights of workers; on the distribution of goods and work in our world; on evangelisation and mission; on inter-faith dialogue and ecumenism, on the gospel of life and a civilisation of love. The Pope stresses that the acknowledgement of this divine presence in every human being is the way the Church has to follow in the years ahead.

In today's text from the Acts of the Apostles, Peter says it in another, more simple, way: "The truth that I have come to realise is that God does not have favourites, but that anybody of any nationality who fears God and does what is right is acceptable to him."

To work is to fast
C10. Ash Wednesday

Joel 2:12-18

2 Corinthians 5:20-6:2

Matthew 6:1-6, 16-18

Lent is thought of as a time of fasting, when Christians prepare themselves for the festival of Easter. Fasting traditionally involved abstaining from eating, or at least from eating certain meals or certain foods. It was a discipline that often required considerable self-sacrifice and hardship. Today, many Christians choose to fast simply by giving up something that is not that essential to them – something that we consider to be a mild "vice", such as indulging in chocolate or drinking alcohol. When we decide on what we are giving up as our Lenten fast, we frequently tell our friends and family, as if to say, "Aren't I good!" This is exactly what Jesus warns against in today's reading from Matthew.

In general, fasting as a serious religious discipline to help us concentrate on our spiritual life appears to be in decline. Over the years, the perception as well as the practice of fasting seems to have changed. The way many saints used to fast – mortifying themselves with hairshirts and flagellating themselves – is now more likely to be seen as a sign of an unhealthy mind rather than as a healthy sign of piety!

Our modern attitude to religious fasting is not helped by the fact that the secular Western world seems have taken over the idea of "fasting" and the "mortification of the flesh": dieting of one kind or another seems to be the "lifestyle" choice of many people, while disciplining the body and putting it through all kinds of trials is commonly practised by those who strive to stay in peak condition or improve their appearance to achieve success in sport and business, or simply in their social life.

But there are other ways of fasting: as well as giving something up for God, we can also do something extra – that is, put extra effort into doing God's will. In today's extract from Saint Paul's second letter to the Corinthians, Paul is asking us to discipline ourselves in order to become "fellow workers" with Jesus Christ. Why not make Jesus' work our fast?

To consider work as fasting is nothing new. Older readers may be able to recall the time when "hard" work discharged labourers of the obligation to restrict their food intake during Lent. Not all work qualified for that dispensation – it all depended on why and how the work was done.

In a recent poll, law students in the USA were asked why they had decided to study that particular subject. The majority replied that their choice had been determined by the amount of money they could earn once they were qualified. Others spoke of the prestige they hoped their future profession would give them. Thirty per cent answered that they studied law because they were interested in a more righteous world, and it is this type of work that corresponds to the asceticism in the life of Jesus. It is an asceticism that Pope John Paul II stressed in his writings to prepare us for the Great Jubilee.

Of course, we work for our daily bread, but that should not be the defining characteristic of our work. We are engaged in something much broader than simply working to achieve a decent standard of living for ourselves and for others. We are co-workers of Jesus Christ. This means that we are to work at establishing God's kingdom here on Earth. We should carry out everything we do – both professionally and voluntarily – in the true spirit of one of Jesus' labourers. If we see all the difficulties we encounter in our jobs as part of the work of Jesus, then we will find real meaning in our work.

Tempted leadership
C11. First Sunday of Lent

Deuteronomy 26:4-10

Romans 10:8-13

Luke 4:1-13

Bishops and priests frequently take it upon themselves to share their responsibility and stimulate what some of them would call the "empowerment" of all the faithful. The Church as a whole did that during the Second Vatican Council, and this initiative produced many important local developments throughout the world. However, such initiatives are often obstructed by the Church's bureaucracy, which has difficulty in appreciating the conscientisation of the laity. They can also be thwarted by the unwillingness of people at the grass-roots level to accept the shift of responsibility from church leaders to themselves.

Paul writes to us all: "The word, that is the faith we proclaim, is very near to you, it is on your lips and in your heart" (Romans 10:8). We should pay attention to this, because leaders are often tempted to think that the word only sounds from their own mouths, and there are plenty of followers who simply want to be told what to do. Jesus warned us against such attitudes.

In today's gospel reading, we see a Spirit-filled Jesus standing at the cross-roads of his life. The devil knows that when Jesus leaves the wilderness he will embark on his public ministry, so now is the time to try and seduce him away from his mission.

First the devil encourages him to make bread from stones to satisfy his hunger. Later in Jesus' life, hungry people will come to Jesus asking him to guarantee them their daily bread. Then the tempter challenges Jesus to take over all political power. Later on, people will ask Jesus to be their king. Finally, the evil one asks Jesus to give a sign of his power by jumping from the top of the Temple so that he can be miraculously saved by his angels. In the near future, people will ask Jesus again and again to give them a sign by performing a spectacular miracle. Jesus refuses to give in to any of these temptations, declining the opportunity to play roles that would take responsibility away from others.

Far back in Old Testament history, God did exactly what the devil is challenging Jesus to do now – God had taken over and solved peoples problems for them. Just look at today's reading from Deuteronomy, which says, in effect: "My father was a wandering Aramaean. He was ill-treated, but we called on Yahweh, and Yahweh's mighty hand brought us out of Egypt with great terror, and with signs and wonders." However, the time of that kind of divine intervention is over: no generation has understood that more than our own in this post-Holocaust era.

Jesus was tempted to take over from us. Thank God he overcame that temptation! If he had not done so, we would never have found the word on our own lips and in our hearts. We would have remained like children, always needing someone to work miracles for us and tell us what to do.

One of Rabbi Mosche Leib's disciples asked him why God allowed so much wickedness in the world. The old rabbi answered: "So that you will never be able to let someone starve whilst consoling him with heaven or telling him to trust in God. You, yourself, have to help him as if there were no God at all – as if you were the only one able to help. You and no one else. That is why God tolerates such wickedness."

When the word is in our mouths and hearts, God expects from us a maturity and a willingness to accept responsibility for our lives.

A long journey
C12. Second Sunday of Lent

Genesis 15:5-12, 17-18

Phillipians 3:17-4:1

Luke 9:28-36

Luke describes Jesus' life as a journey towards the kingdom of God. Early in Jesus' public ministry, Luke tells how Jesus "resolutely took the road for Jerusalem" (9:51). Jesus' journey is the thread onto which Luke threads the key events of Jesus' life, like pearls on a string. Jesus is not the only one who makes a journey in Luke's gospel: Mary, for example, hastens to Elizabeth, the shepherds come to Bethlehem, Joseph and Mary go to Jerusalem and return without him, and so on.

Even after Jesus' resurrection, Luke sticks to this narrative pattern. Jesus walks with two of his disciples, one of whom is Cleopas, as they make their way home to Emmaus. It is late afternoon, and as they walk they tell Jesus of their disappointments, doubts, and sadnesses. He enlightens their minds and warms their hearts, but for some reason they do not recognise Jesus until he breaks their bread. As soon as they realise who he is, he vanishes. Although it is not long since they arrived home, they set out again immediately for Jerusalem – disregarding the dangers of the night – to tell the apostles what has happened (Luke 24:13-35). It seems that an encounter with Jesus always results in people setting off on a journey!

Before Jesus ascends to heaven, he instructs his disciples to go to the ends of the Earth with the Good News. That is exactly what Luke did himself. He travelled the length and breadth of the then known world, from Macedonia to Syria, Palestine, Malta, and even Italy. His book Acts of the Apostles is one long story about the apostolic journeys of Peter, Paul, and many others. Luke describes how the Good News travelled from the mother church in Jerusalem to Judea, Samaria, Damascus, Phoenicia, Cyprus, the Roman provinces of Cilicia, Galatia, Achaia, Asia, and finally Rome itself – "the end of the Earth".

Today's gospel reading is another episode on Jesus' journey. Jesus takes Peter, John, and James to the top of Mount Tabor. As Jesus begins to pray, Moses and Elijah appear with him. Jesus radiates and shines as he discusses with his two predecessors "his passing which he was going to accomplish in Jerusalem" (Luke 9:31). The word Luke uses for that "passing" is the Greek word exodos. It is an exodus from the old, diseased world to the new, healthy world of the kingdom of God; it is an exodus from the dark night into bright daylight.

All Jesus' disciples are invited to accompany Jesus on this exodus journey, which leads to the glory they suddenly see shining from within him there on the mountain. The light at the end of the journey is important, because one would not want to walk out into the dark night without the certainty that day will soon dawn. We all need that "light at the end of the tunnel".

Three times Luke refers to the path Jesus calls us to follow as the "Way" (Acts 9:2; 19:9, 23). As far Luke is concerned, whenever we encounter Jesus we are set on our way towards the light of a new human life. It may be a long journey, but we are assured that it will be a rewarding one.

Sickness and healing
C13. Third Sunday of Lent

Exodus 3:1-8, 13-15

1 Corinthians 10:1-6, 10-12

Luke 13:1-9

We know from Paul's letter to the Colossians that Luke was a Greek doctor (Colossians 4:14). Although Luke's gospel does not specifically mention the profession of its writer, the traditional assumption is backed up by the precise way in which the symptoms of diseases are recorded: we see the miraculous healings performed by Jesus through a medical eye.

Being a doctor himself, Luke portrays Jesus as a healer. In fact, in Luke's account of Jesus' first public appearance in the synagogue at Nazareth, Jesus says: "No doubt you will quote me the saying, 'Physician, heal yourself'" (Luke 4:23).

Doctor Luke looked at the symptoms shown by the world in which he lived, and pronounced it to be chronically sick. His gospel lists at least 24 different diagnoses of people with moral aberrations, from heartless priests and lazy servants to money-lusting farmers and corrupt lawyers.

Luke's gospel shows how Jesus came to heal this sick world. When the imprisoned John the Baptist sends his disciples to ask Jesus whether he is "the one who is to come", Jesus' answer is about that healing:

"Go back and tell John what you have seen and heard: the blind see again, the lame walk, lepers are cleansed, and the deaf hear, the dead are raised to life ..." (Luke 7:22).

Healing is a curious process. Is it really the doctor who heals, or the patient? If you go to the doctor when you are sick and ask, "Do you think you can heal me?", a smart doctor will not answer with an unqualified "Yes". What that doctor will tell you is that he or she can trigger off a healing process by stimulating something within you. The doctor can treat symptoms and create a situation in which healing can occur, but the process can only be completed by the actions of your mind and body. So healing can be initiated from outside, but it is ultimately accomplished from within.

The second question most sick people ask is: "Why am I ill? How did I get this disease?" In some circumstances, this question may be little more than a coded version of: "Who gave it to me? Whose fault is it?"

Today's gospel story addresses those questions. Jesus is told of two terrible recent tragedies: some Galileans have been murdered in the Temple at Jerusalem, while in Siloam, a tower has collapsed, killing 18 people. Everyone seems to agree that, in each case, there is a connection between those tragic events and the moral disease in their midst. Who is to blame? Did the victims bring this fate upon themselves?

Jesus says that the people who perished were no more guilty or sinful than anyone else – no one can wash their hands in innocence. He explains that it is more helpful to know how to get rid of their misery, rather than to apportion blame or cast judgement on others. The remedy is that all must repent and convert. In Luke, Jesus' work centres around a formula for healing the world: a conversion, a reconciliation of the past, and a healed continuation of life.

The story about the barren, sickly fig tree in a vineyard illustrates that process. The earth around the fruitless tree will be turned and manured once more in the hope that the next season fruits will be produced. All kinds of things are done to make the tree fruitful but, in the final instance, the outcome depends on the tree. If that fig tree remains insensitive and unresponsive to all the care it is given, and still produces no fruit, then the tree is past hope. Alas!

Accepting ourselves
C14. Fourth Sunday of Lent

Joshua 5:9-12

2 Corinthians 5:17-21

Luke 15:1-3, 11-32

The parable of the prodigal ("recklessly wasteful") son has probably

106

provoked more discussion than any other parable told by Jesus. It has been painted, dramatised, put to music, and commented upon in myriad different ways. It is such a well-known story that practically everyone recognises it immediately, even those who are not church-goers. This parable can sometimes have dramatic effects upon its readers, as the following story shows ....

A young man in our parish who was the child of an alcoholic father was going through a deep personal crisis, so he decided to go on a marathon 30-day retreat. It was a bold but important step. Happily it paid off, because the young man came back changed, and he wanted to share his experience with the rest of the parish. He explained how the story of the prodigal son had given him the impulse he needed to recover. To help him meditate on the story, he had used a picture by Rembrandt, which shows the Father embracing the wayward son. The young man said that as soon as he identified with the returning son, he understood that God loved him very deeply.

Suddenly, he almost jumped from his chair as he had a new insight into the picture. He realised something that had not even crossed his mind during that 30-day retreat: it was not only the Father who forgave his son, but the son also forgave himself. Until that moment, the young man had never been able to love himself – this was the "shadow side" to his personality. Then and there he decided to accept himself as he was and to thank God!

In explaining his experiences, the young man used the old King James translation of the Bible, which describes how the wayward son "came to himself" in the stench and squalor of the pigsty and confronted himself with his failings. The "shadow side" to his personality was that he really craved the responsibilities and duties (and hence the esteem in his father's eyes) that his older brother had. Once he understood this, he decided to return to his father.

When the eldest son saw how his disreputable brother was received by his father, he was upset, jealous, and puzzled. "I have slaved for you and never once disobeyed your orders," he said to his father in all truthfulness, but not without some bitterness. His father praised him for his obedience and fidelity, but added: "We should celebrate and rejoice, because your brother here was dead and has now come to life ...."

In reality, both brothers were lost until they faced up to their shadow sides. The older brother's overwhelming sense of duty made him suppress any thought of pleasure or enjoyment for himself, while his younger brother's exaggerated sense of fun led him to repress his sense of duty. They were like two sides of the same coin!

We all have a little of both brothers within us. We must accept our duties and responsibilities and carry them out in a way that shows our love for others and for ourselves. Only then will we be able to truly enjoy our lives and be able to live with real integrity.

107

On the side of the people

C15. Fifth Sunday of Lent

Isaiah 43:16-21

Philippians 3:8-14

John 8:1-11

The Pharisees ask Jesus to take sides in a contentious situation: should the adulterous woman be stoned to death, according to the Mosaic Law? They know that Jesus could not possibly stand by and watch her being stoned, and they hope that his answer will give them ammunition to use against him. They are flummoxed by Jesus' ingenious answer (John 8:7). He takes sides against no one, but in favour of the woman.

Jesus always acts in a way that preserves the unity of God's family. When Jesus dismisses the woman, telling her to "go and don't sin any more," he is confident that she will not revert to her old ways because he sees something positive and lasting within her – her faith. Not only has the woman been helped to leave her sinful ways behind, but her accusers also go home better people, because Jesus' challenge that only the sinless can throw the first stone has forced them to make an honest assessment of themselves. Jesus is doing what Isaiah prophesied in today's Old Testament reading: "See, I am doing a new deed, even now it comes to light; can you not see it?" (43:19).

The new deed that Jesus brings to the world is to choose the side of humanity every time. He is on the side of Peter and the lame man, of Levi and the prostitute, of the lost sheep and the prodigal son, of Zaccheus, and of the adulterous woman in the gospel story of today. He is always giving hope and helping people on their way. Even when he is nailed to the cross, Luke tells us that he nevertheless prays: "Father, forgive them; they do not know what they are doing" (Luke 23:34). Despite the agony of his crucifixion, Jesus still has compassion on those around him. He tells one of the murderers crucified with him, "Today you will be with me in paradise" (Luke 23:43).

The diary of Etty Hillesum, a young Jewish woman imprisoned in a Nazi concentration camp during World War II, echoes Jesus' sentiments. In her diary, Etty concludes that God, whom she found in the deepest part of her inner being, can be found in every person. One evening, she writes: "I will have to pray tonight for that German soldier ... he is suffering, too ... on both sides of those borders [between human beings] people are suffering and one should pray for all of them. Good night."

In Ravensbrück concentration camp, an anonymous prayer written on a piece of brown packing paper was found on the body of a dead child. The poem notes: "O God, do not think only of the women and men of good will, but think also of those of bad will. Do not only think of the suffering they caused us, but also of the fruits that suffering produced: our comradeship, our fidelity, our humility, our generosity, and the greatness of heart that has been growing out of all this. When they come to judgement, let the fruits we rendered be their forgiveness."

So we see that the good and the bad, the oppressors and the oppressed, the rich and the poor are not separated – they are all kept together by Jesus in God's family. This is because God has made a choice, and that choice is unity, coherence, and the final goodness of life.

Death threats
C16. Palm/Passion Sunday

Isaiah 50:4-7

Philippians 2:6-11

Luke 22:14-23, 56

In about 1970, a small Christian community formed in San Salvador. They had no water, no electricity, and no school. The people were poor, hungry, and without hope. Some of the men and women had realised that, despite the atrocious conditions in which they lived, every person in that community harboured many God-given possibilities within them that were just waiting to be realised.

They started a prayer group together and focused on the themes of light and dark in John's gospel. In the beginning there were only a few, but the group soon grew. As people found inspiration and hope in the word of God, they began to tackle the problems in their lives – their alcoholism, their debts, their despair, and their suicidal thoughts. Eventually, they became confident enough to start a credit union, and then a building society. They argued successfully with the authorities to connect them to the water and electricity supplies. They combated their greed, egoism, and machismo. Little by little, the whole community was beginning to heal.

As the community became more and more organised, the authorities became more and more suspicious. The community leaders were labelled progressive and dangerous. Arrests, interrogations, disappearances, and persecutions followed, and three priests in the group – Trutiullio Grande, Alfonso Navarro, and Ernesto Barrero – were murdered between 1977 and 1978.

Their archbishop, Oscar Romero, was convinced that the priests had been shot because of their pastoral work and pointed an accusing finger at the authorities. Romero himself was killed on 24 March 1980, while celebrating the Eucharist. Some days before, he had written: "I often get death threats; I honestly confess that as a Christian I don't believe in death without a resurrection. If they murder me I will rise in the people of El Salvador ... and when they execute their threats I will offer my blood to God for the salvation and resurrection of El Salvador." Today, more than 15 years later, that prophecy is fulfilled: Romero's portrait hangs in countless shops, living rooms, churches, and markets throughout El Salvador.

The message of this story is that we cannot make the option for the poor without suffering ourselves.

When Jesus entered Jerusalem on a donkey (Luke 19:28-40), the poor and oppressed, to whom he had given so much hope, cried out: "Blessings on the King who comes in the name of the Lord!" They shouted as loud as they could, hoping that the authorities, the priests, the Romans, and their own political leaders would hear them. They understood that they had to support him because he would have to undergo much suffering for their sake. The Pharisees reproached Jesus for their behaviour, saying: "Master, check your disciples!" Jesus refused to silence the crowd, knowing that only those who are prepared to shout and cry about the state of the world will be willing to work for change.

Whenever and wherever you promote justice, peace, and love in the name of the kingdom of God, you will encounter resistance from those in authority. Jesus had no illusions about this, and neither did Oscar Romero. In Luke's gospel, there is never a doubt as to what the outcome of Jesus' ministry will be: death. For Jesus, death was no tragic anti-climax. Indeed, it was the beginning of a new hope – the same hope that sustained Romero in the face of death.

Jesus rode into Jerusalem knowing that the echoes of the "Hosannas!" and "Alleluias!" around him would soon be replaced by the piercing shouts of "Crucify him!", but still he rode on.

Recognising Jesus
C17. Easter Sunday

Acts 10:34, 37-43

Colossians 3:1-4

Luke 24:13-35

In Luke's gospel today we encounter two desolate travellers on their way from Jerusalem to Emmaus. They had given up hope, because they had thought that Jesus would solve the world's problems.

Before they had left the rest of Jesus' followers in Jerusalem to walk the long road home, they had heard something about his empty tomb, but they did not see that it was significant. Even if Jesus had risen from the dead, so what? He would not have been the first: they could think of Lazarus and the son of that widow in Nain just for a start. Had those resurrections changed the world? Not in the slightest! Sure, they were grandiose signs, but of what? They explained to the lonely traveller who had joined them on the road that the world needed to be redeemed, not resurrected. They felt cheated, let down, and deceived.

Their complaints revolved more around what they had expected Jesus to do than around Jesus himself, although their fellow traveller politely tried to put them right by explaining what their holy scriptures had prophesied about Jesus.

It was only when they broke bread with the traveller that they realised exactly who he was. Had Jesus told them on their on their journey that the Messiah had come to Earth to break bread with humanity? We cannot be sure, but there must have been a connection between what Jesus told them on the road and what they suddenly understood and felt when he broke bread in their presence.

Today, we celebrate not only that Jesus overcame death victoriously, but also that the lifestyle Jesus introduced is still alive and thriving, and will never die. We celebrate the risen life of the Lord in ourselves, in others, and in the world around us.

This risen life is at the core of Luke's book The Acts of the Apostles. Luke has his own personal reasons for wanting to record the risen life. In a sense, the Emmaus story is Luke's own resurrection story. He is probably the only one of those first evangelists who never saw Jesus. Luke came to Jesus through his contact with Christian communities he met in his work as a travelling physician.

Luke was touched by the kind of life those communities lived. He was struck by the way they cared for widows, orphans, sick people, lepers, and the poor. He also was struck by the unity within these communities, which centred around the breaking of bread. For Luke, the ways in which the Christian communities acted and reacted to the world in which they lived were signs of God's kingdom among us. He believed he was seeing Jesus' risen life being lived out by the communities of his followers.

Luke wrote to Theophilus that he wanted to tell him about "the events that have taken place among us" (Luke 1:1). Of course, he wanted to tell the story about Jesus – and he did so in his gospel – but he also felt compelled to write another account to explain what had later happened to Jesus' disciples under the influence of the Holy Spirit. For Luke, the Lord Jesus did not disappear to another dimension: he remains in our midst, revealing himself to us every time we break bread with one another.

The Thomas test
C18. Second Sunday of Easter

Acts 5:12-16

Revelation 1:9-13, 17-19

John 20:19-31

Just like last Sunday's gospel story about the road to Emmaus, today's resurrection story is about recognising Jesus. Recognition of Jesus was a problem for the disciples in almost all the resurrection stories. Even when the figure before them looked like Jesus, they still had difficulty assuring themselves that it really was him.

It was only natural that some doubt remained – after all, the disciples had only recently been mourning his death! On one occasion, Jesus dispelled that doubt himself by asking for some food to eat. Unfortunately, Thomas was not present to see the proof. He heard the story later from the disciples, plus the one about how Jesus gave them his greeting of peace and breathed the Holy Spirit upon them. Despite all this, Thomas was not convinced.

Thomas was thinking of another test. He knew that sometimes our eyes can deceive us, so he decided that the only ultimate proof was to touch the wounds on Jesus' hands and the wound in his side. He wanted direct evidence that the person the disciples said was Jesus was the same one who suffered and died on the cross. If he could not do that, he said, he would refuse to believe.

Eight days later Jesus appeared among them again. This time, Thomas was with them. Jesus beckoned Thomas towards him: "Put your finger here; look, here are my hands. Give me your hand, put it into my side. Doubt no longer but believe." Even before he touched those wounds, Thomas knew that the Lord was standing before him.

Thomas was right: you only can recognise Jesus and his spirit when faced with the hard facts – that is, the scars of the wounds that result from trying to realise the kingdom of God here on Earth. The "Thomas test" is not only valid in Jesus' case. It is a test that applies equally to the community he left behind, and to every disciple of Jesus, and to every human being.

Thomas is often is called "doubting" Thomas, and is used as a model for the unbeliever. However, we should ask what exactly Thomas doubted about Jesus, and why he doubted. The traditional portrayal of Thomas as someone who did not believe in Jesus is inaccurate: what he said was that he did not believe that the others had seen him. Thomas certainly believed in Jesus. At the moment that he saw his wounds there was not a trace of doubt left. He pronounced the shortest possible act of faith: "My Lord, and my God!"

Why would Thomas have doubted what the disciples had said? Was it that their story just did not seem to add up: why, if they really had seen Jesus, did they remain in that room instead of rushing out and telling the world? Would it not have changed their lives completely? Maybe it is here that we touch upon the deepest reason of the unbelief of our world. It is not so difficult to believe in Jesus – even Karl Marx is said to have believed in him – but it is much more difficult to believe in his disciples! If we had, as we claim, met the risen Christ, would we not live totally different lives? Are believers really so different from unbelievers?

There is a story that an old Indian man once asked a missionary: "If what you say about Jesus is true, why is it that you waited so long to come and tell us?" Every Christian will meet the doubting Thomases who test us and ask us to offer proof of what we preach. Be warned, because if you cannot show them the scars and marks of your struggle for peace and justice, they will not believe in you, although they might believe in Jesus.

The last breakfast
C19. Third Sunday of Easter

Acts 5:27-32, 40-41
Revelation 5:11-14
John 21:1-19

It is always nice to go out in the evening, especially at the weekend, when we can put the worries and cares of the week aside. During a candle-lit dinner we can grow very close to each other. The conversation runs smoothly as we eat and drink. As we relax, we feel free to talk about all kinds of things we would not normally mention. Such moments allow us to exchange intimacies in a way that would not be possible amid the hustle and bustle of the day. The evening meal, whether we dine out or at home, can often be one of those cherished occasions when we seem to be able to bridge the distance between us.

In contrast, the breakfast table often seems to remind us of how far apart we are from each other. There is a busy day ahead – tasks have to be allotted, work must be done, and the debris from last's night meal has to be cleared away. In such circumstances, the differences between us become obvious. We are sensitive to the slightest criticisms and become overly defensive. We are reticent, steeling ourselves for the rat-race of the day ahead. What seemed so promising late in the evening, is frequently so compromised early in the morning.

Jesus and his disciples experienced the same thing. They had been so close during the Last Supper, especially at the moment when Jesus broke the bread and passed the cup around to emphasise their unity: one body, one blood, one spirit. Jesus had washed their feet, and opened his heart to them. At the end, they rose from the table singing. Even his warnings about what lay ahead had been forgotten.

In John's gospel this Sunday, we find Jesus at breakfast with a group of his disciples. After the miraculous haul of fish, and after having recognised Jesus, they are sitting together at a charcoal fire. Jesus is toasting some bread for them and cooking some fish. The disciples feel embarrassed, and nobody dares to ask Jesus anything, or even to acknowledge that they recognise him.

After eating, Jesus asks Simon Peter the same question three times. It is a question that is always difficult: "Do you love me?" When Peter answers each time, "Lord, you know I love you," Jesus replies with, "Feed my lambs," then, "Look after my sheep," and, "Feed my sheep." These are the tasks Jesus gives to Peter, and to all those who love him.

According to some commentators, the 153 fish they caught that morning may have something to do with all those sheep Jesus asked Peter to look after. Saint Jerome thought that the number 153 represents the different types of fish to be found in the Sea of Tiberius. If that is the case, the text would run parallel to Matthew (13:47), where Jesus likens the kingdom of God to a dragnet in which fish '"of all kinds" are caught. Furthermore, these texts point to the "mission" texts at the ends of the other gospels and the beginning of Acts, in which Jesus asks us to go to the ends of the Earth to gather in all the scattered children of God. At the core of this mission is Jesus' universal love: when we love him, we will be interested in all those he loves.

It is easy to discuss that mission and pray about it over an evening meal when we feel especially close to one another, just as the apostles felt happy during the Last Supper. At breakfast, however, things are different and reality bites: tasks are apportioned and work has to be done. Peter got his mission, and so did we: whether it is fish, sheep, or people, they are all entrusted to our loving care.

The Messianic secret
C20. Fourth Sunday of Easter

Acts 13:14, 43-52

Revelation 7:9, 14-17

John 10:27-30

It was winter, John writes (10:22). In the Temple at Jerusalem that cold, damp morning, a group of people gathered around Jesus. "How much longer are you going to keep us in suspense? If you are the Christ, tell us openly," they asked. Jesus did not give them a straight answer to their question. In his cagey reply, Jesus talked about himself as being a shepherd, and about the "sheep" that listened to his voice, and about those that did not.

Jesus hinted at his identity without expressly declaring it. He revealed himself as the Messiah only to a few close friends, and even they were asked not to tell others. This is what is often called "the Messianic secret". If we are to understand this phenomenon, perhaps it would be useful to try and imagine ourselves in Jesus' predicament and consider how we might have reacted.

That chilly morning, Jesus was surrounded by a group of people who had a clear idea about the Christ they wanted to redeem them. If Jesus admitted that he was, indeed, the Messiah, they would have expected him to behave in line with their expectations. He knew that they would try to appropriate him and use his Messiah-ship as a way of making themselves distinct from others. Jesus's aim was quite the opposite: he came to break down all differences and barriers between peoples and nations.

Jesus had learned this lesson when he presented himself in the synagogue at Nazareth some time before. Initially, the villagers applauded him enthusiastically when he told them that he had come to liberate prisoners, to make the blind see, and to announce the Great Year of the Jubilee. However, when he added that he was going to do this for everyone, not just for them, they were outraged and even tried to throw him off a cliff. They did not need a Messiah like that – they wanted their own, exclusive, tailor-made Messiah.

Jesus simply could not confess himself to one group of people without doing an injustice to all the others. Consequently, he was unable to give a direct answer to his questioners in the Temple. He described himself as a shepherd because a shepherd keeps the flock together. Jesus had come to "gather together in unity the scattered children of God" (John 11:52), the end result of which we see in the second reading of today:

"I saw a huge number, impossible to count, of people from every nation, race, tribe, and language; they were standing in front of the throne and in front of the Lamb, dressed in white robes and holding palms in their hands" (Revelation 7:9).

Jesus would probably use the good shepherd metaphor today if he were asked to which Christian denomination he belonged. If Jesus returned to Earth, have you ever wondered where he would go? Would it be to the Pope in Rome, the Secretary of the World Council of Churches in Geneva, the Patriarch of Moscow, Billy Graham in the USA, the Kimbanguists in Zaire, or to a basic Christian community in Brazil? Wherever he went, some people would to be upset that he had not visited them first! Who knows, as Jesus is the Messiah of the whole of humanity, not just of Christians, he might choose go to an Ashram in India or a Mosque in Beirut?

Do we, too, sometimes try to appropriate Jesus' love for ourselves, instead of spreading it to others?

Love revolution
C21. Fifth Sunday of Easter

Acts 14:21-27

Revelation 21:1-5

John 13:31-35

It was night, and Jesus' fate had just been sealed – Judas was on his way to betray him for a handful of silver. All human beings know that they are going to die, but Jesus also knew how, when, and where his death would occur. His mission was reaching its fulfilment, so he began to describe how the events that were fast approaching would glorify both himself and his Father.

The first time Jesus spoke of his glory in John's gospel was when he was visited by a party of Greeks in Jerusalem, just before the Last Supper (12:20-22). That incident is the turning point in John's gospel (see B17: The hour has come). For a long time, the Jews had viewed the Greeks and their Hellenic culture as the greatest enemies of the Jewish tradition and religion. The way the Greeks were welcomed by Jesus and his followers was a radical statement about the nature of God's love.

Jesus had been waiting for this moment since his mission on Earth first began. It was a signal that God's love was all-inclusive. The scope of God's love suddenly expanded a thousand-fold to include people's of all races and nations. Jesus later described God's love as a huge house with room enough for everyone (John 14:2).

The visit of the Greeks was hard evidence that the beginnings of a new world, a new Earth, and a new heaven were taking root. It was proof that a universal love and a global solidarity were at last being planted in the heart of the human family. As Jesus says in today's gospel text:

"My little children, I shall not be with you much longer. I give you a new commandment: love one another; just as I have loved you, you must also love one another. By this love you have for one another, everyone will know that you are my disciples" (John 13:33-35).

Up to that point, love and solidarity had always been restricted to one's own familiar circle – people of one's own kind or persuasion. The new commandment Jesus gave to his followers demanded that their circle of love should include the whole human race within its circumference. Like Jesus, they were to stretch their arms around the entire globe in a loving embrace.

This love revolution cost Jesus his life, just as it has cost the lives of so many of his followers since. It is in this context that he said: "Unless a wheat of grain falls on the ground and dies, it remains a single grain; but if it dies it yields a rich harvest" (12:24). As we nurture the seed of God's universal love within us, others will see Jesus and God glorified in our lives.

Years ago, a Dutch priest visited a Christian hospital in Northern Zaire. The priest asked the Belgian director how the hospital's Christian identity was made evident to others. The doctor smiled and pointed at a nurse and said: "Every time a nurse like that is willing to help a patient of another ethnic group, our Christian identity is manifest." It is at such moments that God's glory becomes visible in the world.

The divine ombuds-person

C22. Sixth Sunday of Easter

Acts 15:1-2, 22-29

Revelation 21:10-14, 22-23

John 14:23-29

The phrase, "It has been decided by the Holy Spirit and by ourselves ..." (Acts 15:28), concludes a discussion among the apostles and elders on a point of discipline: should the newly baptised non-Jews adopt the Judaic heritage of Jesus' first disciples?

Paul sympathises with the newcomers, who were far from eager to accept alien customs and obligations (15:7-10). The men, understandably, did not want to be circumcised simply because they had been baptised. James, however, foresees some problems. Would the older Jewish Christians not feel betrayed? Did not the reluctance of the new believers to be circumcised suggest that they thought that their elders were wrong in following that Jewish practice? There is no doubt that Paul and James are passionately dedicated to Jesus' cause; their disagreement arises simply because of their different ages and cultural backgrounds.

Luke notes that the discussion was lengthy and difficult. The apostles involved the whole community in the decision-making process. They treated the question in that way because they believed that the Holy Spirit was not only given to their leaders, such as Peter and James, but also to the entire assembly of believers. They did not think the Spirit's presence was greater in some people than in others – all had been given the Spirit in equal measure.

How is the Holy Spirit given to us? That question is at the root of the disagreement that has kept the Christian community divided along east-west lines for more than 1,000 years. We in the Western Church believe that the Holy Spirit is given first to the individual, and then to the community via the individual. However, in the Eastern Church, one believes that the Spirit is given first to the community, and then to the individual via the community.

This difference of opinion has had a profound influence on society as well as on the Christian Church. Some years ago, the presidents of the most powerful nations on Earth made live television broadcasts to each other's nations on New Years Day. Ronald Reagan told the Soviet people that his main interest was to assure their individual human rights, while Mikhail Gorbachev told the Americans that his main worry was to avoid a conflict in the human community.

The two interpretations complement each other, because they are the two halves that make up the whole. The Holy Spirit is a gift to each of us as an individual person, and it is also a gift to us in our inter-personal community. The true way of addressing any contentious issue within the Christian community is summed up by the phrase: "It has been decided by the Holy Spirit and by ourselves ...."

John gives the Holy Spirit a name in our gospel reading. He calls it paracletos, which is a word that does not translate very well into English. It means "helper", "advocate", "consoler", or "counsellor". Perhaps the best translation would be something like "ombuds-person". These different translations all point to the same thing: that the Holy Spirit will help us to realise the kingdom of God here on Earth. For that reason, the Spirit is also called the "in-between God", or the "connective God". Through the Spirit's work and inspiration, peace and unity will be established among us.

"Peace be with you," said Jesus as he breathed on them the Spirit that would bring us together into one body, and one peace.

Responsibility
C23. Ascension Day

Acts 1:1-11

Ephesians 1:17-23

Luke 24:46-53

It must have been a difficult day for Jesus' followers – and a sad one, too. It had finally dawned on them that Jesus was leaving them for good. Strangely, Jesus had told them that they should be glad, and that his leaving was good for them. If he did not go, they would never discover that they themselves were equipped with the Holy Spirit (John 16:7), and that they would be able to do even greater things than he did (John 14:12).

G. K. Chesterton once wrote that the genuinely great person is the one who makes others feel great. Another British author, H. G. Wells, stated that the real test of someone's greatness is how much responsibility he or she entrusts to others. Wells added: "That is why Jesus is the greatest one among us!"

These two authors merely confirm what we experienced in our own lives when others transferred responsibilities to us for the first time. Can you remember how good you felt the first time you were allowed to go to school without being accompanied by your parents, or when you were first allowed to drive the car by yourself, or when you were entrusted with the care of a baby for the first time?

God has treated humanity like that right from the very beginning, when he created Adam and Eve and entrusted the whole created world to them. In Jesus, God renews that transference of responsibility and power. It is not only Jesus who is going to be the light of the world and its yeast and its salt. We, too, are entrusted with the responsibility of being the world's light, yeast, and salt.

Jesus' ascension is the final divine answer to the questions we repeatedly hear: "How can God allow such awful things to happen in this world? Why doesn't God interfere? Why can't God do something?" Well, God did interfere and transferred the responsibility for the world to us. And God gives us the Holy Spirit, which provides us with all the power, force, and the energy needed to shoulder that responsibility.

The ascension was the moment when God assigned this responsibility to us. Jesus left the disciples and journeyed up to heaven; whenever his followers accept that responsibility, they embark upon that journey with him.

Unity
C24. Seventh Sunday of Easter

Acts 7:55-60

Revelation 22:12-14, 16-17, 20

John 17:20-26

Stephen had been brought before the Sanhedrin council and falsely accused of blasphemy. The high-priest had asked Stephen whether he really thought that Jesus would destroy the Temple and end its practices. Stephen's answer was rather abstract and theological. He gave them a lecture on the whole history of salvation, explaining that the Temple had never really been part of God's plan, and that the building of it had been a misunderstanding, resulting from the stubbornness of the priesthood. Stephen pointed out that you cannot lock up, limit, or restrict God, because God's Spirit is present in all of us and not reserved for an elite group of people. He then launched a stinging criticism of the council members: "You stubborn people ... you are always resisting the Holy Spirit, just like your ancestors used to do."

Today's reading from Acts joins the story just as Stephen has finished answering the high-priest. Suddenly, heaven opens for him and he sees Jesus in God's glory. This is no abstract theological theory – this is reality! All the pieces finally fall into place, even though Stephen is on the point of death. At that moment, heaven and Earth are connected: Jesus is not only there in heaven, but Stephen can see him from the Earth as well. In an instant, Stephen understands it all: humanity and the whole of creation are united through Jesus. That is what Jesus speaks about during today's text on the Last Supper from John's gospel, when he says that he will remain in the world with us and in us after his death and resurrection.

The members of the Sanhedrin council are so outraged that they chase him out of the city to stone him. The vultures gather in the distance as the murderers hand their clothes to Saul. When the stones begin to rain down upon him, Stephen prays an amazing prayer for unity: "Lord, do not hold this sin against them." This is almost identical to Jesus' prayer on the cross: "Father forgive them; they do not know what they are doing." In such prayers, there is no longer a distinction between friend and foe.

120

It is astonishing how even in the most extreme circumstances people manage to find the strength and love to call for such unity. Martin Luther King said of those who threatened him:

"Do what you like, we will go on loving you. Throw us in prison and we will continue loving you. Send your masked terrorists to our families in the dark of the night, let them beat us leaving us half-dead, we will continue loving you."

Etty Hillesum, a young Jewish woman killed during the World War II, discovered during her time in a concentration camp that she could "listen in" to God in her inner being. Once she had become aware of God's presence within herself, she concluded that God must be present in everyone, whether friend or foe. This revelation changed her world. She kept the whole of humanity together in her heart, praying for all of them.

People who discover the wholeness and unity of God's family and creation pray as Jesus and Stephen did. The power and influence of the Holy Spirit helps them to remain faithful to Jesus' command to love their enemies. In doing so, they fulfil Jesus' prayer that "they may be so completely one" (John 17:23). Remember: God lets his rain fall over the good and the bad alike (Matthew 5:45).

One world, or no world at all

C25. Pentecost

Acts 2:1-11

1 Corinthians 12:3-7, 12-13

John 20:19-23

At Pentecost, we do not celebrate something that happened to Jesus. From now on, the story is about how Jesus' life and power are shared by humanity through the Holy Spirit. There have always been differences of opinion over this issue. To understand how they arose, we need to examine the Pentecost story in relation to the gospels.

There are three different sets of people present when the Holy Spirit comes upon them at Pentecost: the Twelve (now reduced to the Eleven!); the group that included Jesus mother, Mary; and the crowd of about three thousand Jews and foreigners in the streets. There are also two different occasions on which the Spirit was given to Jesus' followers: on Easter day (John 20:22-23), and at Pentecost 50 days later. We also find three ways by which the Holy Spirit is given to people: through Jesus' breath (20:22); through tongues of fire (Acts 2:2); and by the water of a baptism (Mark 1:9-11). With so many different aspects to consider, it comes as no surprise that the relationship of the Holy Spirit to the believer has always been a "hot topic" in the Christian Church.

Indeed, it determines the difference between Catholics and Protestants: does the Holy Spirit speak to the heart and mind of every believer, or only to the Pope and his bishops and priests? Likewise, it is at the core of the dispute over liberation theology between Latin American theologians and the Roman prefects: is the Holy Spirit present when basic Christian community members read and interpret the Bible, or does authentic inspiration only come from the Church's hierarchy? The inter-faith dialogue also turns around this issue: is the Holy Spirit the exclusive prerogative of the Christian believer?

Underlying all this lies a more fundamental issue: does the Holy Spirit come upon people from without, or does it arise from within a person?

In 1945, a farmer in Egypt found a set of old books, now known as the Nag Hammadi Library. It contained many texts – some older than our four gospel texts – that threw new light on how the early Church thought about this issue. In one of the books, called the Gospel of Thomas, Jesus says: "There is light in every human being, a light that illumines the whole world." Could it be that the smouldering embers of the Holy Spirit within us suddenly burst into bright flames when we are first touched by Jesus' life, death, and resurrection, illuminating a part of our inner being that was previously hidden? Is the Holy Spirit not given to us at the very beginning of our existence?

This last year of preparation for the Great Jubilee is dedicated to the unifying work of the Holy Spirit – how, then, can we let ourselves be divided over such an issue? In his letter to the Corinthians, Paul explains the apparent confusion by saying that there are various gifts, services, and tasks, and all are equally valid and have a rightful place. Our assignment is to form out of all those gifts the one body and the one Spirit of Christ in the world. It is, indeed, a question of either one world or no world at all.

Dance and play
C26. Trinity Sunday

Proverbs 8:22-31

Romans 5:1-5

John 16:12-15

In our reading from Proverbs, Wisdom says that she was at the side of God during the creation of heaven and Earth: "I was by his side, a master craftsman, delighting him day after day, ever at play in his presence, and at play everywhere in his world, delighting to be with the children of humanity."

Saint Epiphanius noted centuries ago that Moses taught about God's oneness, that the prophets speak about a divine two-some, and that it is only in the gospels that we meet the three-fold God. In our Proverbs text we find the two-some God: Yahweh and the personified divine Wisdom. The two persons of God are dancing, playing, and singing. Their dance brings forth the whole of creation.

When our concept of God changed to a Trinitarian one, to do full justice to the way God relates to God's own self and to us, the idea of dancing and playing remained. The leaders of the early Church meditated upon what God would be doing for all eternity and came up with the word *perichoresis*. This difficult word indicates that one person of the Trinity encompasses two others, and that each person of the Trinity is present in the other two. However, it also has another interpretation. The root of this word is derived from the Greek *khoros*, meaning "dance" or "chorus", telling us that the life of the Trinity is a dance, a play, and a joyful refrain. This dance and play is the core of the divine life, and consequently should be at the core of our own lives.

In the mid-1900s, the first Lutheran missionaries in Rabai, Kenya, invited the local population to their initial service. The congregation was treated to a German service translated into their own language, Kiswahili. It was full of words, endless prayers, a long sermon, much sitting and standing, and some rather a-rhythmical German hymns! The missionaries asked their guests whether they would return next week. The answer was an emphatic "No", because nothing in the service related to their understanding of worship. When the missionaries asked how the service might be changed, the reply was: "You should do it as we do it – eating, drinking, and dancing." Their exuberant worship was an expression of their gratitude for the life God had given them.

Our Western societies are beginning to recover that old exuberance. For almost all youngsters, going dancing is the high point of the week. It is a celebration of your life and it bonds you to others – it is heaven!

A while ago, I was sitting on a train to New York when a young couple sitting opposite began to study a map of the city. The young man next to me asked them if it was their first visit to New York. "Yes," they answered, "What do you recommend we should do?" He replied that if they only had the time and the money to do one thing in New York they should go to a certain night-club. "You have to pay a small fortune to get in," he told them, "but you mustn't miss it – the music, the atmosphere, and the dancing are incredible! It's like I imagine heaven to be!" This was hardly a theological comment, but it definitely embodied a biblical insight.

The three persons of the Trinity are engaged in a joyful dance. We, too, should try to get in step with the divine dance.

They have no wine

C27. Second Sunday of the year

Isaiah 62:1-5

1 Corinthians 12:4-11

John 2:1-12

Bible scholars have great difficulty with the story of the wedding at Cana – there seem to be too many unanswered questions and loose threads. What is the real point that John wants to make with this story? Does Jesus change Mary's role from mother to bride, making her a symbol of the Church? And what of the wine? The new wine is said to be better than the old, so does that mean that the old wine is no good? Besides, the water that Jesus changes into wine is not ordinary water – it has been poured into casks used for Jewish purification rites. Does this suggest that Jewish customs should be written off, together with all other pre-Christian traditions?

In the light of these questions, it is easy to understand Jesus' dilemma on that occasion. If we can sense the symbolic implications of this event, 2,000 years on and in a very different culture, how much more obvious would they have been to the people at the wedding feast?

The story has a simple enough beginning: the wine at the wedding feast has run out because too many unexpected guests have arrived. The custom is that guests bring their own drinks, but some people have obviously – and rather selfishly – not done that, so now there is a problem.

Mary tells Jesus: "They have no wine." Jesus knows what she wants him to do, but he realises that anything he does will be seen to have symbolic overtones. He explains to her that to provide wine now would invite misunderstanding. The hour is not yet right for such gestures. However, he later relents and goes to the kitchen to make all the water blush into wine. The wine is so good that the master of ceremonies complains, asking why the best wine has been kept back until last. Jesus' fears are proved right: his gesture has been misunderstood!

The Cana story is not about wine: it is about a wedding, and it is about love. God loves us as a passionate husband or wife loves his or her spouse. From ancient times, the prophets had been speaking about a time when the relationship between God and humanity would be so intimate that you would be able to speak of it as a marriage, with God as the bridegroom of the people, as we read today in Isaiah:

"... you will be called 'My Delight' ... Like a young man marrying a virgin, so will the one who built you wed you ... and the bridegroom rejoices in his bride, so will your God rejoice in you."

Jesus, too, spoke about the wedding feast that would take place at the end-time (Matthew 22:3). Many prophetic descriptions of that time speak of the abundance of food and drink at that wedding feast. One apocryphal document dating back to the time of John's gospel mentions that the wine harvest will be tenfold. Every vine will have a thousand branches, every bunch of grapes will have a thousand grapes, and every grape will render hundreds of litres of wine. In comparison, the six hundred litres at Cana pale into insignificance!

In Cana that day, a young married couple were sitting at the table of the wedding feast. The names of this bride and groom are not mentioned, but we can be pretty sure that they were eagerly waiting for the end of the festivities and the departure of the guests! Did they understand when they drank that miraculous wine that they had become a symbol of the love that meets us when we encounter Christ?

The year of the Jubilee
C28. Third Sunday of the year

Nehemiah 8:2-6, 8-10

1 Corinthians 12:12-30

Luke 1:1-4; 4:14-21

This is a great Jubilee text! Jesus goes to the Sabbath service in the synagogue at Nazareth on Friday night, as is his custom. His reputation has spread throughout the countryside, and many have come to see him, curious about what he might say. After all the miracles he has been performing in other places, he really ought to explain himself.

Jesus stands up to do the reading. They hand him the scroll that contains Isaiah's text (Isaiah 61:1-2). Jesus rolls the scroll open to the text he has chosen, which tells of the anointed one who is coming with good news to liberate prisoners, free the oppressed, and announce a period of grace – the Great Jubilee. When he has finished reading, he sits down again. The crowd are agog. There is such tension that you could cut the atmosphere in the synagogue with a knife. Finally, Jesus says: "This text is being fulfilled today even as you listen."

Many liberation theologians use this text to explain that Jesus' mission was to announce here on Earth the beginning of the final Year of Jubilee. We still celebrate jubilees today, but they are far removed from the old Jewish tradition, according to which a rams-horn (*jobel*) was

125

sounded at the beginning of each 50th year. During this year, all slaves were freed, debts were forgiven, and all property – land included – was reapportioned among the people.

Not surprisingly, people were never completely faithful to the principle of Jubilee, but the custom was at least partially put into practice, as we see in today's Old Testament reading. Because of the somewhat half-heartedness of the approach to the Jubilee, the prophets began to speak of God's own Jubilee year in which all would genuinely be accomplished. In Nazareth, Jesus identifies himself as the one who was going to institute "the Lord's year of favour". No wonder that the people in his village were enthusiastic!

Harold Miller, an African-American, lived for with the nomadic Gabra people of north-eastern Kenya for many years. Every 50th year the Gabra celebrate a Jubilee, redistributing their cattle among the people, forgiving all debts, and ending all disputes, so that everyone can start afresh. Miller was living with them for their Jubilee celebrations, and could not believe his eyes when he saw what they were doing. The people told him that they, in turn, could not understand how anyone could to survive in a community that did not practise such a custom. The differences in wealth and status would become so great that the community or society would collapse. The gap between the rich and the poor, the successful and those who failed, would become unbearable and the debts unpayable. We cannot deny those truths when we look at our societies and the global capitalist economy.

In our first reading today, Ezra reminds his people of Moses' Law. Back in their own country after their exile in Egypt, they have lost their vision. When the people hear what they should do, and how they should organise themselves, they break out in tears! Ezra tells them not to weep and mourn. He asks them to react more positively, in a manner appropriate to the celebration of the Jubilee. He tells them to go and eat and drink, taking care that they share what they have with those who have nothing.

The task Ezra gave his people is the task Jesus gives us today as we prepare for the Great Jubilee – "the Lord's year of favour".

Refusal
C29. Fourth Sunday of the year

Jeremiah 1:4-5, 17-19

1 Corinthians 12:31 –13:13

Luke 4:21-30

Today's gospel text is the concluding part of the story we looked at last Sunday. If you remember, Jesus has announced in the synagogue at Nazareth the promised Jubilee, which he calls (in the words of Isaiah) "the Lord's year of favour". The people listening to him in the synagogue are wildly enthusiastic about the prospect. The words he speaks are pure grace!

Suddenly the whole mood changes. By the end of today's reading, they are so set against him that, for the second time in his life, he is in mortal danger. (The first time when Herod tried to kill the infant Jesus in Bethlehem.)

What was it that happened to make the crowd turn against him so quickly? To understand what was going on, try to put yourself in the place of the crowd that evening. They had been upset because Jesus had been working all kinds of miracles and healings in Capernaum and other places, leaving the sick in his home town of Nazareth in their suffering. Jesus admits this, but he does not apologise. In fact, he makes it worse by telling them that his work and the "Lord's year of favour" will not be restricted to them, but will extend to non-Jews and pagans. He reminds them of two non-Jews blessed by God in their scriptures: Naaman, the Syrian, and the widow from Zarephath, a Sidonian town.

The crowd will not accept that they have to share this wonderful prospect with others. They want to keep the best things in life – that is, God and God's favours – within their own closed little circle. This same stance lies at the heart of nationalistic and racist attitudes, and religious separatism.

Simone Weil, the French Jewish activist, who died in London in exile in 1943, had a unexpected mystical experience during Holy Week in a Benedictine Abbey in France. In her own words: "Christ himself came and invaded me." She had never read any book on mysticism, and nothing she had heard about it had ever interested her. "God in his grace had kept me away from the mystics, so that it would be evident to me that I had not invented this unexpected contact by myself," she later wrote.

When she told a friend who was a priest what had happened to her, he advised her to get baptised. It was, according to him, the only logical conclusion. Simone hesitated, because she knew that she could only be baptised in a denominational church, and that meant that she would belong to one particular group of Christians. Like all Christian groups, they would probably find ways of excluding Christians of other denominations from their celebrations of the Eucharist, not to mention non-Christians. "How can you sit in the name of Jesus Christ at a table that excludes others, condemning them?" she writes to her friend, "Did Jesus not come to begin an open table service?" She concluded that she would not find the type of baptism Jesus left us in any Christian Church.

Jesus' fellow villagers display their lack of openness to others by pushing him out of the synagogue. They are about to hurl him down the hill when he turns around. Looking his persecutors in the eyes, he walks out of the circle they were trying to close around him. He walks away to continue his work and his journey. This journey will lead him to Jerusalem, where, for exactly the same reason, the people will thrust him out of town and crucify him.

Catching people, not fish
C30. Fifth Sunday of the year

Isaiah 6:1-8

1 Corinthians 15:1-11

Luke 5:1-11

Some years ago, a meeting of the Young Christian Students (YCS) at an African university was discussing the political situation in their country. They followed the method introduced by Cardinal Cardijn, their founder: "See, judge, act". Suddenly, a student leader who had a reputation for being "left-wing" (which in fact only meant that he was somewhat better informed about the political situation than the others!) leapt up and referred to the gospel text of today:

"Why is it that we Christians don't seem to be able to do anything about the injustice and the poverty in our country? Just because Jesus said; 'I will make you fishers of men,' the Church has made it its sole task to drag those fish out of the disturbed waters of society – to catch them and bring them safely to the shore. But nobody ever thinks of doing anything about calming the troubled waters, and the 'saved' ones will perish on the shore once they have been fished from the waters that threatened them."

The room fell silent. Nobody had even considered that interpretation before!

The story they were discussing occurs twice in the New Testament, once in Luke, which we are reading today, and once in Mark (1:17). The two read differently. In Mark, Jesus says that he will make his followers into "fishers of men" (see B34: Fishers of men).

In Luke's version, Jesus does not say that he will make them fishermen. He simply says: "... from now on it is people you will catch." (Translated literally, the original text says: "From now on you will catch them alive.")

In his book *The Kingdom Within*, the Anglican priest and psychologist John A. Sanford takes a fresh look at this fishing metaphor.

Sandford suggests that the fish are symbols of what is swimming in the dark waters of our inner being. He says that there are all kinds of characteristics, expectations, qualities, and abilities that are ·currently hidden from us because they are swimming around in the deepest, darkest parts of our personalities. These mysterious creatures must be fished up from the depths, caught, and eaten in order to be fully assimilated into our character so that we can attain our full human potential. The apostles are fishermen because they have fished the content of their inner selves to the surface, and because they will help others to do the same.

In the earliest Christian iconography, Jesus was symbolised by a fish, the symbol of the totality of all the inner possibilities that can and should be brought into the light of day. At that time, Julian the African wrote:

"God's source produces continuously a flood of living water, a stream in which there is one fish, caught on a divine fish hook, feeding the whole of the world."

This mysterious, puzzling text becomes slightly more comprehensible when you try to look at it from Sanford's point of view. Jesus is the fish that swims in the dark waters of humanity's inner being. He carries within him all the neglected, ignored, and repressed elements of the human psyche. By fishing him out and consuming his body, we can – individually and collectively – assimilate him into our lives and become whole, as God always intended we should be.

Level ground
C31. Sixth Sunday of the year

Jeremiah 17:5-8
1 Corinthians 15:12, 16-20
Luke 6:17, 20-26

In the gospels by Mark and Matthew, Jesus climbs a mountain or hill before he gives the eight beatitudes. This seems to imply that what Jesus has to say comes from above (ie from heaven) and that it is also above us – that is, it represents an ideal to strive for or a prize to be won after a long struggle. In Luke's gospel, by contrast, Jesus comes down from the mountain before he gives the crowd his blessings, to the level ground where the crowd is waiting for him.

The crowd have come a long way – from Judea, Jerusalem, Tyre, and Sidon – to hear Jesus and to be healed. Jesus looks at the crowd; he then looks at his disciples and says: "How happy are you who are poor: yours is the kingdom of God. Happy you who are hungry now: you shall be satisfied. Happy you who weep now: you shall laugh. Happy are you when people hate you, drive you out, abuse you, denounce your name as criminal, on account of the Son of Man."

On first reading, it might appear that Jesus is suggesting that poverty, and all its consequences: hunger, sickness, vermin, lack of education, prostitution, infant mortality, and misery, should make someone happy! Of course, this is not what he means. Jesus was talking to people who had come to him to be delivered from that type of wretchedness.

They have come not only to see and hear him, but also because they consider themselves to be poor, hungry, thirsty, and frustrated and oppressed. They have come because they want change in their world. They long for justice and integrity, and for more satisfaction and joy in their lives. Jesus sees that hope in them, and praises and blesses them for it.

Jesus tells them that they are the hope of the world, not because they have come to him, but because they realise that the current situation is intolerable. They have left everything behind in search of change and a better future. They have come because they thirst for a transformation. They know at first hand the cruel fate of so many in this world, and they are sure that there must be an alternative.

This dynamic impetus for change is what has brought Jesus into the world, and he recognises the same thing in the crowd before him: the people assembled here are moved by the same thing that moves Jesus.

Jesus then speaks about those who have remained at home – the rich and replete, who are laughing now, patting each other on the back in their self-satisfied smugness. Such people have no sense of reality, and as a result will one day discover with great bitterness how they have deceived themselves. Their sadness will be awful, he says.

Jesus' ideas that morning are not really so surprising. They are plain statements that we all know to be true in our heart of hearts – hence the symbolism of all this taking place on "'level ground". This level ground represents our common, everyday human experience. Jesus leaves us in no doubt that change is going to come – it is inevitable, although not everyone can see it from where they are – and it will arise out of the hope, expectation, and determination of people from the underside of our society.

Love your enemies
C32. Seventh Sunday of the year

1 Samuel 26:2, 7-9, 12-13, 22-23

1 Corinthians 15:45-49

Luke 6:27-38

130

Sometimes when we pick up the Bible it seems such an old, *passé*, and irrelevant book. Its stories are so well-known that everything in it has that feeling of *déjà vu*.

When we feel like that, we are completely missing the point, because the Bible is a book that is yet to be completed. When we read the ends of the four gospels, we realise that they all finish with Jesus talking about a commission and a new beginning. What began in those books is still continuing today.

It is important to understand that Jesus left us not a story to tell and retell throughout the ages, but a lifestyle to live. It is a lifestyle that is as pertinent to the modern world as it has been to ages past. Take today's gospel text: "Love your enemies, do good to those who hate you, bless those who curse you, pray for those who treat you badly." To Jesus, these were not merely words, they were a code for life. Jesus lived what he proclaimed and taught, and his followers are expected to do the same. It would be wrong to think that Jesus' lifestyle ceased to be relevant to the world when Jesus ascended into heaven.

Not so very long ago, I heard a preacher state that the time of martyrs is past. How can anyone say such a thing when our own generation has witnessed the deaths of Martin Luther King Jr, Oscar Romero, the Maryknoll sisters in Nicaragua, the Jesuits in El Salvador, the sisters in Liberia, the Benedictines in Algeria, and so many others! Pope John Paul II rightly suggested, in his preparatory document for the Great Jubilee, *Tertio Millennio Adveniete* that it is time the Church rewrote the Martyrology, the book in which it traditionally lists the names of all its martyrs.

I would like to tell you the story of one such modern martyr who fearlessly lived out Jesus' command that he should love his enemies. Early one morning during the time that Idi Amin ruled Uganda, some soldiers raided the house of the Anglican bishop Janani Luwum in Kampala, Uganda. They threatened the bishop with their revolvers, turned the whole house upside-down, and terrorised his children. The bishop told them: "There are no arms in this house, we pray for the President and we pray for his troops." After several hours, the soldiers had found nothing, so they gave up. As they left, they even had the nerve to ask the bishop to open the gate for them! The bishop's wife told him not to, and to let the soldiers go out the way they came in. Janani replied: "We are Christians, we have a purified heart, and as a witness to that I will open the gate."

Only 10 days later, Janani Luwum disappeared. He was most probably shot during a meal to which he had been invited by President Amin. After his house had been searched, Janani knew how dangerous it would be to accept the invitation, but he still went to the meal. He thought that he should not miss an occasion at which he might be able to do some good.

Like the Bible, Janani's story has not yet ended. He is dead, for sure – Amin let him burn to ashes, and those ashes were thrown out somewhere in the bush – but his witness lives on in the people of Uganda. Janani's loving, non-violent reaction to the violence used against him won him the battle over his enemies, because he broke through the cycle of violence.

Discipleship

C33. Eighth Sunday of the year

Sirach 27:4-7

1 Corinthians 15:54-58

Luke 6:39-45

The disciple asks: "Holy scripture tells me that I need a good teacher to make spiritual progress. Is that true?" The teacher answers: "It is necessary in the beginning. After that, it is the teacher in yourself who plays the role of spiritual director."

Jesus says practically the same thing in today's gospel text: "The disciple is not superior to the teacher, but the fully trained disciple will always be like the teacher." Elsewhere, Jesus promises his disciples that the Holy Spirit will tell them everything they need to know when he has gone. In effect, the Spirit will be our spiritual director. There is the divine spark of the Holy Spirit is in all of us, as any Christian should know. However, that does not mean to say we will never encounter any difficulties, or that we necessarily see everything in the right perspective.

At the beginning of 1989, I attended a lecture by a philosopher from Russia. His paper had been sent on to the audience from Moscow in advance. However, when he arrived at the lecture theatre, he told us that he had since written a new paper! During his brief time in the West, he had been struck by the tremendous importance placed upon personal freedom and individual independence, and it was about this that he now wanted to talk. He explained that "The Western Christian is convinced that he or she carries a divine spark." This view, he said, had resulted in Western secular society placing a one-sided, if not decadent, emphasis on individuality and privacy.

The ensuing discussion was polite, but fierce. One person accused him of underestimating personal freedom. He retaliated by saying that our blinkered attitudes did not take into account the limits of the individual and the needs of society. In effect, both camps accused each other of being blind to the truth. Each could see the splinter in their opponent's eye, but not the plank in their own!

One thing became clear: even a pious belief in the presence of the divine spark of the Holy Spirit can turn out wrong. Although this belief gives us the power of Jesus Christ, we still need the wisdom to use that power in the correct way. There are plenty of stories of disciples who became as powerful as their teachers, but who misused that power. In Acts, we read of Simon the Magician, who wanted to buy from the apostles the power to pass on the Holy Spirit, not because he wanted to build up the Christian community, but because he thought it would make him rich and famous (Acts 8:9-25).

Perhaps that is why Jesus took great pains to explain to his disciples the nature of the disciple-teacher relationship. For example, when he had finished washing and drying their feet at the Last Supper, he asked them:

"Do you understand what I have done to you? You call me Master and Lord, and rightly, so I am. If I then, your Lord and Master, have washed your feet, you should wash each other's feet. I have given you an example so that you may copy what I have done to you" (John 13:12-15).

Then he told them that they should eat their bread and drink their wine in such a way that they formed together one body and one blood. If they did all these things in unity, equality, and love, they would remain true to the Spirit of Jesus, and the difference between disciple and teacher would disappear from their midst.

The prayers of strangers
C34. Ninth Sunday of the year

1 Kings 8:41-43

Galatians 1:1-2, 6-10

Luke 7:1-10

From the prayers Solomon prays at the opening of the Temple in today's Old Testament reading, we get the feeling that he is unsure whether he has been right to build it. The priests were in favour of a Temple, of course, but the Prophets had always been against it: after all, how can you enclose God, for whom even the sky is too small, in any building built by human hands? Is not the very act of building a temple unjust and unfair to all those who do not happen to belong to your particular religious persuasion? Building our own house for God seems to imply that we do not want God to live with others. While praying, Solomon tries to solve the problem by asking God to listen to the prayers of those strangers as well.

Listening to the prayers of a stranger is exactly what Jesus does in the story from Luke. We see how Jesus turns around, astonished, when the friends of the Roman centurion explain why the man has not come himself to ask Jesus to heal his servant. The centurion feels himself so much of an outsider that he dare not approach Jesus. He sends some Jewish elders to Jesus on his behalf, and then some friends. Having listened to those friends, Jesus heals the man's servant and says to the crowd: "I tell you, not even in Israel have I found faith as great as this" (Luke 7:9). It is a story many missionaries and evangelists recognise from their own experience.

In July 1988, the International Association of Mission Studies met in Rome. One of the workshops at that meeting focused on the question of religious plurality. The discussion began with an exchange of personal experiences. Again and again, the participants expressed the same astonishment that Jesus had in the story from Luke. One of the participants said, "When I left the Princeton Seminary, I never expected that the Hindus I would meet would walk so closely with God. It was a complete surprise for me to realise that they, too, live in God's presence!"

The final report of the workshop began by acknowledging that religious pluralism was the reason for their original missionary activity – they wanted to reach people of other faiths with God's love. However, they admitted that:

"In many cases, that missionary experience changed our own exclusivity. We discovered that others, too, walked with God ... we outgrew a certain religious provincialism and discovered that the reign of God is larger and wider than the Church ... Most of us consider this plurality ... as an expression of the Will of God ...."

Not everyone agreed on the parallel that was drawn between their own experience and that of Jesus. Is Jesus really amazed when he hears of the faith of the Roman centurion? Some commentators, afraid of the theological implications if they were to admit that the man was a real Roman and therefore a pagan, suggest that he might have been one of the Romans' Hebrew collaborators. That is why, they argue, the man did not dare to come to Jesus himself.

For Luke, at least, the text is a turning point in his story of Jesus. For the faith of the centurion, Luke uses the same word (*pistis*) he used for the faith and expectation of Jesus' mother, Mary. Just as God's presence is never restricted to one temple, humanity's faith in God is not limited to only on group.

Death overcome
C35. Tenth Sunday of the year

1 Kings 17:17-24

Galatians 1:11-19

Luke 7:11-17

Why does Luke tell the story of the widow of Nain? Surely there is more to it than the return of a son to his mother?

Luke has another intention: he tells the story to provoke in us a similar reaction to those who witnessed this miracle: "A great prophet has risen up among us! God has visited his people!" It is a tale about the gracious power of God, which is manifested here in Jesus and also in the prophet Elijah in the reading from the first book of Kings.

According to the Greek text, the widow of Nain's son was her only child. Despite the obvious tragedy of the death of her only child, in such a traditional society it would have been an even more catastrophic loss, because it meant the end of her family's life-line. In those times, life was not so fragmented as it is today. Every person was considered a vital link in the chain of life that had streamed down through the ages from God, through the ancestors, and into each new generation. What happens in the gospel reading is that a complete break in the family's life-line occurs, the ending of all the widow's hopes and dreams for the future.

We all know from experience how sad it is when someone you love dies; consider how devastating it must be to have to bury your own child. The widow at Nain is not so different from your friend whose daughter died of cancer, or whose son died in a car accident. The feeling of profound hopelessness that strikes at such a moment is akin to the sadness the widow felt in today's story.

We human beings can overcome many difficulties, and medical advances have enabled us to extend our lives as never before. However, death remains: it is the one obstacle we cannot overcome. It is at this point that our story gives us hope, because it shows that death is not all powerful – God can overcome death!

This what the bystanders must have understood when they heard Jesus say to the mother: "Don't cry!" Jesus went up to the bier and touched it. The bearers stood still. All eyes were fixed on Jesus. The silence was broken when Jesus said to the dead body: "Young man, I tell you to get up." He sat up, and I imagine that he looked with a slightly bewildered expression at Jesus and then at his mother, and then began to talk. At the moment Jesus gave him back to his mother, the assembled crowd started to shout: "God has visited his people!"

God breaks through the hopelessness of this world, offering new opportunities. The way is open in front of us: our life is, indeed, assured and guaranteed by God. That is what today's story is about, and it applies to everyone confronted with death. God has overcome not only physical death, but also all the other forms of dying that accompany us on our way through life: marriage break-up, losing a job, disappointment when you have to give up your plans and expectations; and so on.

We must continue telling these stories of how God overcomes death whenever bereavement and sadness threaten to overwhelm us. This is how we know that "God has visited his people!"

Forgiveness
C36. Eleventh Sunday of the year

2 Samuel 12:7-10, 13

Galatians 2:16, 19-21

Luke 7:36-8:3

The woman who entered the dining room was a sinner in the opinion of everyone in town – including herself! She herself must have felt this even more acutely in the house of a Pharisee – someone who obeyed the Law to the letter. She realised that she was neither welcomed by the host nor his guests.

Jesus, too, recognised the woman as a sinner, but he turned to Simon, his host, and said: "Simon, you see this woman ... she has poured out her tears over my feet and wiped them away with her hair ... For this reason, I tell you that her sins, her many sins, must have been forgiven her, or she would not have shown such great love." In another translation of this text, Jesus' meaning is more ambiguous. His words to Simon are given as: "For this reason I tell you: her sins are forgiven, and you can see that because of the love she shows."

In the first version, it appears that the woman was forgiven because she showed tremendous love for Jesus, and this is the traditional explanation that is found even in the oldest commentaries. However, this is not necessarily the best explanation, and certainly it makes what Jesus said next a little confusing. When Jesus added that: "It is someone who is forgiven little, who shows little love," he seemed to be saying that the love a person shows depends on the measure to which they have been forgiven. This turns everything around, so that the woman loved Jesus because he forgave her – that is, she loved Jesus because he loved her. She anointed Jesus feet, dried them with her hair, and covered them with kisses because she was loved, forgiven, and accepted by Jesus.

The woman had been reminded of her sinfulness day and night for years, and she had come to loathe herself. With that mind-set, she was unlikely to have tried to wash Jesus feet to earn forgiveness, because her low self-esteem would have made her view her own actions as worthless. What she really needed was to be forgiven and accepted for who she was.

Just imagine that you have seriously offended someone you really love. When you meet the person in question, she says: "I forgive all the things you did to me!" However, this does not make you feel much better about yourself, because only your wrong actions have been forgiven. What you really need is to be forgiven yourself. Only then will the bond between you and the person you have wronged truly be restored, and only then can you forgive yourself. The initiative to forgive in that way can only come from the offended party.

When we hear and use the word forgiveness, we so often think just about the forgiveness of sins or the pardon of a punishment. That is not what forgiveness really is about – true forgiveness means not that your wrong deeds are negated, but that you are accepted as you are. It means to be taken up again wholly and unconditionally into the life of another.

As long as that woman did not feel herself accepted by God, she could neither love God nor herself. When she entered the Pharisee's house, she already knew that she was forgiven and accepted by Jesus. That is why she loved him so much.

Anointed by God
C37. Twelfth Sunday of the year

Zechariah 12: 10-11

Galatians 3: 26-29

Luke 9: 18-24

In the gospels, the question "Who is he?" is muttered and whispered wherever Jesus goes. Everyone who meets Jesus seems to ask that question. He is obviously someone who makes an immediate impression on whomever he encounters.

In today's gospel, Jesus himself poses the question to his disciples: "Who do you say I am?" After some silence, Peter speaks up: "The Christ [anointed one] of God". Peter is correct, but Jesus then describes himself as the Son of Man. Jesus is not trying to contradict Peter, but to make a specific point about himself and his followers.

"Son of Man" is a term Luke uses no less than 26 times. He used up a lot of ink on it, and many New Testament commentators have since followed his example, trying to fathom exactly what the term "Son of Man" means. I am not suggesting that all that ink was wasted, but still no one seems to know the precise answer!

Maybe we should look at what Jesus tells us about the Son of Man in the gospel reading. He says of the Son of Man:

- He will suffer grievously.
- He will be rejected.
- He will be killed.
- He will be raised from the dead.

These defining characteristics apply to Jesus, but they are also meant to apply to his followers. Jesus adds: "If anyone wants to be a follower of mine, let him renounce himself and take up his cross every day and follow me."

Why on Earth should God's anointed one have to suffer, be rejected and killed, and then rise again? Why is Jesus' suffering (and, by implication, the suffering of his followers) unavoidable? Why is it that, through the ages, so many of his followers have died so young, and endured such violent deaths?

The answers to these questions revolve around the dynamism of God, as revealed in stories such as the exodus from Egypt. If you read the exodus story, you see how God opted for the Hebrew nation in their exile, oppression, and slavery, thereby demonstrating that our divine parent is an ethical God who sides against injustice. Opting for the poor and the oppressed means that you express your preference for those who know from bitter experience that the world – with all its oppressive business, political, and religious structures – is fundamentally unjust and needs to change.

People whose work sustains those oppressive structures will see such an option as being directed against them personally. Jesus is not afraid to identify who these people are in his own time: the elders, the high priests, and the scribes. They are afraid that they will lose their power and influence. They cannot see that a just world would be to their own advantage, and they are willing to use violence if necessary to maintain their position.

When Jesus explains that the Son of Man is going to suffer, die, and rise again, he is trying to make clear the likely consequences of being anointed by God. To be anointed means that you are seized by that divine and irresistible dynamism. Jesus explains that in order to be his follower you have to renounce yourself, take up your cross every day, and follow him.

This is undeniably a hard and difficult task, but it is not an impossible one. If we take up our cross and follow Jesus, God will give us strength and anoint us with the divine dynamism, so that we are fully equipped to join Jesus in his non-violent struggle for the establishment of the kingdom of God.

The Jerusalem road
C38. Thirteenth Sunday of the year

1 Kings 19:16, 19-21

Galatians 5:1, 13-18

Luke 9:51-62

"Now, as the time drew near for him to be taken up to heaven, he resolutely took the road for Jerusalem ...." This is a defining moment in Luke's gospel: Jesus' decision to go to Jerusalem determines his fate and fixes the course of the rest of his life. It changes his character completely, and we notice that he even begins to speak differently and becomes more demanding of his followers. He will not be on this Earth much longer, so he must make it clear to his disciples that now is the time to sink or swim.

Then Luke refers to Jerusalem as being Jesus' destiny, all kinds of images and metaphors are conjured up. Jerusalem is a woman's name meaning "peace", "owner of peace", or "in whom peace is at home". It is also the geographical name of the city where Jesus' life and ministry will find completion in his death and resurrection. It is in Jerusalem that the new human life will break through into the old world.

Elsewhere in the Bible, we find Jerusalem being used as a metaphor for humanity: she is described as a beautiful bride who is full of life and waiting for her bridegroom (Revelation 21:2). The name Jerusalem is also used to denote the kingdom of God or heaven – the eschatological and mystical destination of humanity's long pilgrimage (Hebrews 12:22). At the end of time, Jerusalem will be the place where the whole of humanity will come together to celebrate the final realisation of God's kingdom (Revelation 21:26).

Jerusalem is what you might call the bottom line in life. The journey to Jerusalem is the final one we will make. That is why Jesus becomes so absolute in the demands he makes of those who want to follow him. Things that were once of primary importance to us – such as housing, clothing, food, burying your parents, contact with your family – lose their importance once you are on the Jerusalem road. We have set our sights on the kingdom of God, and nothing must distract us from that.

At some time in our lives, each of us will reach the point where we have to choose whether or not to take the road to Jerusalem. It is an all-or-nothing moment, with no room for compromise, and we must accept the consequences of the choice we make. Someone who understood this was the former Secretary General of the United Nations, Dag Hammerskjold, who died in an unexplained air crash while on a peace mission to Zaire. He wrote in his spiritual diary, *Markings*:

"I don't know who – or what – put the question; I don't know when it was put. I don't even remember answering. But at some time I did answer 'Yes' to someone – or something – and from that hour I was certain that existence is meaningful and that, therefore, my life, in self-surrender, had a goal. From that moment I have known what it means 'not to look back', and 'to take nought for the morrow.'"

Jesus resolutely took the route to Jerusalem. Deliverance comes when we take the unavoidable suffering of human life with us on our way to Jerusalem. It will come as no surprise that Pope John Paul II intends to visit Jerusalem at the beginning of the Great Jubilee!

Togetherness
C39. Fourteenth Sunday of the year.

Isaiah 66:10-14

Galatians 6:14-18

Luke 10:1-12, 17-20

The non-Jewish evangelist Luke is the only one who tells us the story about the sending out of the 72 (in some documents there are only 70). Numbers in the Bible are sometimes very significant. It is not difficult to guess that the number of apostles, 12, refers to the 12 tribes of Israel that have to brought together again. However, the meaning of the number 70 or 72 is not so obvious.

In Genesis (10:1-32), we are told how Noah had 70 or 72 grandsons. (The Hebrew version of Genesis gives the names of 70 grandchildren, but the Septuagint, a later Greek translation, gives 72 names. Hence the difference in numbers.) Eventually, those grandsons and their families left their ancestor's homestead to spread out all over the world. In many Bible translations, this is called: "The dispersal of the peoples".

Luke's 72 must have referred to those different grandsons. It is not difficult to guess why Luke tells this story: as a non-Jew, Luke had a good reason to explain that the mission Jesus gave his disciples is not just to gather in the 12 tribes of Israel, but also to harvest the whole of the world's population.

According to Luke, the Good News is for the whole world, and not reserved for one exclusive race, culture, or group of people. Luke notes that the first disciples of Jesus kept having difficulties with this notion.

140

Right up until Jesus left them, they were fixated on that mission to Israel. Even at the very last meeting they had with Jesus, just before his ascension into heaven, they were still asking him; "Lord, has the time come for you to restore the kingdom to Israel?" He answered them by saying, "you will be my witnesses not only in Jerusalem but throughout Judea and Samaria, and indeed to the ends of the Earth," (Acts 1:8).

The non-Jew Luke is a universalist. He expresses that universalism with some urgency in his story about the 72: they were not to be burdened themselves with heavy trunks, money, sandals, or any other luggage. There was not even time for idle chit-chat on the way. Their greeting to everyone was to be a simple "peace". They were not to expect to be fêted wherever they went, because the kind of peace they were announcing would not be welcome everywhere. This was a peace that meant the end of racism, fascism, apartheid, and every other kind of discrimination or divisiveness. They were sent out like lambs among wolves.

When they returned, they proudly told Jesus of their success in performing miracles and casting out evil spirits. Jesus warned them that those things were not the real issue: the important thing was to proclaim the peace of the kingdom of God and to gather in all the nations of the world. Jesus explained that to refuse God's peace is even worse than to sin morally. On the final day, the fate of sinful Sodom will be more tolerable than the fate of those who refuse the peace of the kingdom, because rejecting God's peace violates the unity of God's family.

Who is my neighbour?
C40. Fifteenth Sunday of the year

Deuteronomy 30:10-14

Colossians 1:15-20

Luke 10:25-37

A lawyer comes to test Jesus. He asks Jesus a theoretical question on a practical issue: "Master, what must I do to inherit eternal life?" Jesus is determined not to be disconcerted, and simply directs a question back at the lawyer in reply: "What does the Law say about it." It is as if Jesus is saying: "You know the theoretical answer to this jolly well – after all, you are a lawyer!" The lawyer answers:

"You must love the Lord your God with all your heart, with all your soul, with all your strength, and with all your mind, and your neighbour as yourself."

At that time, it was probably quite rare to combine the command to love God from Deuteronomy (6:5) with the text in Leviticus that instructs you to love your "neighbour" (meaning a fellow-countryman, but not a non-Jew) as yourself (19:18). Jesus then tells his interrogator, somewhat unenthusiastically, to obey that law.

Embarrassed about this abrupt end to the conversation, the lawyer asks a second question to try once more to engage Jesus in a discussion: "Who is my neighbour?" We have seen how Leviticus answers that question, but Jesus' story rules out any exclusive interpretations of the term "neighbour". The priest and the Levite in the story ignore the beaten stranger by the roadside, even though he is a fellow Jew; in contrast, the Samaritan, who is from a different and despised people, shows the injured man the love demanded in Leviticus.

Jesus does not define who the lawyer's neighbour might be, but tells him a story instead. This is a common ploy Jesus uses when faced with such a question. He does not like others to hide behind his ideas and moral insights: he would rather people thought out their own opinions about the issues he discusses. Jesus tells a story, gives examples and speaks in paradoxes, and it is up to the listener to draw his or her own conclusions. Jesus is no writer of encyclicals, laws, or rubrics. In fact, only once do we see him writing, and that is in loose sand, which would have soon disappeared in the breeze.

Jesus always ends up returning questions to the people who asked them in the first place. He does this because it is in ourselves that we have to find the answers. Moses expresses this in today's Old testament text from Deuteronomy:

"For this law that I enjoin on you today is not beyond your strength or beyond your reach. It is not in heaven ... Nor is it beyond the seas ... No, the word is very near to you, it is in your mouth and in your heart for your observance."

Morality, ethics, politics, economics, a great master plan, and so on, – Jesus leaves it all to us. It is his intention to show us that we can find it all in our own hearts.

The lawyer does not get the neat definition of a "neighbour" he so desired; instead, he gets the story about the good Samaritan. Listening to that story, you cannot but form your opinion. Jesus instigates a process within us that helps us to find the answer in our own hearts. By the end of our reading, this process has even led the lawyer, who had come to "disconcert" Jesus, to a full knowledge of who exactly is his neighbour.

The one body of Christ
C41. Sixteenth Sunday of the year

Genesis 18:1-10

Colossians 1:24-28

Luke 10:38-42

In his letter to the Colossians, Paul writes that he is responsible for announcing a mysterious secret to them, something that has been "hidden for generations and centuries". Paul often mentions this in his letters: to the Colossians, he says that the mystery is that Christ is in all of us; to the Ephesians, he writes that the secret he has to reveal is that all human beings together form one body and one family, and that all – Jew and Gentile alike – share in Jesus' promises.

We often forget that a secret is not something entirely new - it already existed, but was simply hidden or not publicly known. To reveal a secret or solve a mystery is consequently a process of disclosing or uncovering. When the truth that we are all one in Christ is disclosed to us, we realise that this has always been the case, even though we never knew it.

The oneness of humanity in Jesus is the Good News of the kingdom of God. It remained a secret for generations and centuries until Jesus revealed it himself through his life and work. In John's gospel, we read that the whole of creation is formed as God's offspring through Jesus Christ.

In January 1989, a young Australian woman named Ruth Henderson told me that she had been a passenger on a hijacked TWA aircraft in 1985. She sat next to a man named Robert Dean Stehem, who had been beaten up and tortured by the hijackers. His head and back were bleeding, and his wrists were bound together so tightly that he had lost the feeling in his hands. His knees and ribs were bruised and aching.

Ruth did not know what say to comfort him, but she began talking to him, anyway. They talked about unimportant things such as his love for scuba diving and his travels in Greece. Talking about those normal, everyday things seemed to help Robert to forget his pain. He told her that it was perhaps best that it was he who going to be killed, because he was the only one of the hostages who was not married. He said this without hesitation. He knew that it was highly unlikely that all the hostages would get out alive. The highjackers needed a victim, he said, and he was prepared to be that victim in order to help the others escape. Robert was later shot after further gruesome torture.

Robert felt compassion for others, he identified with them. At such a moment, the barriers between us fall away, and we become one. Christ identified himself with humanity in the compassion he showed for us, which had its most profound expression in his death and resurrection. It is through that compassion that Jesus becomes one with each of us.

143

Together, we form the unified body and Spirit of Jesus here on Earth.

Schopenhauer found his inspiration in Buddhism, but the insight is revealed to us in its totality in the person of Jesus Christ.

How to pray
C42. Seventeenth Sunday of the year

Genesis 18:20-32

Colossians 2:12-14

Luke 11:1-13

God has heard of the terrible sins being committed in Sodom and Gomorrah. Together with two companions, who later in the story prove to be angels, Yahweh decides to go and investigate. Abraham is asked to guide them to the two cities along the shortest route. When the cities are in view, the angels carry onwards, but Abraham is dismissed and can go home if he wants. Yahweh tells Abraham that if the bad things he has heard about the two towns prove to be true, then severe measures will have to be taken against them. Abraham remains standing there before Yahweh, thinking about what he has just heard.

Abraham has a question for God, and it is a difficult one - dare he ask it of the Almighty? He is worried, because he knows that the stories are true and he fears the worst for the populations of Sodom and Gomorrah, including his brother Lot and his family. Is Yahweh going to punish the town in the old fashioned way - that is, collectively, so that no distinction is made between guilty and innocent. What about the children, and the unborn babies still in their mothers' wombs?

Surely those days are past? Abraham is convinced that God could not do a thing like that any more - it would be so unjust. He puts his question to God, pleading for the innocent to be spared: "Are you really going to destroy the just person with the sinner? ... Will the judge of the whole Earth not administer justice?"

We are accustomed to approaching God reverently, piously, humbly, and silently, with closed eyes and bowed head. Abraham's approach is different. He is bold and forthright, and almost cheekily reminds God of God's good name and nature, as if to say: "If you really are a just God, you will surely spare the innocent." If we look at other Bible texts, we find that this bold approach to prayer was also used by Moses and Jesus.

In today's gospel text, Jesus teaches us how to pray. He tells us to begin by reminding God of God's holiness and sovereignty: "Father, may your name be made holy, your kingdom come!" Having done that, we are to ask for a new start to life and all that is needed for that new beginning, such as bread and forgiveness. We should tell God, without beating about the bush, that God should forgive us as we forgive others, and we should ask God to prevent us from being misled, and to guide us along the right path in life.

Jesus not only tells us what we should pray for, but also how we should pray. We should pray no-nonsense prayers, forgetting long words and "highfalutin" phrases and explaining in simple terms what we expect from the one who put us on this Earth, and whom we trust through thick and thin.

This approach is the core of the story that Jesus tells after instructing the disciples about prayer. A guest arrives in the middle of the night and is hungry, but the host has no food in the house, so he goes to his friend to ask for some loaves. We are told that the loaves are not handed over out of friendship, but because of the host's "persistence" (Luke 11:8). However, in the original Greek, the word used is *anaideia*, which literally means "shameless". To pray for something in a modest, unassuming way is not Jesus' recommendation. If we take this to heart, it will transform our prayer life!

Vanity
C43. Eighteenth Sunday of the year

Ecclesiastes 1:2, 2:21-23

Colossians 3:1-5, 9-11

Luke 12:13-21

Luke is very interested in the poor. He shows how Mary sings, even before Jesus' birth: "The hungry he has filled with good things, the rich he has sent empty away" (Luke 1:53). Luke is the only one who tells us how the first visitors at Jesus birth were shepherds – people who were on one of the lowest rungs of the social ladder (2:1-20). He also reveals that Joseph and Mary could only afford to pay the tariff laid down for the poor (two turtle doves) when paying for Jesus' circumcision (2:24). It is only in Luke's gospel that we hear John the Baptist shouting that those who have food and clothes should share them with those who have none (3:11).

Luke has pity on the poor and also, it may surprise us, on the rich. Luke's gospel carries 18 warnings on the dangerous power of riches. Luke fears that the rich will miss their true vocation because they are so obsessed with their own wealth. This is also Jesus' concern, which is why he tells the story we read today of the rich farmer, who puts all his confidence in his money and the value of the crops in his barns instead of in God. This is not only sinful, but also unwise and idiotic.

In the reading from Ecclesiastes, the attitude of the rich towards their wealth is called "vanity". The original word, *hebel*, means "a gust of wind". The rich farmer's attitude is so short-sighted, because his life and riches are as stable as a gust of wind. People who consider their property as a kind of life-insurance are, according to both Luke and the author Ecclesiastes, just plain foolish. Their money is wasted money, as it is not used to promote the kingdom of God.

Having understood this, we should not think Jesus had an unqualified respect for poverty, because that also has its dangers. When you are poor, you can be so taken up by your daily worries and the basic struggle to survive that you are hindered from trusting in God. The same greed that often makes the rich so mean, can also drive the poor to bitter envy.

Jesus does not seem to differentiate much between the rich and the poor. The fact that one is rich or poor almost seems to Jesus to be an accidental circumstance of life, although Jesus does expect the rich to use their wealth in a way that is pleasing to God. The essential thing, whether rich or poor, is to be of Christ – that is the real pearl, the priceless treasure. The new life of Christ asks us to end our idolatry of money and possessions, to love and care for one another, and to promote justice and peace.

The inter-denominational Church of the Saviour in Washington DC, USA, has many wealthy members, many of whom are members of a group called the Ministry of Money. The group meets regularly to see how they should invest their money to promote the welfare of humanity. An example of their work is their decision to invest in companies that research into sicknesses and disease among poor people. This is an area that is often overlooked by the large pharmaceutical companies, because there is no money in it. Luke would have had no difficulties with those rich people!

In transit
C44. Nineteenth Sunday of the year

Wisdom 18:6-9
Hebrews 11:1-2, 8-19
Luke 12:32-48

In the reading from Luke's gospel, Jesus gives an exacting command: "Sell your possessions and give alms." It is no longer only the rich who are expected to do this – it applies to all those who choose to follow Jesus.

In Acts, Luke tells us how the early Christian communities took those words literally. That first, noble attempt to realise the kingdom of God here on Earth faltered because the time was not right. The problems they experienced were the result of the tension caused by the "already/not yet" nature of the kingdom, which we know to be with us, but for which we still wait expectantly. This tension will also cause us difficulties, but the kingdom should still be our aim in life. Because we have not yet arrived there, we are told to keep our belts done up and our lamps lit. We are living on a promise that has not yet been fulfilled.

The author of the letter to the Hebrews compares our situation to that of Abraham and Sarah. They realised that they were like strangers in this world. They were nomads travelling through life looking for the country God had promised them, knowing that they would one day reach it, even though they could not yet see it. They invested all they were and had - including their only son Isaac - in the hope and expectation that God's promise would be fulfilled.

Abraham and Sarah are our models. We too are nomads on this Earth. Perhaps we should print the word "traveller" or "in transit" under the names on our business cards or letterheads, because we are all on a journey. Abraham and Sarah could not look beyond the horizon of their own lives, and so never saw the promised land. We are more fortunate, because we can see the promised land mapped out for us in Jesus' life, death, and resurrection.

Jesus invested everything he was and had in the kingdom of God, putting his whole existence at stake. That is what he asks us to do when he speaks about selling everything we have and giving it to the poor. Instead of taking it literally, we should understand it as an appeal to devote ourselves to the final outcome of the great divine-human adventure.

In 1968, the Amsterdam police arrested a girl, Koosje Koster, for obstructing the traffic. During the interrogation, the police asked her what she had been doing. She replied: "I was handing out currants to the passers-by from a paper bag." Why did she do that? "To make them all eat at least once out of the same brown paper bag." Why did she give them currants? "Because that word [in Dutch] reminded me of Saint Paul's letter to the Corinthians, in which he writes about eating together" (1 Cor. 11:18-34).

Jesus would probably have approved of her symbolic actions. Jesus himself describes the culmination and final destination of our journey through life as a banquet or an enormous feast. We have a "taster" of this huge heavenly get-together in our Eucharist celebrations with fellow believers. In the same way, the celebration of the Great Jubilee should give us a foretaste of the wonderful common future that lies ahead for humanity in the presence of God!

Dove and hawks
C45. Twentieth Sunday of the year

Jeremiah 38:4-6, 8-10

Hebrews 12:1-4

Luke 12:49-53

The pacifists among us – the "doves" – are serious people, because once you have renounced violence there is no possible compromise. That is also true of the "hawks" among us, who believe in the efficiency of violence. The doves often have difficulty in coming to terms with today's reading from Luke. After all, if Jesus did oppose violence and if he was the Prince of Peace, how do we explain his words to the disciples?

To answer this question, let us read Luke's account of the arrest of Jesus (26:47-53). When the chief priests and elders come with the Temple guard to take Jesus away, there is a scuffle. We can guess that Jesus' followers group round him like a kind of body guard. Luke writes how they ask Jesus: "Lord, shall we use our swords?" At the mere suggestion of it – and even before Jesus is able to answer the question – their swords are swinging through the air, cutting off the ear of one of the high priests' servants.

Jesus' whole mission is at stake, because to sanction violence at this moment will demand a reinterpretation and revaluation of all he has been saying and doing to promote the kingdom of God. That is not what happens. Jesus tells the disciples to "Leave off!" and they put away their swords. He touches the man's ear, and heals him. Jesus then turns to the high priests and the captains of the Temple guard and blames them for the incident because they came for him with swords and clubs.

It is against that background that we have to read today's text. Jesus tells the disciples that he has come to bring a fire on the Earth, and that he hopes it will set everything ablaze. He explains that he will have to undergo a baptism of blood, and that he is distressed by the prospect of it. Then he asks them, rather sadly: "Do you suppose that I am here to bring peace on Earth?" Knowing Jesus, the disciples naturally assume that the correct answer is "Yes".

Of course, the disciples were right, but as Jesus carried out his public ministry, it became clear that he was simply too much for some people. His mere presence was enough to divide families into those who were in favour of him and those who were against him: father against

148

son, daughter against mother, mother-in-law against daughter-in-law, and so on. For many, the thought of following Jesus was just too subversive. Others simply considered it extremely risky, an attitude that is confirmed by Jesus' words to his disciples on the evening he was arrested: "... if you have no sword, sell your cloak and buy one" (22:36). That is how dangerous it had become to be in his company!

Jesus came to bring peace. The Hebrew word for peace is shalom, which is the same word Jesus tells his disciples to use as their greeting on their travels. Shalom means "whole". A plate or a cup is shalom as long as it is not broken. Shalom encapsulates the kind of wholeness Jesus came to bring to this world. However, this wholeness is something that people willingly have to practise, not something that you can force upon them. There is no middle way with this peace, because it is a peace that has to be chosen. You are either for it or against it – you are either a "dove" or a "hawk".

Choose peace, choose life!

Answers and questions
C46. Twenty-first Sunday of the year

Isaiah 66:18-21

Hebrews 12:5-7, 11-13

Luke 13:22-30

Jeopardy is one of the most popular quiz-shows in the United States. The essence of the game is that the contestants are given answers, and have to guess what the questions are. This is much more difficult than you might think. If you have all the answers but do not have the questions, you will lose.

Luke, who promised in the introduction to his gospel to give an ordered account, brings together a set of four answers to a question asked of Jesus: "Sir, will there be only a few saved?" The answers are:

- Enter by the narrow door.
- The ruler of the house may close the door on some people.
- The saved ones come from all over the world.
- The last ones will be the first ones.

Even if you had these answers before you, you would still find it well-nigh impossible to guess the original question, because Jesus does not answer it directly. He is not prepared to play a numbers game regarding how many will enter the kingdom of God. For Jesus, the issue is not how many people will enter the kingdom; the issue is how we react to the invitation to enter that kingdom.

The traditional interpretation of this gospel text is that it is about the after-life: it is about heaven and (as there is a mention of "weeping and grinding of teeth") hell. If we are saved, we are taken up to heaven: the narrow door is the door to heaven. Jesus is the one who opens the door of heaven to the saved, and closes it against the un-saved. Salvation is open to people from every race and nation.

Is this a correct interpretation of Jesus' meaning? Is being saved something that happens in the after-life, or is it something that occurs here on Earth?

At one point, Jesus describes how the door is left ajar, so that we can look inside and see Abraham, Isaac, Jacob, and the prophets. They are, of course, sitting there in heaven because of the roles they played here on Earth. It is on Earth that they devoted themselves to establishing the kingdom of God, and it is on Earth that they struggled for justice and peace.

The status of being "saved" is just as valid now as will be in the after-life. It is in this life that you are either in the kingdom of God or out of it. When all you do is eat, drink, and consume, you are not building the foundations of God's kingdom. You may well be waving your baptismal certificate, your missal, or your prayer book, but they will not help you if you are not engaged in Jesus' efforts. You will not be given the chance in the after-life to enter what you refused or neglected to enter while here on Earth. You may well be ready with the right answer when you knock at heaven's door, but the question will no longer be being asked! The door-keeper will say: "I don't know where you come from." You might protest, "But I ate with you, you taught me!" Sadly, the response will be: "I don't know you."

To speak about what is awaiting us after this life is difficult, because the traditional images that were used hardly mean anything to us today. However, if you do not have a dimension to your life that transcends your earthly existence, you will remain stuck in it. At the end of your life, you may no longer even know yourself where you came from.

At table
C47. Twenty-second Sunday of the year

Sirach 3:17-20, 28-29

Hebrews 12:18-19. 22-24

Luke 14:1, 7-14

One of the more important Pharisees invited Jesus to eat with him. Jesus knew that he was not just being invited out of kindness. His host had another intention: he could not make Jesus out, so he wanted an opportunity to observe and study him at close hand. Jesus accepted the invitation, not just out of politeness, but because he, too, had a hidden agenda. Jesus wished to show the Pharisees who he was and what he wanted. To start with, Jesus highlighted the seating arrangement at the table "because he had noticed how they [the guests] picked the places of honour" (Luke 14:7).

Jesus also remarked on the fact that his host had only invited his friends, his family, and his rich neighbours. This was certainly not the guest list Jesus would have drawn up: he was known for sitting at table with different types of people – that is, the poor and the marginalised. Jesus let them know what he was thinking by telling a parable. He mixed in some pieces of advice that were more than just rules of courtesy – they constituted a radical change of table policy.

Jesus' table conversation is often used to help define our "option for the poor". This option has become quite a trendy, fashionable concept in the Church today: theologians use it in their liberation theology; bishops during their synods; religious and missionaries during their chapters; parish councils in their meetings; and even some politicians in their speeches. With so much talk, it is easy to overlook how radical and revolutionary this option is.

The injustice, oppression, and exploitation in our world are inextricably linked to the way our economy, politics, media, and religious institutions are organised. The majority of the population is engaged in maintaining those structures, either directly because of their jobs or indirectly because of their lifestyles. The change will have to come from somewhere else – from those who are (to use Jesus words) weeping and mourning, thirsting for justice and hungry for peace. These are the people who are marginalised by our societies: the unemployed, the homeless, the refugees, the exiles, the persecuted, and the oppressed. (Luke would probably call them the poor, the disabled, the crippled, the blind, the widows, and the orphans.) A radical option for these people would, indeed, overthrow the existing world "pecking order" at the global table.

As Christians, this option means that we must open our social circle to include those wounded and hurt people, and invite them to our table. In our personal lives, it means that we have to accept at the "psychological" table within us all those human characteristics that have remained underdeveloped in us, that we have repressed, or that have become atrophied. In our relationships with others, it means that we must open the windows and doors of our heart and soul to all our human brothers and sisters. In our Church, it means that we respect everything that is "feminine" and "motherly", and that we take those dimensions seriously and inclusively. In our ecological context, it means that the animals, plants, and the environment must no longer suffer because of our wasteful lifestyles.

The "Son of Man" Jesus came as the model of created wholeness. His example shows us that we should find places at a common table for all the underdeveloped, wounded, neglected, exploited, and abused elements of God's world.

The price we have to pay

C48. Twenty-third Sunday of the year

Wisdom 9:13-18

Philemon 9-10, 12-17

Luke 14:25-33

The crowd around Jesus is growing larger with each day that passes. They come because they are curious to see and hear him; because they want to be healed, because he is famous; and for all sorts of other reasons. They flock to Jesus in the same way that people today go out of their way to get a glimpse of a TV celebrity, a sports personality, or a head of state.

Jesus suddenly turns around and faces the crowd, which must cause some consternation. They are quite willing to walk behind him, but they feel a bit uneasy when he stands there gazing intently at them. They avoid his gaze in embarrassment.

There is a story by the Danish philosopher Soren Kierkegaard about Jesus visiting a church in Denmark one Sunday. The parishioners are singing that they are Jesus' followers, when the sacristan suddenly rushes from the vestry and whispers something in the preacher's ear. Jesus is sitting in the sacristy right now, and he would like to see everyone personally! Jesus has been drawn to the church by the singing. The parishioners file into the sacristy one by one, where Jesus asks each of them the same question: "Are you really my follower?" Nobody dares to answer the question, neither with a "Yes" nor a "No", but as soon as they are back in the safety of the church again, they bravely continue singing their hymn!

In the gospel reading, Jesus tells the crowd what it costs to become one of his followers: you have to carry his cross from day to day; you have to give up your possessions; and you have to hate your father, mother, children, brothers, and sisters – and even your own life.

That last condition seems too high a price to pay. However, in Hebrew "hate" was an emphatic way of expressing total detachment from something. When you quarrelled with your family when you were younger it was because you did not "hate" them enough. You fought with your father, you struggled with your mother, you resented the success of your brothers and sisters simply because you were not yet your own person – you were still emotionally and psychologically dependent upon your family. You have to grow out of those dependencies before you can be your true self.

John A. Sanford, an American author, illustrates this point by telling the story of Albert. Albert is in his early 40s. He has a job that offers no creative, financial, or promotional opportunities. He is deeply depressed and goes for some counselling. It becomes apparent that Albert is a very creative person who has given up all hope of further personal growth because he feels that his first duty is the care of his family. Behind that sentiment hides the powerful personality of his domineering mother – a very conservative and emotionally manipulative woman.

The problem is that Albert does not "hate" his mother sufficiently. He is so emotionally bonded to her that he has never become his own man. He has spent his whole life running around after her without asking himself what he was doing or why he was doing it. In a sense, Albert is like all those people who follow Jesus around unthinkingly, without considering what it takes to become one of Jesus' real "followers".

In Luke's text, Jesus uses the Greek word *apotasssestai*, meaning "say farewell to"(14:33). Without saying a metaphorical "farewell" to all those people and things upon which you have become dependent, you will never come to yourself, and you will never really follow Jesus.

Lost and found
C49. Twenty-fourth Sunday of the year

Exodus 32:7-11, 13-14

1 Timothy 1:12-17

Luke 15:1-10 (or 1-32)

Today's gospel story is about one sheep and one coin. The sheep belonged of a flock of one hundred and the coin was part of a set of ten. We usually pass over the numbers we find in the Bible without giving them a second thought, unlike Saint Augustine, who was very intrigued by their use. He wrote in his book *The City of God*: "We should not look down on numerology, that science is in many cases an excellent help to the attentive Bible commentator."

Perhaps we should pay more attention to the numbers we find in scripture, because we often imbue numbers with special significance in our daily lives. For example, we often ponder what the numbers that occur in our dreams might mean, and we feel reluctant to buy something trivial with a £100 note, because it is almost as if we are "breaking" a precious unit. Once that large note is divided up into smaller notes and coins, the money seems to disappear much more quickly, like sand trickling through our fingers.

This insight might explain the behaviour of the shepherd in Jesus' story. Who, for heaven's sake, would leave 99 sheep on their own to look for a single maverick? And why is the woman so frantically joyful when she finds a coin worth only about ten pence? She calls her friends together and tells them: "Rejoice with me, I have found the drachma I lost!" Are we just supposed to laugh at this, or is there some deeper meaning hiding behind all those numbers?

In the oldest human communities, the number ten was very important, and the multiple 1000 was considered a divine number. It stood for everything, including God. Methodius wrote: "The number 1000, consisting out of 100 times ten, is a full and perfect number ...." When you think of ten and 100 as elements of the divine number, the losses of the sheep and the coin are disasters: they must be found! Without the lost sheep or the coin, both numbers are incomplete – the symbolic units are broken.

Gregory of Nyssa wrote that the lost drachma represents "our lost humanity". He thinks that the lost coin is the heart and the soul of the woman herself, and that the lamp she lights is "without any doubt our consciousness that throws its light on hidden depths." The lost coin can only be found "in our own house, that is in ourselves." The woman in question is no longer herself, as part of her disappeared in the dark of her existence. She lights a lamp to find the part of herself she has lost. No wonder that she is so glad when she finds her treasure!

Is this too far-fetched an interpretation or too psycho-analytical? Gregory goes even further when he adds that "the parable refers to our king [Jesus], not yet hopelessly lost, but hidden under rubbish." According to him, Jesus is hidden in every human being as the one who redeems. If we do not find him, we will never be our true selves. This will be more than just a tragedy, because we will become like the lost sheep in the first part of the story and then the whole of the flock – the whole of humanity – will suffer by not being complete.

The treasure, the kingdom of God, is in each one of us. You can also call that presence Jesus Christ, our brother who is too often lost within our inner selves.

Perhaps there is something in numbers after all!

154

The astute steward

C50. Twenty-fifth Sunday of the year

Amos 8:4-7

1 Timothy 2:1-8

Luke 16:1-13

The parable about the unjust steward (or accountant) is a tricky one. It is the story of a steward who squanders the property of his master and who, when accused of this, is intent on assuring his future after his dismissal. At the end of the parable, Luke adds on some snippets of advice from Jesus on the use and abuse of money, although they do not offer much that helps us to understand its meaning.

It is generally accepted that the steward makes provisions for his future in a fraudulent way. Note, however, that his dishonesty is established before he begins to take steps to secure his future. It is not explicitly stated that the measures the steward then takes are in themselves dishonest.

According to some experts, it was the custom of the time that a steward controlled the sums his master gave out as loans. He was also the one who determined the commissions paid on the loans. In many cases, those commissions were the only way to make money, because the Jewish Law forbade usury – that is, the charging of interest. To avoid any legal difficulty, the amounts mentioned on the invoices were often higher than the money that was actually handed out. In other words, the commission was added to the total figure on the invoice.

An example might help: the historian Josephus noted how King Herod Agrippa borrowed money from a banker in the Near East through an agent called Marsyas in the year ad 33. In order to get the money, he signed an invoice stating that he borrowed 20,000 Greek drachmas, even though he actually received 2,500 drachmas less. The difference was Marsyas' commission. When bartering goods in kind, such as grain, wine, salt, oil, or beer, that "hidden" commission would often amount to between 50 and 100 per cent.

If we apply this knowledge to our story, it may well be more accurate to assume that the steward simply subtracts the commissions – which are probably his, in any case – from the amounts due to his master. If this interpretation is correct, then we cannot say that the steward is doing anything dishonest in these transactions. This would seem to be supported by the way his master praises him for his "astuteness". Perhaps the master agrees in advance to the reductions made by the steward?

155

The story is about more than the wise use of money – it is also about a "conversion". A man who is guilty of squandering and mismanaging money assumes he will be dismissed from his post. In order to face the future, he converts and becomes astute, rather than fraudulent, in the handling of money. The "unjust steward" is thus a model for Jesus' disciples, not because of his dishonesty but because of his prudence.

If this parable helps us to know how best to react when confronted with a crisis, then it will have taught us a useful lesson.

The distance between us
C51. Twenty-sixth Sunday of the year

Amos 6:1, 4-7

1 Timothy 6:11-16

Luke 16:19-31

Commentators tell us that the parable of the rich man and Lazarus is derived from an old story that goes back to ancient Egyptian mythology. Whatever its historical origins, we cannot simply label this as an "old" story, because it is also a story of our own age. That is, perhaps, why the rich man has no name: he is a universal figure for all times. The poor man at his door, who is too sick and enfeebled to ward off the rich man's dogs that lick his wounds, does have a name: Lazarus, which means "God-helped".

In 1975, at the meeting of the World Council of Churches in Nairobi, Kenya, a Dutch delegate said that he thought Kenya was a magnificent country, but that he would be glad to be back to the Netherlands. He added: "I don't have this poverty at my doorstep at home. I wouldn't be able to stand it in the long run." The man was wrong to assume that he would not have to deal with the problem if he went home. The poor people would still be lying at his door; only the distance between them would be different.

The gospel story of today is precisely about that distance between the poor and us. We know that Lazarus is lying at our gate, as well as at the gate of the rich man. If we can say that about ourselves, then Amos would be able to add:

"Lying on ivory beds, and sprawling on their divans, they dine on lambs from the flock, and stall-fattened veal; they bawl to the sound of the lyre, invent new instruments of music like David, they drink wine by the bowlful, and use the finest oils for anointing themselves, but about the ruin of Joseph they do not care at all" (6:4-6).

In the gospel story, Lazarus dies first and the rich man second. The rich man gets a beautiful funeral. The poor fellow remains unburied, but angels carry him into Abraham's lap. When the two see each other in the after-life, their positions have been reversed because God has intervened. The one thing that remains the same between the two men, and which is fixed forever, is the distance the rich man put between himself and Lazarus while they were on Earth. It is apparent that he must have been aware of Lazarus' suffering during his life, because he recognises him and mentions his name. Nevertheless, the distance remains between them, and it cannot be bridged.

The rich man, who burned his tongue on the sumptuous food he ate on Earth and who now cannot get a drop of water to cool it, asks Abraham to send Lazarus to warn his rich brothers. When Abraham answers that the warnings of Moses and the prophets should be sufficient for them, the rich man insists, saying: "Ah no, father Abraham, but if someone comes from the dead, they will repent." Abraham replies that if they do not listen to Moses and the prophets, they are unlikely to listen even if someone should rise from the dead.

Jesus, the one who is telling this story, rose from the dead for us. However, the distance between the rich and the poor is increasing all the time. The number of starving people at the door of the rich is growing every day. One-third of the world's population owns almost everything, leaving the other two-thirds to suffer. The crucified one rose from the dead to tell us to do something about it. Was Abraham right when he said that we would not listen?

Ungrateful servants
C52. Twenty-seventh Sunday of the year

Habakkuk 1:2-3; 2:2-4
2 Timothy 1:6-8, 13-14
Luke 17:5-10

Paul's second letter to Timothy is strange to read, because it is all about Paul himself: his contribution, his principles, his words, and his imprisonment. It all sounds like a grand exercise in self-promotion, especially when thought of in the context of today's gospel, in which Jesus calls us "merely servants".

Perhaps we should note that many Bible scholars think that the two letters to Timothy were not written by Paul, but by one of his "fans". The letter is thus to be valued not simply because Paul is its author, but because it was much used in the early Church.

The letter attributes a lot to Paul, which is what happens when you write about someone whom you admire. However, the people you admire often talk about themselves in a completely different way. You might talk admiringly about the talents of a great artist, and then be shocked to hear him confess that he has no idea how he achieves his great works, or where his inspiration comes from.

Paul knows that the inspiration for his work and teaching does not come from himself. He never forgets that he is nothing more than a mere "servant". One of the things Paul repeats over and over again in his letters – except, that is, in his letters to the Galatians – is his gratitude for what he has received.

In the film *Amadeus*, the court composer, Salieri, confesses that he is most probably the cause of Mozart's death. He hounded him to his death because of something he never understood: how was it possible that Mozart, who to Salieri appeared a vulgar and superficial person, seemed to be packed with such phenomenally beautiful music? Salieri, a pious and God-fearing person, had the greatest difficulty in composing mediocre music, and yet all that rascal Mozart had to do was to sit down in front of a piece of paper and out poured the most enchanting music!

Luke's gospel text is about that kind of free gift, or "gratuity". The faith Jesus' disciples ask for is the capacity to be inspired and animated in such a way that everything will be possible for them. Jesus reminds them that it is God who sends us gifts like that. When such gifts are given, they are to be used for the benefit of all, not simply to serve our own needs and wants. We should remember that we are, primarily, God's servants.

Salieri thinks that he deserves such a gift, because he devotes himself to God. Salieri believes that you can earn your grace, and yet he fails where Mozart succeeds. Salieri is not grateful for the gifts, talents, and abilities he already has. Comparing himself to Mozart, he thinks that he should be endowed with more and better gifts from God. Mozart lives without these worries and simply just composes, full of joy and pep!

The mistake Salieri made can also be made in reverse. For example, Milicent, a widow in her fifties, visits one of her friends who has a very painful sickness. She feels suddenly inspired to lay her hands on her sick friend, who immediately feels that a healing process is beginning within her. She tells that to Milicent, who withdraws her hands at once, saying: "It is impossible that God would give a gift like that to a sinner like me." Just as in the case of Salieri, we can thwart God's gifts by not accepting what we have received and by not being grateful.

It is difficult to be a servant!

Keeping Jesus in mind

C53. Twenty-eighth Sunday of the year

2 Kings 5:14-17

2 Timothy 2:8-13

Luke 17:11-19

"Remember the Good News that I carry," writes the author of the second letter to Timothy. Remembering and forgetting are also the themes of today's gospel story of the healing of the ten lepers. When only one comes back to Jesus praising God for his healing, Jesus asks: "Were not all ten made clean?" Did the other nine forget so quickly what had happened to them?

At the Last Supper, Jesus tells his disciples to keep him in mind always, for all times to come. This is what we do when we celebrate the Eucharist. The breaking of bread keeps alive his memory – a memory that forms the bedrock of our existence. It is almost unimaginable that Jesus could be forgotten, and yet it does happen: a teacher in London noted recently that some children have no idea what they are celebrating at Christmas. We should not be complacent: anything can be forgotten. The Bible tells us how the Hebrews, returning from their exile, had forgotten the whole of the Law until Nehemiah (8:5) finds the scrolls and the people – with tears in their eyes – listen to the text as Ezra reads to them.

When we forget something, it no longer forms part of our consciousness, and thus fails to influence our lives. The wise ones among us do their best to keep their old memories alive – the failures and disasters, as well as the successes. Certain things should never be forgotten, such as World War II, the Holocaust, and the atomic bombs that were dropped on Hiroshima and Nagasaki. To refuse to forget the past or to be consoled over it can also be prophetic: just remember the lament that was sung after the murder of the innocents in Bethlehem, when Matthew quotes Jeremiah (31:15): "A voice is heard in Ramah, lamenting and weeping bitterly: it is Rachel weeping for her children, refusing to be comforted for her children, because they are no more." She does not want to forget or to be consoled.

Sometime ago, a missionary who had spent many years in Africa was giving a talk to a group of parishioners about her experiences in that continent. When they asked her what Africa needed most, she answered: "Memories". To her audience, who were geared up to offer practical or financial help – something "concrete" – this sounded rather ridiculous. She explained what she meant: "I have been in so many African countries where only one solution to their problems is ever considered: guns. After so many years of dictatorial and violent regimes, the people have forgotten the traditional, peaceful ways of solving conflicts and disputes."

To forget something implies that you are losing part of yourself – something that you did, experienced, learned, saw, or heard. It is your memory that keeps your personality together through the years. Just flick once through an old photo album, and you will know what I am writing about. As soon as you see the pictures, something in yourself knits everything together into a coherent record of your existence, like a spider weaving a web. When you look at the web, you are reminded of who you are. Your memory is the mortar between the events of your life.

Paul writes: "Remember the Good News I carry." Remember Jesus – never let him be forgotten. If you do, you will lose not only him, but also yourself. Remembering Jesus in the sign he left us – the breaking of the bread – also helps us to remember who we are.

Pray until the end
C54. Twenty-ninth Sunday of the year

Exodus 17:8-13

2 Timothy 3:14 – 4:2

Luke 18:1-8

Luke gives more space to the topic of prayer than any of the other gospel writers. This probably has something to do with the fact that Luke was introduced to Jesus through the Christian communities he met on his travels. His descriptions in Acts of the men and women he met in those communities show that they made a deep and lasting impression on him. They are living under the influence of the Holy Spirit, and are constantly receiving direct instructions from the Spirit: "Do not go to Bythinia ..." (16:7), "Let Asia wait ..." (16:6), "Go to Cornelius ..." (10:20), and so on.

Luke showed that these first Christians were led by the Spirit through Holy Scripture, visions, dreams, and even by throwing dice! Their main inspiration, however, wells up in their hearts while they are praying. According to Luke, they are living in a new time – the era of the Holy Spirit. Luke stresses the role of the Holy Spirit up to eighteen times. He does that from the very beginning of his gospel, when he writes that Mary conceives by the Holy Spirit, and when he describes how the embryonic John the Baptist is filled with the Spirit when he leaps up in the womb of his mother, Elisabeth.

160

Jesus is constantly shown praying in Luke's gospel, including at his baptism; in the desert; in the mountains before choosing his apostles; alone with his disciples; during his transfiguration; when his disciples return from their mission; in connection with Simon's temptations; on his own in a secret place; in Gethsemane; and on the cross. There is also the model prayer – the "Our Father" – and four parables on prayer. Luke does his best to emphasise that prayer is necessary to touch the Spirit and to live under its influence.

The kingdom of God is the work of the Holy Spirit, which is why you should "pray continually and never lose heart," as Jesus reminds his disciples. He illustrates this by telling the parable about the unjust judge, who had neither fear of God nor respect for anyone, and a widow who insists that he gives her justice. In the end, the judge is afraid that she might slap him the face or give him a black eye, so he relents and gives her the justice she craves!

Jesus tells us that if we are persistent and insistent in our prayer, then God, like the judge, will not fail to grant us our requests:

"Now, will not God see justice done to his chosen who cry to him day and night even when he delays to help them? I promise you, he will see justice done to them, and done speedily."

Until the kingdom of God is fully realised on Earth, we have to continue praying and never lose heart – right until the end.

Tax collector or Pharisee?
C55. Thirtieth Sunday of the year

Sirach 35:12-14, 16-18

2 Timothy 4:6-8, 16-18

Luke 18:9-14

Whichever way you look at it, Jesus had something against the Pharisees. Some Bible scholars say that he himself was a Pharisee, which is why he could address and criticise them with such aplomb.

Today, the words "Pharisee" and "pharisaic" are terms of reproach in the English language. The term "pharisaic" might be compared with the term "jesuitical", which Jesuits do not like because they know it is not meant in a positive or complimentary way. They also know in their hearts that there are sound historical reasons for it gaining these negative associations. The original meaning of the word Pharisee escapes us. Some specialists think that it means a person who is "put aside" or "separated". The Pharisees attitude was very much "holier-than-thou", thanking God that they were not grasping, unjust, and adulterous sinners like anyone else. Today, we would call them "religious snobs".

In the gospel reading we find a Pharisee and a tax collector in the Temple. We must allow for a bit of authorial licence here, because in reality, the Pharisees did not go to the Temple – they were synagogue people. Their main concern was with the Law. They loved the Law so much that they even did more than the Law prescribed! If you do more than the Law prescribes, they thought, you surely cannot go wrong.

Whenever there was a doubt about the application of the Law, they always decided in favour of the strictest interpretation. They tried to remain "pure" and formed cliques that only eat with each other and did business amongst themselves. Their actions were designed to make them different from other people, on whom they looked down with disapproval. In their own eyes, they were the only true believers.

Jesus was often seen in their company. Several times he was invited to eat with them, and he willingly accepted those invitations. He often used these occasions to tell them what he thought of them. Their ideas were certainly not his: he was against their interpretation of the Law, their exclusivity, and their pettiness. He called them "white-plastered tombs" (Matthew 23:27). His sympathies were with those whom they despised.

You had to be in good standing and well-off to be a Pharisee. With their money and their influence they were always capable of putting themselves above the masses. Jesus simply could not stand that attitude, and he reacted against it. Jesus hardly reacted against the monstrous tyranny and organised crime of his days; he seemed to think that it was more important to do something against the ordinary, everyday hypocrisy around him. He forcefully opposed the religious hypocrites and bullies who terrorised their own neighbourhood and churches.

With whom do we identify when we listen to Jesus' story of the two men in the Temple? After all we have heard, it cannot be with the Pharisee! Does that mean that we would like to be the far-from-popular tax collector? Or would it, after all, be better to identify with the Pharisee? Are they just as bad as each other? Jesus' parables often contain this kind of teasing ambiguity. The answer is that we are neither like the Pharisee nor the tax collector, but if we are honest we will admit that we can see something of each of them in ourselves.

An amusing conversion

C56. Thirty-first Sunday of the year

Wisdom 11:23 – 12:2

2 Thessalonians 1:11 – 2:2

Luke 19:1-10

Children love the story about Zaccheus, because it is such a crazy story. We often take the gospel stories so seriously that the humour in them escapes us. We are so concerned with teasing out the allegorical and symbolic meanings that we do not notice their humour.

Who talks about a splinter in the eye of your sister and a beam in your own, without a chuckle? Who can suppress a laugh when Jesus compares John the Baptist – that knotty man in his smelly old camel skin, his far-reaching voice and his sombre prophecies – with a reed swaying in the wind and a dandy at the king's court (Luke 7:24-25)? What about Jesus' suggestion to light a lamp only to put it under the bed, or a camel trying to creep through the eye of a needle – ludicrous! Then there is the story about the man who knocks on his neighbour's door in the middle of the night to ask for three loaves of bread; his poor neighbour is in bed and claims that he cannot climb over his wife and kids to fetch him some food (11:8).

The people around Jesus must have laughed wildly at those stories. You could say that Luke has a rather deadpan sense of humour, because he does not make much of those comical situations. Even Luke's down-playing of the comic side to Jesus cannot spoil the playfulness that often comes through his stories. Do you remember the widow who wanted to wallop the unjust judge in the eye (18:4-5)? Misplaced ecclesiastical solemnity disguises the fact that Jesus was once surrounded by people who enjoyed him and his stories! They would not have hung around him for so long if he just spoke doom and gloom all the time.

Children see the humour better than we do, because they come to the stories afresh. Just try asking them to make a drawing of Zaccheus after having told them the story. Forget all the exegetical, semiotic, text-critical, demythologising, and post-modern deconstructivist approaches – the scene with Jesus looking up to Zaccheus through the leaves and branches of the sycamore tree, asking whether he can stay for lunch, is a winner!

The story of Zaccheus is one of four examples Luke uses to show the effect a meeting with Jesus has on a person's life. The others are the story about Peter (5:1-11); the episode of the "sinful" woman in the house of Simon the Pharisee (7:36-50); and the parables about the lost sheep, the lost coin, and the prodigal son in chapter 15.

In our story, Zaccheus climbs up a tree to see Jesus, about whom he has heard all kinds of stories. As a top boss in the Revenue service, he is not exactly the most popular citizen, and this is compounded by his collaboration with the Roman forces.

While all the people around call Zaccheus a sinner, Jesus highlights the positive things he sees in him, saying: "...this man, too, is a son of Abraham." He affirms Zaccheus as much as he can, and it triggers something off in Zaccheus that had been hidden up to then. There is nothing mystical or abstract about the way Zaccheus reacts. Instead, he is hard-nosed and practical, as you might expect from someone of his position: "I am going to give half my property to the poor, and if I have cheated anybody I will pay him back four times the amount."

The crowd around must have erupted into cheers. Jesus looked at them, smiled, and said: "That is why I came."

Heavenly faithfulness
C57. Thirty-second Sunday of the year

2 Maccabees 7:1-2, 9-14

2 Thessalonians 2:16-3:5

Luke 20:27-38

The Sadducees come to Jesus to discuss the issue of resurrection. The conversation that follows is one of the more interesting in Luke's gospel. It is not only about resurrection, but also life after death, and how married people will relate to each other in that state. They are intriguing questions to put to someone who claims to come from God, who is not married, and who consequently cannot refer to his own personal experience of marriage.

It was more than thirty years ago that I, as a young priest, used to take Holy Communion to a very ancient, bed-ridden widow who lived in a decrepit old farm. She lay in a large wooden bedstead, and on the wall opposite the foot of her bed hung a life-size portrait of her surly looking husband. It was a slightly blurred photo and a little yellowed. In the middle of his face were a number of dead flies that had managed to creep behind the glass of the frame.

On the last occasion that I gave her communion and extreme unction, just before she died, she pointed with a wrinkled finger to the photo and said, as her voice broke with emotion, that she was on her way to be with him. Her husband represented heaven to her. She wanted to be with him again, just as she had been in her married life, through all the ecstasy, joy, and sadness. In an interview in 1985, when he was 84 years old, the philosopher Jean Guitton said that barriers come tumbling down whenever a couple embrace. As they embrace, they leave the Earth for a brief moment to have a "pre-experience" of the future risen life.

The Sadducees who come to Jesus put a question to Jesus: what happens after death if a woman has had several husbands? Such a woman would not be able to be intimate with several men at the same time,

164

would she? Objections such as these are the reason the Sadducees do not believe in the resurrection.

When they hear the question, the people around Jesus must understand what it is about – not just older ones, but also the younger ones who have just given each other a stealthy kiss. Is the fidelity of love only something temporary, something that lasts until death parts us? Jesus looks at them with an ironic glint in his eye, and says that in this world you marry, but in the next world you do not, because there you never die.

Death divides us from those we love in this world. The risen life is to be lived not with one, two, three, five or ten others, but with everyone. Heaven means no longer being separated from others, and no longer being divided in yourself. Heaven means that God's children are one in God's presence.

We cannot imagine what this will be like, but Jesus did use a few metaphors to help us grasp this idea: we together form one vine, in which all the branches, roots, leaves, flowers and fruits constitute one life; we form together the one tree of life; we will sit together at one banqueting table. Jesus even asks us to eat ourselves into one body, and to live on one blood. This is but a foreshadowing of the at once personal and universal intimacy that will characterise our life after death.

The Lord is no God of the dead, but of the living; for to him everyone is alive.

Sun of righteousness
C58. Thirty-third Sunday of the year

Malachi 3:19-20

2 Thessalonians 3:7-12

Luke 21:5-19

In today's extract from Luke's gospel, Jesus foretells the destruction of the Temple. A desperate rebellion against Roman rule broke out in ad 66, and culminated in the Romans recapturing and laying waste to Jerusalem in AD 70. The Temple was plundered and burned to the ground, fulfilling the prophesy Jesus has made several decades before. The historian Josephus describes the event in his book *Bellum Iudaicum* in quite some detail. He noted: "The flames thanked their beginning and cause to God's own people."

Although Jesus predicted the end of the Temple, you did not have to be a great prophet to foresee that its days were numbered. The hypocrisy and corruption of the religious elite threatened its structures from within and invited God's judgement. The Romans saw the Temple as a powerful symbol of Jewish resistance, and were no doubt waiting for a convenient pretext to put an end to it.

Mark wrote his gospel before the destruction of the Temple, and it is clear from his book that many Jews and Judeo-Christians believed that the end of the Temple would also mean the end of the world. Paul, too, wrote most of his letters before this event took place. His letters to the Christians in Thessalonica, for example, are dated around the years AD 50 and AD 60. The feeling that the end was nigh was obviously something that preoccupied many believers in the early Church. Paul tells the Thessalonian Christians that they should go on working, notwithstanding their forebodings and misgivings about the future.

When Luke wrote his gospel, the Temple fire was part of history. One of the main sources Luke used was Mark's gospel. Knowing that the Temple had been destroyed – not by a direct intervention from God – and that the world had not ended, Luke rewrote this element of the story to link the fate of Jerusalem with the coming fate of the world. Jerusalem now stands for the "temple" that is God's world. The local disaster is reworked with cosmic dimensions: earthquakes, famine, plague and cancer, wars and frightening developments will strike the Earth; there will be signs in the heavens; and the just will be persecuted, arrested, and sometimes even executed. Luke invites us to view the prophecies of the end-time by the light of the flames that Josephus described consuming the Temple.

It is not difficult to see some parallels between this doomsday scenario and our world today. You do not need to look far to see how we are destroying the Earth. Our environment is polluted, trees are dying, animals become extinct, the air is charged with lead and other toxins, the water stinks, the ozone layer is punctured, and the peoples of the world scramble for what is left over of our natural resources. When you think of the greenhouse effect and global warning, you might even say that we have set the whole world on fire.

In our reading from Malachi, however, we find a genuine promise of hope: "The sun of righteousness will shine out with healing in its rays" (3:20). We should take heart, because every day thousands and thousands individuals and groups put their lives on the line for the sake of human rights, peace, and justice. Those groups have been there since the very beginning: thousands have been martyred the world over. With the help of the newest communication technologies, this "healing movement" continues to grow.

Luke, who initially diagnosed the world around him as terminally ill, changed his opinion when he met men and women who were full of the "sun of righteousness" that is Jesus' Spirit. Rest assured: the old and sick world disappearing in the light of that sun. A new dawn is coming! Amen!

166

Mission impossible!
C59. Thirty-fourth and last Sunday of the year

2 Samuel 5:1-3

Colossians 1:12-20

Luke 23:35-43

The people look on as Jesus hangs from the cross between two murderers. They can see how the soldiers are fixing a notice above his head in three languages (Greek, Latin, and Hebrew) which reads: "This is the King of the Jews". His friends – who still love him, despite his sad failure – ask themselves how they could ever have believed he would accomplish his bold mission.

The magistrates and priests jeer and the soldiers mock him. In these circumstances, the little sign with the word "king" on it seems ridiculous. His followers wonder how that man, bleeding from all over his body, will ever be able to recover, saying to themselves: "How will we ever get over a disaster like this?"

That question was not only asked at the foot of the cross; it was also the question that was asked after the Holocaust and after the atomic bombs fell on Hiroshima and Nagasaki. It is the question that is still asked every day throughout the world: how can our world heal the traumas and wounds of slavery, ethnic cleansing, racism, apartheid, child abuse, discrimination, drugs, genocide, corruption, and deceit?

Doctor Luke suggests forgiveness as a remedy. Jesus shows forgiveness twice in Luke's passion story. The first time is in verse 34, the last verse before the beginning of our gospel text today. In that verse, Jesus prays: "Father, forgive them; they do not know what they are doing." The second time Luke shows Jesus' forgiveness is in verses 42-43, when one of the murderers next to Jesus looks up at him and says: "Jesus, remember me when you come into your kingdom." Jesus answers: "... today you will be with me in paradise." The murderer's question is rather vague ("when you come"), but Jesus reply is very precise ("today"), because he knows he is about to complete his mission, and usher in God's kingdom.

Forgiveness is the only way we can possibly restore the past and heal the wounds of the present. It is the only way – it is Jesus' way. According to John, the first thing Jesus says to his disciples when he appears to them after his resurrection is, "Peace". He then adds, as he gives them their commission to spread the Good news across the globe: "For those whose sins you forgive, they are forgiven" (John 20:23).

It is not easy to forgive; in fact, it is impossible if you refuse to acknowledge that you ever committed any wrong yourself. When you face up to your own sinfulness and need for forgiveness, then it becomes not only possible to forgive others, but also necessary. How could we live together if we were unable to forgive and be forgiven?

In Luke's gospel the words of the good murderer are the last words Jesus hears. It is his last human consolation and affirmation. When that murderer turns to Jesus, the foundation stone of the new world is laid. Practically all his followers have left him, but the words of the murderer on the cross form a bridge between his kingdom and the Earth.

Jesus prays for one final time: "Father, into your hands I commit my spirit." The sky becomes pitch black, and the sun is dimmed. The old world is gone, and the new one begins. Proficiat!

1999: The Year of God the Father
Year A of the Liturgical Cycle

Spiralling towards the light

A1. First Sunday of Advent

Isaiah 2:1-5

Romans 13:11-14

Matthew 24:37-44

This Sunday we start the final liturgical year of preparation for the Millennium, with Matthew accompanying us in most of our gospel readings. It is still too early to get our Christmas decorations out of the boxes, even though many of the department stores and shopping malls did that weeks ago. But it is time to prepare our advent wreaths, blowing off the dust, weaving in some fresh fir and holly, and replacing last year's burnt-out candles with four new ones.

We are also at the beginning of a new three-year liturgical cycle – a cycle that seems to be as round and closed in on itself as the advent wreaths we bring out each year. Season follows season – in the same order and without interruption – year by year. This endless cycle seems to have patterned our thinking. We are so accustomed to it that we sometimes apply it to ourselves, especially when we feel depressed, saying things like, "There's nothing new under the sun."

Complaints like that are as old as the Bible. You can find them in Ecclesiastes: "What was will be again; what has been done will be done again ... Take anything of which it may be said, 'Look now, this is new'. Already, long before our time, it existed" (1:9-11). It is as if all we ever do is go round in circles.

Fortunately, the very first reading of this new liturgical year assures us that this is not true. In Isaiah's vision, the nations of this world are not running around in circles – they have an aim and a destiny. They are on a pilgrimage towards each other and towards God, converging from all sides on the mountain of the Temple of Yaweh.

The Jesuit philosopher Pierre Teilhard de Chardin saw this in another way. Writing in the early part of this century, he looked at humanity's pilgrimage on Earth from an anthropological standpoint, pointing out that early people probably spread out across the globe from somewhere in East Africa. Teilhard de Chardin explained that they had no idea of what their final destination would be. They were also unaware that they lived on a globe, so they could not have imagined that they would one day meet again to continue together towards their goal. They armed themselves against the dangers they would face on their travels, and especially against each other.

Isaiah foresaw that they would gradually begin to understand what their journey was all about, and that they would eventually decide to beat their swords into ploughshares and their spears into sickles. When they reached their final destination, there would be no more need for war.

The human family is not running in a circle, but is on its way to a common destiny. A lot in our history does repeat itself, but the pattern it forms is not a circular one but a spiral – a spiral that moves us steadily upwards, progressing ever onwards towards our goal.

Since the beginning of his pontificate, Pope John Paul II has been asking us to view the years that precede the year 2000 as a time of Advent. He hopes and expects that by the end of the century the world will be nearer to its final realisation of the kingdom of God.

We cannot celebrate this Christmas exactly like we did last year's, because we have moved on since then. Too much has happened in our lives to think of our existence as a repeating circle. Spiralling forwards and upwards, we will one day step out of all darkness, because the night will be over and the light of God's love will shine upon us.

The coming retribution
A2. Second Sunday of Advent

Isaiah 11:1-10

Romans 15:4-9

Matthew 3:1-12

In today's gospel reading, John the Baptist tells the Pharisees and Sadducees that they will not be able to escape from the coming retribution if they do not repent. This strong message is meant to be taken seriously.

If we were to apply John's warning to ourselves, we might realise that we, too, need to repent. We might feel that we have incurred God's wrath by not taking responsibility for one another and for creation. And we might conclude that we ought to do something to appease God, who in anger now threatens to punish us with all kinds of disasters.

This line of thought makes God appear to be the real the problem, but that is not true. It is true that we are living under a great threat and that the world is in danger, but it is not because God is angry. The root cause of the trouble is our own behaviour. We have been mismanaging our relationships not only with one other, but also with animals, plants, and even the Earth's mineral resources. The situation is now so bad that the Earth is struggling to survive.

Even in those far off days, John was preaching that the end was near. It is an end that we ourselves will not be able to avoid if we do not change our ways. John likens it to an axe ready to fall on the roots of trees. The axe is not there because God is going to destroy those trees, but because we are. The sick trees in England's New Forest, in the Black Forest in Germany, in the mountains in the USA and Canada, and in so many forests throughout the world are not dying because God is killing them. They are sick because we have poisoned them by turning the rain that falls on them into a deadly acidic downpour.

Neither is human society threatened by God's anger. The dangers we face are the results of our own actions. Just think of the ever-widening gulf between the rich and the poor. The booming private security business that protects the rich and their belongings from the poor is a sure sign that we cannot go on like this without causing conflicts.

John the Baptist asks the Pharisees and Sadducees, "Who warned you to fly from the retribution that is coming?" When Luke tells his version of this story (Luke 3:1-18), he makes it clear that John is speaking not just to the Pharisees and Sadducees, but also to all who have come to see and hear him. When they reply, full of fear, "What should we do?" John's answer is not that they should do penance or start to pray. Instead, he tells them to change their whole lifestyle, to be honest, and to share their belongings with others: "If anyone has two tunics he must share with the one who has none, and the one with something to eat must do the same" (Luke 3:11).

The people who have come to hear John need to change, otherwise they will perish. John can do nothing more but warn them. He can prepare those who repent by baptising them in the waters of the River Jordan. But baptism alone is not enough. For their real conversion, someone else is needed. This person will be much more powerful than John, and will baptise with the Holy Spirit and with fire, burning away everything that needs to be cleared out, and giving new life in its place. This person is Jesus. He is the one we need to meet again this Christmas.

Life from within

A3. Third Sunday of Advent

Isaiah 35:1-6, 10

James 5:7-10

Matthew 11:2-11

From his dark prison cell, John the Baptist sent his disciples to Jesus with a question. Well, it was more of a complaint or an objection than a question. While John was being kept in the darkness of the prison and threatened by a frivolous king, Jesus was walking free as a bird outside in the sun with his "Good News". John found the situation difficult to cope with – after all, how would you feel if you were in prison and a member of your family was walking around working miracles, but doing absolutely nothing to help you? John himself had preached that Jesus would grow in stature, and that he himself would diminish in stature, but surely this was taking things a bit too far!

Of course, being a prophet, things were not quite so simple for John. He was probably more concerned about the welfare of the people around him than for his own liberation. These were the people who had come to him at the river Jordan, and who had remained with him, waiting for Jesus. Yet something was not quite right.

John had foretold that a winnowing fan would be used to sift the whole of humanity, but nothing of the kind had happened. The fire he had expected Jesus would use to purify the world had not been lit. And the axe at the roots of the trees had not even been lifted. The divine power and might of which he had prophesied – putting his own life on the line in the process – had not come. So what was Jesus doing?

John soon got his answer: "The blind see again, and the lame walk, lepers are cleansed, and the deaf hear, and the dead are raised to life, and the Good News is proclaimed to the poor." The Good News is what happened in the lives of all those wounded women, men, teenagers, and children. Something within them had been touched by Jesus, beginning a new and healing life in each one of them.

Although John had warned people that they had to convert from within, he nevertheless thought that the change Jesus came to bring would come from without. According to John's expectations, Jesus would use that winnowing fan, setting fire to the chaff of humanity. It was Jesus who would bring the axe down on the roots of the tree. Salvation would come as a deus ex machina.

We often think that problems of our world and our society should be sorted out in a similar way – that someone else should act and impose a solution. We say things like:

- "If only the government would take some drastic action."
- "If only the Church leaders would speak out more strongly."
- "What about strengthening the police force, or giving harsher punishments for crimes?"

With this kind of reasoning, we forget that real change can only come from within ourselves. There is no other solution. No lasting change can ever be imposed from outside. It is doomed to fail. Human history – with all its wars, concentration camps, and mass graves – is a sad testament to that. A genuine rebirth can only come from within the roots of our own lives.

Meister Eckhart once asked in one of his Christmas sermons: "What would the birth of Jesus from Mary mean to me, if he had not also been born from within me?" The answer is obvious: it would mean nothing. The new life is born from within us. And for all those for whom this process seems much too slow – as it seems to have been for John, or at least for his disciples – Jesus adds: "And happy is the man [or woman] who does not lose faith in me!" (Matthew 11:6).

A changing family
A4. Fourth Sunday of Advent

Isaiah 7:10-14

Romans 1:1-7

Matthew 1:18-24

Why did Matthew write his gospel? Mark had already written his account of the life of Jesus, and Matthew must have been aware this. He would also have been familiar with the strong oral tradition of story-telling, which both he and Mark probably used as a source. So why write another gospel? The answer is that Matthew has his own specific background, his own intentions, and his own audience to address.

In his encyclical *Redemptoris Missio*, Pope John Paul II emphasises the differences between the gospels. It is worth remembering and appreciating these differences. If you were to try to harmonise the four gospels or blend them together, as you might different foods in a mixer, each would lose its own characteristic flavour, colour, and style.

Matthew was from a Jewish background and wrote for an audience of Jewish Christians in the wake of the destruction of Jerusalem. He wanted them to understand Jesus. That is why he tried to show how everything that happened to Jesus had been foretold in the sacred Hebrew scriptures.

One of the ways in which Matthew shows this is by using the Hebrew name "Emmanuel". We hear it twice this Sunday, first in the reading from the prophet Isaiah and then in the gospel reading: "The virgin will conceive and give birth to a son and they will call him Emmanuel, a name which means 'God-is-with-us'" (Matthew 1:23). Matthew not only begins his gospel with this name, but he also ends his gospel using it: "And know that I-am-with-you always; yes, to the end of time" (28:20).

In between those two names he structures his gospel as a kind of roof or shelter above all Jesus does, as if it were home for the whole of humanity. Matthew explains how, in Jesus, God came to live with us, inviting all of us into God's home – the kingdom of God.

It is as "Emmanuel", or "God-with-us", that Jesus will help us out of our difficulties. Everything in Jesus' life – his mission, teaching, miracles, and healing, his chasing away of evil, and all the events of his last days, including his cross, death, and resurrection – are simply an expression of this "God-with-us". No wonder that many commentators judge the name "Emmanuel" to be the core and at the same time the summary of the Good News according to Matthew!

One of the weaknesses of Matthew's gospel is that it is coloured by the ideas of the patriarchal, male-dominated society into which both he and Jesus were born. It was the only type of society Matthew knew. The tradition was that the man was the head of the family – and there was an end to it!

We can see this clearly when Matthew tells the story of Mary and Joseph. The angel does not go to Mary first, but to Joseph. It is Joseph who is given the message: "Joseph, do not be afraid to take Mary home as your wife, because she has conceived what is in her by the Holy Spirit. She will give birth to a son, and you must name him Jesus ..." (1:20-21).

In the gospel by the more travelled and more "liberated" Luke, Mary is placed firmly the centre of the story. However, in Matthew's version, not a single divine word is addressed to Mary. The story focuses on Joseph. It is interesting to note how, in order to fit in with the society of his day, Matthew's telling of the story goes against Isaiah's prophecy. Isaiah had foretold how the woman would bear a son, and how she would call her child "Emmanuel". Luke is faithful to Isaiah's prophecy, but Matthew tells us that Joseph must give the child the name Jesus – although he adds later that he would also be called Emmanuel.

One thing is certain: things are going to change under the new roof that is being built over all of us, including the relationships between men and women!

God's gifts
A5. Vigil Mass of Christmas

Isaiah 62:1-5

Acts 13:16-17, 22-25

Matthew 1:1-25

Christmas is about gifts and presents. On Christmas eve, the shops are filled until late in the evening with shoppers who delayed buying their gifts until the last moment. Perhaps they had been determined not to buy anything at all this year, but had suddenly changed their minds. In the end, hardly anyone can escape the pressure to buy gifts for others.

Christmas is about one particular gift, but it is not the type you can buy in a shop. It is about the gift that was given to Mary, Jesus' mother. An angel came to tell her that she was full of the Holy Spirit. Celebrating Christmas means sharing in what happened to Mary at that moment. How often are we aware of being with the Holy Spirit? And when and where should this happen?

The annunciation by the angel to Mary has always been one of the best-loved subjects for Christian artists. Most depict Mary on her knees in a chapel-like room, suggesting that the angel met Mary while she was at prayer. The gospel gives no hint as to what Mary was doing when the angel arrived. Was it because she was at prayer that the angel told her that she was full of grace?

Many people have told me that they have prayed for years and years without ever having felt the presence of the Holy Spirit in themselves. The Greek Orthodox bishop Anthony Bloom wrote a book about that problem. In his book, he tells the story of a woman who complained to him that she had dedicated herself to prayer for over 14 years, without ever feeling God's real presence in her life. No divine light, no signs or signals – nothing. She remained stuck in the dark night of the soul. The bishop gave her his advice.

After some time, the woman returned to him. She told him that she had followed his advice. She had gone home and sat down in her most comfortable chair with a cup of tea. She had started to knit. Eventually, she felt totally relaxed. She glanced at the crucifix on the wall and a picture of Mary. She looked out of her window at the beautiful garden, which was full of plants, flowers, and birds, and watched some children passing by on their roller-skates. She gazed at the sun in the bright blue sky, and the tiny white clouds. She listened to the sounds in the street, the excited voices of the playing children, and suddenly ... it was given to her!

We tend to limit God's presence in our lives to the times when we are at prayer. It is one way of getting God out of the rest of our lives! We only allow God to enter our lives when we are in a church – kneeling with our eyes closed and hands folded. By only giving God access to those parts of our life we consider to be "holy", we are reversing the roles, so that God's presence in us does not depend on God, but on us.

To celebrate the 65th birthday of a world famous Bible scholar, his friends organised a party as a way of thanking him for all he had done to enlighten others about God's word. One of his friends told him that there was one thing he had never understood. Why had this man – known all over the world for his Bible studies – never visited the Holy

Land? He answered, "I always avoided doing that, to make it clear to myself that Jesus is present here and now in my daily life. My own life is the 'holy land' where I meet him."

The Holy Spirit, announced so long ago to Mary, wants to be reborn in us and in our world. It was in her body, in her work, in her house, and in the extra-ordinary "ordinariness" of this Palestinian woman, that she was faithful to what was given to her: Emmanuel, God-with-us.

Jesus the stranger
A6. Midnight Mass (Christmas)

Isaiah 9:1-7

Titus 2:11-14

Luke 2:1-14

The world had no place for Jesus on the night that he was born. Mary was in labour, and Joseph had no-one to turn to for help. He had to think of so many things at once: they needed hot water, and thus a fire; they needed something like a towel; and where were they going to put the baby? Fortunately, there do not seem to have been any complications. In time, the child started to cry, was detached from his mother, and then washed and swaddled in some pieces of cloth, according to the not-too-healthy custom of the time.

It was only when it was all over that they noticed how quiet it was – there was a deathly hush. No one showed the slightest bit of interest in what had happened. Everyone in the world was busy with other things. There were no flags, parades, demonstrations, processions, fireworks or anything like that. Just an almost absolute silence. No midwife to help, and no relations to comfort and congratulate the young mother. There was not even a cradle in which to lay the baby. In the end, it was God who broke the silence by sending first one angel, and a then a host of them, to shepherds sleeping in a nearby field.

We have many beautiful hymns about those shepherds, and our nativity scenes are full of idealised shepherd figures. But in Jesus' time, shepherds were regarded as a kind of underclass, and were viewed as untrustworthy, unreliable, antisocial, and as dangerous tramps. The rabbinical tradition of that time classified them in the same category as prostitutes and tax-collectors!

There was no real place in the world for these people, just as there was no real place for the new-born child. And yet it was to them that the angels came. God contacted people whom the world ignored, just as it ignored the birth of God's son. God had given humanity a paradise, and they had changed it into a hell: Cain murdered Abel; they built a tower to compete with God; Joseph was sold into slavery by his brothers, just as the so-called First World sells the developing world into economic slavery today; and the list goes on.

God had become a stranger in God's own world, just like the prophet Jeremiah had warned them long ago: "O you hope of Israel, saviour in time of trouble, why are you like a stranger in the land, like a traveller ...?" (Jeremiah 14:18).

God came into this world as a homeless person, feeling at home with the homeless and the disadvantaged. It explains the presence of the shepherds, and also Jesus' attention later in his life to the marginalised, the neglected, the poor, and those regarded as strangers. Luke's story could not have been clearer on this point. The world needed a new beginning, and that new beginning occurred with the birth of Jesus. It was such a new and radically different beginning that it could only be described using such insights as the "immaculate conception" and the "virgin birth".

Jesus came into this world as a stranger. Today, many people feel as though they are strangers in the world in which they live. Many of these "strangers" withdraw from society or live rough, like the shepherds who felt more at home in the open air. Often they are really men and women around whom the glory of God shines, just like it did around those shepherds in the field.

From word to deed
A7. Christmas (Day Mass)

Isaiah 52:7-10

Hebrews 1:1-6

John 1:1-18

Four different gospel readings are used from the Christmas Eve vigil of yesterday evening to the Day Mass today. John's gospel is the one used in the Day Mass. If you look at the official ecumenical Christmas reading cycle for this year, you will find that it is the only one used by all denominations. Perhaps this is an indication of the importance of this text, which is a prologue to John's gospel story.

Is not the easiest of readings to comprehend. We might prefer a more simple text, like the ones by Luke and Matthew – texts that are full of angels and stars, a stable and a cradle, good and bad rulers, shepherds and magi, sheep and gifts, and all the other items we like to put in our nativity scenes. Having reminded ourselves of the familiar details of the

Christmas story, we eat and drink, give each other presents, and we are as glad as small children. And it is possible to do all that – as we so often do – without ever giving a thought for the divine mystery we are celebrating.

If you celebrate Christmas somewhere in Africa, Latin America, or Asia, or in New Zealand or Australia, it is even more obvious that the paraphernalia of Christmas decorations, customs, and traditions often obscure the main point of the whole event. In hot climates and in the countries of the southern hemisphere, where Christmas falls in the middle of their summer, it seems very strange to see imitation snow on the shop windows and in cafeterias, or artificial frost on imported Christmas trees. No wonder that liturgists and theologians sometimes say that it might be better to abolish all those old Germanic and Celtic customs, which date from the pre-Christian celebration of the winter solstice in Europe.

John's Christmas text does not deal with any of these all-too-familiar Christmas details, but focuses on the central issue of Christmas. It is a text in which you cannot dodge the mystery of the incarnation. It may be a bit difficult to grasp for us in today's world, but it was not always like that. Biblical scholars in general agree that the core of this prologue to John's gospel is based on an old hymn – one that was sung long before the celebration of Jesus' birth was fixed as 25 December. In other words, it is not a real "Christmas" song, as we often think of them, but a hymn about the birth of Jesus. The Christians who sang that hymn were expressing their joy that God's Word had become flesh.

John does not explain what the "Word" (*logos* in Greek) means. The people for whom John was writing would not have needed any further explanation, but perhaps we do. The text of the second reading may help. There we read: "At various times in the past and in various different ways, God spoke to our ancestors through the prophets; but in our own time, the last days, he has spoken to us through his Son" (Hebrews 1:1-2). In short, a word has become a deed. A promise has been fulfilled in the form of a human being. God has been born among us as Emmanuel, or "God-with-us".

Our joy does not depend on us, on how we feel or what mood we are in; it depends on God. It is God who makes us happy. God's light has come into the world, and that is good news indeed!

Something of that goodness and new light can manifest itself in our own lives through our solidarity with those less fortunate than ourselves. We can talk endlessly about helping others, such as the poor, and about how we sympathise with them. But it is only when we share in their poverty that they will be able to say: "You became one like us." It is at such a moment that all those words on solidarity become a deed, just as God did when God's word had become flesh.

The Holy Family
A8. Feast of the Holy Family

Sirach 3:2-6, 12-14

Colossians 3:12-21

Matthew 2:13-15, 19-23

Matthew tells the story about Jesus' flight to Egypt to show that Jesus was like a second Moses, coming out of Egypt to free his people. I must admit, it is not the most appropriate text to choose for the Feast of the Holy Family, at which we celebrate the family of Joseph, Mary, and Jesus, and look to it as an ideal for our own families.

The word "family" is a very broad term, meaning different things to different people. What may seem like a "normal" family to one person may seem very strange to someone of a different nationality, culture, religious faith, or social background. The first time I experienced this was when I was a part of an international community of students in a House of Studies in the Netherlands. I lived together with Canadians, Germans, Frenchmen, Italians, Americans, and Ugandans, to name just a few of the nationalities present. As you can imagine, many difficulties arose out of cultural misunderstandings between the students.

One evening, the superior of the house called us all together to sort out the problems once and for all. He told us that from then on we had to consider our community as one large family, with him as our common father. What he had forgotten was that we came from very different families. Some of the students were from patriarchal families, in which everybody stood up when the father entered the room, while others were from egalitarian families, in which all decisions were taken democratically and even the youngest had their say. The poor superior soon realised that his solution would not work when a student brashly entered his room without knocking while the superior was shaving in front of his mirror! The students began to act as though they were at home with their own families, leading to just as many problems as before.

The first time I preached in a suburban American parish, after spending many years in Kenya, I was surprised to hear that more than 50 per cent of the people in the parish were not living in "normal" Christian families. Some were divorced or separated, others were simply living together unmarried, and very many had decided to remain single. According to the statistics of that time (1985) only 23 per cent of Americans lived in "normal" Christian families. I wonder whether Jesus, Mary, and Joseph would qualify as a "normal" Christian family under today's statistics! They remain, however, our, model.

Jesus seems not to have specifically blessed the concept of the family. He came to ask us to be reborn, and that rebirth means establishing new types of relationships. For Jesus, there are spiritual bonds that are more important than those of blood: "Anyone who does the will of my Father in heaven ... is my brother and sister and mother" (Matthew 12:50).

In Matthew's gospel, Jesus insists that we have to free ourselves from our normal family ties (4:22; 8:21-22) if we are to be part of the kingdom of God. Rebirth involves choosing which family we are part of: our blood relations, or the family of our God? Matthew is keen to show us that Jesus' real family is not made up of blood relations, but of those who belong to the house of Emmanuel. Together with "God-with-us", these people form the family of God.

Mary, mother of God
A9. Octave of Christmas (1 January)

Numbers 6:22-27

Galatians 4:4-7

Luke 2:16-21

"As for Mary, she treasured all these things and pondered them in her heart" (Luke 2:19). A text like this can be read in many different ways, depending on your situation. Because these words are often read in the quiet of a room, a church, or a chapel, they are usually thought of as an expression of the Mary's piety.

But does this explanation really do justice to the text? The relationship between this mother and her extraordinary child was unique and must have been very difficult at times – especially since Joseph seems to disappear from the story altogether. These days, we are all acutely aware how a child's early experiences can affect the rest of its life. If you go to a psychiatrist with a problem, he or she will almost certainly get you to talk about your childhood, and examine the influence of your father and mother.

In his book *The Gospel According to Jesus*, the American Bible translator Stephen Mitchell noted how Mary hardly ever features in Jesus' words and deeds, just as the mother is not mentioned in the story about the prodigal son. When Mary does get a mention, it is usually in difficult or painful situations. The same is also true for the rest of Jesus' family. He hardly ever seems to have a good word for them!

In Mark's gospel (3:31-35), we read how Jesus' family arrive to take him forcibly back home, because they think that he is "out of his mind".

We are not given many details about the incident, but we are left in no doubt as to Jesus' reaction. When he is told that his mother, brothers, and sisters are outside, he asks: "Who are my mother and my brothers?" Looking around him he says: "Here are my mother and my brothers. Anyone who does the will of God, that person is my brother and sister and mother." That must have been hard for Mary to accept.

Luke seems to suggest that Jesus was beginning to grow away from Mary even at the age of twelve, when he remained behind in the Temple at Jerusalem (Luke 2:41-52). Perhaps the circumstances of his birth caused problems between them. John's gospel hints that people kept on reminding Jesus that Joseph was not his legal father (John 8:19, 41).

These are awkward texts to deal with, and we often overlook them because they do not fit into the way we like to think about Jesus. But we should not avoid them, because they smack of all the stresses and strains of real-life relationships. Perhaps the problem is that we do not really believe what is said about Jesus – that he is equal to us in all things but sin (Hebrews 4:15).

In truth, we know very little about Jesus' early years and home life. One thing we do know is that he was rejected by the people in his home town of Nazareth. A Zen Buddhist teacher named MaTzu (b.709–d.788) wrote these lines more than 1,200 years ago:

"Do not return to your place of birth,
You cannot teach the truth there.
At the village well there is an old woman
Who calls you with the name of your childhood."

Although MaTzu had never heard of Jesus, these words are remarkably relevant to Jesus' situation in Nazareth.

Whatever difficulties Mary experienced in her relationship with her son Jesus, she certainly overcame them in the end. We know this because after Jesus' ascension, Mary decided to remain in Jerusalem with the apostles and the women who had been following Jesus. They prayerfully waited for Pentecost (Acts 1:12-14), when they all felt the Spirit of Jesus being born and growing within them. At that moment, Mary became the "mother" of God in a completely new and spiritual way.

The child
A10. Epiphany (6 January)

Isaiah 60:1-6

Ephesians 3:2-3, 5-6

Matthew 2:1-12

Matthew's gospel reading today is about the child in Bethlehem. The word "child" is mentioned three times in this short text. People are coming from far and wide to see the infant Jesus in Bethlehem. The implication of Matthew 2:16 is that they must have been travelling for about two years before they arrived and unpacked their gifts.

The story of the wise men, or magi, has so gripped the human imagination that it has been embellished over the centuries. The popular version we see in nativity plays and on Christmas cards often includes many details not mentioned in the original story, such as the idea that there were three magi. Matthew's account does not actually say how many wise men come to visit Jesus, but the idea probably arose because the text mentions three different gifts: gold, frankincense, and myrrh.

In many traditions, the three magi were described as kings and were given names: Balthasar, Melchior, and Caspar. They were also assigned different skin colours: black, white, and yellow. On some medieval prints, they are even shown to be of different ages: old, middle-aged, and young. Most bizarre of all, they eventually got their own corpses – they were officially and very solemnly buried in Cologne in AD 1162!

Matthew uses the beautiful story of the magi to show that the Messiah has come to bring light to the whole world – to both Jew and Gentile alike. The coming of the wise men from the east is seen by him as the fulfilment of some of the oldest prophecies in the Hebrew scripture, such as today's Old Testament text, in which Isaiah describes how all the nations will come towards the shining glory of Yahweh. It also echoes Isaiah's vision of all the people of the world climbing the holy mountain to God's dwelling place, recycling their weapons into more useful tools so that there will be no more war (Isaiah 2:2-5).

Isaiah foresaw how a child would lead us in all this when he prophesied that all the natural enemies in creation will live together in harmony "with a little boy to lead them" (11:6-10). It might seem difficult to accept that text as a serious reference to the Messiah. How can a child possibly be the symbol of all our hope, and the herald of our final reconciliation with God and with each other? It is, however, a theme taken up by Jesus himself, when he says that we have to welcome the kingdom of God like small children (Mark 10:15). Jesus is fascinated by small children, who are more open to the possibilities of God's kingdom because they still have all their human potential intact. The symbol of the child reminds us that all the potential of the kingdom of God is realised through the child in Bethlehem.

Some years ago, the writer Robert Fulghum explained how he had learned everything he needed to know in life from his kindergarten: to share his sweets, fair play, not to try to sit in the same spot as someone else, to forget and forgive, to rest when he was tired, and to ask for help when he needed it. The world would undoubtedly be a much happier place if everyone were to adopt these simple attitudes as guidelines for living.

Many authors of books on spiritual matters, such as Anthony de Mello, have noted that we should try to liberate the "child" within us. This is the child-like part of our inner selves that we silenced as we grew older. Is it possible that the heart and mind of a child could lead us through our complex modern lives? The wise people from the east were led a long way by the child in Bethlehem. They came to honour him, because in that little child they saw God. Perhaps we would all benefit from taking to heart some of the wisdom of children.

Justice and righteousness
A11. Baptism of the Lord (Sunday after Epiphany)

Isaiah 42:1-4, 6-7

Acts 10:34-38

Matthew 3:13-17

Matthew leaves us in no doubt about the agenda for Jesus's life and work. He makes that clear in the very first words we hear from the mouth of Jesus. When John the Baptist hesitates to baptise Jesus in the River Jordan, Jesus tells him: "Leave it like this for the time being; it is fitting that we should, in this way, do all that righteousness demands" (Matthew 3:15). The word used here for righteousness is *dikaiosune*, which also means justice.

It is interesting to compare those words with the first words spoken by Jesus in each of the three other gospels. Jesus' first words in John's gospel are: "What do you want?" (John 1:38). In Mark they are: "The time has come" (Mark 1:15). Luke records them as: "Why were you looking for me? Did you not know that I must be busy with my Father's affairs?" (Luke 2:49). In a sense, all these words relate to the issue raised in Matthew's gospel – that is, the quest for justice and doing what right-eousness demands.

John is upset when he sees Jesus lining up to be baptised with all the others. What is Jesus doing? Has he forgotten who he is and the role he has to play? Things are not going quite as John had expected. And the nearer Jesus comes, the more John gets upset. When it is finally Jesus' turn to be baptised, John tries to remind him of his proper role, saying: "It is I who need baptism from you, and you come to me!" (Matthew 3:14).

Jesus deliberately steps into the waters of the River Jordan as an act of solidarity with all those who have come to John looking for a better world – looking for justice. And when he steps out of the river, he begins his task of living the kingdom of God in our world. The word *dikaiosune* remains a key word throughout Matthew's gospel. Jesus uses the word seven times in all, five of which occur in the Sermon on the Mount, which is the heart of Matthew's gospel.

But something else might also have been going on in Matthew's mind while he was describing the scene by the River Jordan. Let us not forget Matthew's aim of showing how all the old prophecies found fulfilment in Jesus. Isaiah, for example, records the promise to Yahweh's servant that Yahweh will be with him when he passes "through the seas ... or through rivers" (Isaiah 43:2) – a prophecy that seems to be fulfilled with the baptism of Jesus.

When Jesus steps out of the river, heaven suddenly opens and a voice is heard, saying: "This is my Son, the Beloved; my favour rests on him" (Matthew 3:17). After this divine affirmation, there can be no doubt in John's mind about the role Jesus is going to play in the world. John's role now ends, and he is arrested, while Jesus settles in Capernaum. From there, Jesus begins to preach that the kingdom of God is near. If there is still any doubt about what this really means, just look at today's first reading, a text by Isaiah: "Here is my servant whom I uphold ... I have endowed him with my spirit that he may bring true justice to the nations" (Isaiah 42:1). There is that word "justice" again, this time in the context of the nations of the world, and all those waiting for the revelation of the kingdom of God!

Fellow workers
A12. Ash Wednesday

Joel 2:12-18
2 Corinthians 5:20-6:2
Matthew 6:1-6, 16-18

To fast often means to undergo a privation or to do something extra, something we would not normally do. A lot of extra-ordinary things people formerly did when fasting have now become the in things to do. You hardly meet anyone these days who is not dieting, whether voluntarily or on their doctor's orders. All kinds of people are limiting their intake of sugar, protein, fat, alcohol, and nicotine in order to preserve their health, their looks, or simply their self-esteem. Others put themselves through rigorous exercise programmes that surpass anything people would have done to "mortify" their bodies in ages past.

But there are many others throughout the world – about two thirds of humankind, it is said – who cannot fast for the simple reason that they are living at or even below the level of human subsistence. These people desperately need all the food they can get. The practice of Lent and fasting have to be reviewed if these disciplines are to regain their value and not degenerate into exercises in hypocrisy.

We might use the Ash Wednesday text from Paul's second letter to the Corinthians for such a review. Paul calls himself – and the people he addresses – "co-workers" of Jesus Christ. If were to think of ourselves like that, we would realise that what we have in common with Christ is work. This is no ordinary work. It is the work of Jesus, which means working to make the kingdom of God a reality here on Earth. But how do we become active "co-workers" of Jesus Christ, working for the justice and righteousness of God's kingdom?

For centuries, many Christians have adopted the early-morning custom of dedicating all the work they do that day to the greater glory of God. This is a good and time-honoured practice. But in our day and age, perhaps we should be taking this further, for we now know that everything affects those around us and the world in which we live. Every penny we spend plays its role, and works either for justice or injustice. Any investment we make will have either healing or damaging effects. In this greedy and careless society, it is not always easy to choose which course of action will contribute most to a more righteous world. It certainly requires some asceticism or mortification.

The good news is that whenever we make these choices, we become Jesus' co-workers, working to make the new heaven and Earth a reality. In this way, our lives and our work not only get an "ultimate" meaning, but we also become prepared for Easter, when we celebrate that the salvation Jesus worked among us will be with us for ever and ever.

Temptations in the wilderness
A13. First Sunday in Lent

Genesis 2:7-9; 3:1-7

Romans 5:12-19

Matthew 4:1-11

In today's reading from Genesis, God places Adam and Eve in a fertile, natural wilderness called the garden of Eden. It is pure nature, a territory as yet untouched by humanity. Such places are practically non-existent in the modern world.

Adam and Eve are given the freedom to determine for themselves what is good and what is evil, and what is the right course of action.

They are able do this because they are created in God's image and infused with the Spirit, through which God breathed life into them. Their attitudes are tested, and we all know what happens next! By the end of the story, their relationships to each other and to God have changed dramatically. They have lost their naïveté, which now hides behind two bundles of fig leaves.

In the gospel text from Matthew, we see how the Holy Spirit – God's life-giving breath – leads Jesus into the wilderness. This time, it is not the Garden of Eden but the desert. We all know that deserts are inhospitable places. If you have ever flown over a desert, you will have been struck by the harsh landscape below you. There is no order, no organised pattern – no fences, hedges, or fields – only a vast wasteland of open space, with sand blown into wave-like dunes or rocks eroded into bizarre shapes.

Many of us feel closer to our Creator when we experience at first hand the natural splendour of God's creation, because we can feel far-removed from human society. Likewise, we try to take ourselves into our own inner spiritual desert whenever we go on a retreat. It is to these same wilderness places that Jesus goes to test his attitudes and determine his course of action.

Matthew is not trying to give us a biography of Jesus, full of precise details about his life. His gospel is a reaction to what is happening in the Jewish-Christian community of the time, an attempt to counter its difficulties and answer its questions. He shows his readers that Jesus' temptations are also the temptations of the Church. There is no time that separates the Church from Jesus. These are the same temptations facing every church and every Christian in every age. What we can learn from the story is how to manage our talents and gifts. There are three possibilities. All three are concerned with how we relate to one another, and also how we relate to God, the source of all goodness.

The first temptation is to think of ourselves in a purely materialistic way, concerned only with providing for ourselves and ignoring the needs of others. That is the way most of us live. We concentrate on earning a few more pounds or making a quick profit (changing the stones into bread) and nothing else. The second temptation takes other people into consideration, but in the wrong way. This is the temptation is to use our gifts and talents in a way that makes other people praise us, so that we steal the honour that really is due to God alone. The third temptation goes a step further. The issue is here power: political, military, and economic power. We succumb to this temptation whenever we use our talents and gifts to exploit, plunder, and brutalise others.

Jesus does not give in to any of these temptations. In verse 10, he says: "You must worship the Lord your God, and serve him alone," but he does not elaborate on this. What does it mean to serve God? In the reading from Romans, Paul gives us a theoretical explanation of sin, grace, and redemption, but in the gospel accounts of Jesus' life we find a practical example of how to serve God.

What is required is not a new Adam and Eve who can live again in innocence without fig leaves. Instead of a return to our first naïveté, we need something new: we need Easter and the risen life of Jesus.

Only a dream?
A14. Second Sunday of Lent

Genesis 12:1-4

2 Timothy 1:8-10

Matthew 17:1-9

One gets the impression that Matthew is not really sure how to present the story of Jesus' transfiguration. Did it really happen or was it something the disciples dreamt? The issue is not made any clearer by Jesus' instruction to the disciples not to tell anyone about the "vision" they have had.

It is interesting that at the end of this story, Jesus touches the terrified disciples and when they look up the "vision" is over. Is that not exactly what we do when we try to convince ourselves that we are not dreaming – touch ourselves or get someone else to pinch us?

Dreams are so powerful that they sometimes seem more vivid than real life. We have all woken up with relief from a terrible nightmare. Glad to be in a warm, cosy bed, and gazing at familiar cracks in the ceiling, we think to ourselves, "Thank goodness it was only a dream!" At other times we might wake up with regret, disappointed that a wonderful dream has come to an end. "What a pity life isn't really like that!" we sigh. We know that the events that take place in our dreams are not real, but psychology has taught us that our dreams can tell us a lot about what is going on in our inner selves. Endless books on interpreting dreams reflect the tremendous interest in the subject.

The mysterious events of the transfiguration story resemble a dream more than reality. Jesus takes Peter, James, and John up the mountain, where he is transformed. His face and garments shine with heavenly brightness. Then Moses and Elijah appear with him. A cloud covers them with shadow and a voice from the cloud says: "This is my Son, the beloved; he enjoys my favour. Listen to him" (Matthew 17:5).

If the transfiguration is a dream, what does it mean? The transfiguration is a graphic revelation of what Peter acknowledges shortly before: that Jesus is the Christ and the Son of God (16:15-16). In its symbolism, it looks back to the Old Testament and forward to the events of the resurrection and ascension.

Moses symbolises the Law, and Elijah the prophets. Their appearance with Jesus confirms that he has come to fulfil the Law and everything the prophets spoke of (Matthew 5:17). Both Moses and Elijah had experienced the presence of God on a mountain (Exodus 24:15; 1 Kings 19:8). The cloud symbolises the covering of God's presence (Exodus 24:15-18; Psalm 97:2) and links with the cloud that will hide Jesus from the disciples' sight at the ascension (Acts 1:9) and the return of Christ with clouds (Revelation 1:7). The voice from the cloud echoes the heavenly voice at his baptism (Matthew 3:17), which identifies Jesus as God's favoured Son.

Peter is so amazed by the scene that he offers to make tents for Jesus, Moses, and Elijah. He wants to make the fantastic vision permanent. The voice from the cloud reminds him that the presence of Jesus alone is what really matters. They should listen to him. Only when Jesus has accomplished his mission will they truly understand the significance of this happening. That is why Jesus tells them to keep quiet about it.

After the disciples have been given a glimpse of God's glory, they see "only Jesus". But the voice has assured them that he is sufficient. His life, death, and resurrection will make that glory a reality in their lives. Like the disciples, the full meaning of the transfiguration will be clear to us only when we experience the transforming power of Jesus as a reality of our lives. Until then, it remains nothing more than a nice dream – probably the nicest dream we ever had!

The Samaritan woman
A15. Third Sunday in Lent

Exodus 17:3-7

Romans 5:1-2, 5-8

John 4:5-42

In today's gospel reading, we come across a familiar story of a man arriving at a well where a woman comes to fetch water. One gives the other a helping hand, and many things result from that brief encounter. There are several such stories in the Bible. In Genesis 24:1-67, we read how Abraham sends one of his servants out to find a wife for Isaac. The man arrives at a well and waits for the local women to fetch water in the evening. He prays to God, saying that he will ask for water, and the first woman who replies "Drink, and I will water your camels too," he will ask to become Isaac's wife. When Rebecca replies correctly, he produces gifts of gold from his luggage, and persuades her to become Isaac's wife.

Later (Genesis 29:1-12), Jacob meets Rachel at a well. The stone over the well is so heavy that it can only be lifted by several men. When Jacob sees Rachel, his admiration for her makes him so strong that, to his surprise, he lifts the lid from the well on his own! Then there is the story of how Moses defends the seven daughters of Reuel against some shepherds at a well (Exodus 2:15-21). He ends up marrying the daughter with the wonderful name Zipporah.

And now, in the text from John's gospel, we find Jesus resting at the old well of Jacob in Samaria. When a woman from the town of Sychar arrives at the well to fetch water, Jesus asks her for a drink. She is taken aback, because Jews are usually reluctant to associate with Samaritans. Is he so thirsty that he does not know how to behave? Jesus explains that if she really knew who she was talking to, she would ask him for a drink of "living water". The term was used in the Jewish tradition to refer to the Torah (the Law). Jesus now gives it added meaning. The living water, given by God, is God's Spirit revealed in Jesus.

The two sit there talking by the well in the hot sun, using words such as "Messiah", "salvation", "worship", "God", "truth", and "eternal life". All that in a time when a man would not even address his own wife or daughter in public! The disciples return from the town and are so scandalised by his behaviour that they decide not even to discuss it with him (John 4:27).

Jesus' conversation with the woman is lively and dynamic. They listen and react to each other with great openness and honesty. Jesus amazes her by making a reference to her private life – how could he know such things? Then he makes her feel that her people are wrong in their religious beliefs. This probably angers her. When Jesus says: "You worship what you do not know; we worship what we do know; for salvation comes from the Jews," he must see an angry scowl on her face. He adds, "But the hour will come –" and then, looking at her eyes, he continues, "in fact, it is here already – when true worshippers will worship the Father in spirit and truth ..." (4:23).

Jesus is gradually leading her into the realisation of who he is. From thinking at first that he was a hostile Jewish traveller, she then wonders if he is a prophet, and finally mentions the Messiah. At this point, Jesus admits that he is the promised Messiah (*ego eimi*: "I am he", 4:26). To no-one else does Jesus to reveal himself like this. If John ever makes Jesus open his heart, it is to this Samaritan woman.

She forgets about her water, runs to the town, and tells others what has happened to her. The townspeople go to Jesus and invite him to stay with them for a while. After two days they, too, know what the woman discovered at the well, "that he really is the saviour of the world" (4:42).

191

Honouring God

A16. Fourth Sunday in Lent

1 Samuel 16:1, 6-7; 10-13

Ephesians 5:8-14

John 9:1-41

John must have told his stories about Jesus hundreds of times before he wrote them down in his gospel. Having told them so often, he would have become an expert story-teller, able to recount the stories with the greatest economy of words but to the maximum effect, and certain of exactly how his listeners would react.

Today's gospel story is a good example. It tells how the blind person gradually discovers the identity of Jesus. Through this story, we realise that we are all spiritually blind until we, too, meet Jesus. There are others in the story – the Pharisees – who refuse to acknowledge their spiritual blindness. In their denial, they become more and more lost in the darkness. But it is also a story about the relationship between sin, sickness, and disability, and it raises the question of how we should honour God.

Those of us who consider ourselves to be religious would probably have no difficulty answering that question. We believe that we must honour God in a special building, such as a church or chapel, where the outside world cannot enter. We believe that we should honour God in prayer and in silence. We try to make the time we dedicate to God extraordinary, special, and sacred. We develop liturgies in an exclusive language. We make sure that the things we use in our worship are ritually cleansed. We use special wine in the Eucharist, rather than ordinary table wine, and we use unleavened bread.

In today's gospel story, we see that Jesus honours God through his work. In Jesus' work, there is no time for that sort of exclusive holiness. In healing the blind man, he uses the most ordinary things, rather than anything special or sacred. He spits on the ground, makes some mud from his spittle and the earth, and smears it over the eyes of the blind man. Then he tells him – on the Sabbath, of all days! – to go to the pond at Siloam to wash his face and eyes.

There is something else in this story which is so often overlooked. Before he does anything at all, Jesus says: "As long as the day lasts we must carry out the work of the one who sent me," (q: 4). The word "we" in this text is intriguing. In many translations it is replaced by the word "I", but the original text reads "we". It is a small word, but important, nonetheless, as it implies that we are all involved in God's work. This simple phrase bridges the gulf between the works of God and human activity. No wonder that the clerics around Jesus view him as a threat – so great a threat, in fact, that they eventually decide to kill him.

There is a story of a nurse, who was a faithful member of her parish and worked very conscientiously in a local hospital. One day she decided that she would like to work to promote the kingdom of God. She contacted a religious group working in poor countries. She was interviewed and accepted as a voluntary worker. After a year of spiritual and other training she was sent overseas. Several years later, she returned to her parish and the same hospital in which she had worked before. Both she and her parish community felt that her years overseas had been spent in carrying out the work of God. That is true enough, but she was also doing God's work for all the years she lived in her home town – even if she never realised it!

It never occurs to most of us that our everyday activities can be part of God's work. We can all honour God through our daily work, whether we deliver mail, look after children, repair cars, serve in a restaurant, heal the sick, or whatever else we do. Remember that when Jesus says, "We must carry out the work of the one who sent me", he is including each and every one of us.

Not yet Easter
A17. Fifth Sunday in Lent

Ezekiel 37:12-14

Romans 8:8-11

John 11:1-45

It is probably best not to compare the resurrection of Lazarus with that of Jesus. The danger is that we might think that Jesus' resurrection does not bring us anything new.

Lazarus was called back to his old type of existence. We cannot say whether or not Lazarus actually wanted to come back to life. However, his sisters Martha and Mary desperately wanted him back, and they used his friendship with Jesus as the means to achieve it.

The story of the resurrection of Lazarus is full of drama – and the smell of his tomb! Yet, some time later, Lazarus obviously died again. There is even a legend surrounding Lazarus' second death. In that story, the risen Lazarus cannot stop laughing when he sees the people around him pointlessly worrying about all kinds of things. As he has already died once, he knows what life and death are really about. He sees more clearly than anyone else the real nature of all things: the "vanity of vanities". His laughter eventually becomes so unbearable to the people of his village that they can take it no longer. They stone him to death outside the village.

There is another lesson in the story about Lazarus. It is about the logic of love. Martha knew that Jesus loved Lazarus, because they were such close friends. That is why Martha and Mary were so sure that if Jesus had been there he would not have allowed his friend Lazarus to die. Friends and lovers often each tell one another that their love or friendship is *ad infinitum* – that is, for always.

This kind of logic is also valid in the case of God's love. If God loves an individual, then that person must be immortal. It is the kind of logic the Pharisees in Jesus' time were familiar with. They did not see God's love merely as a love for the nation of Israel, but rather as a love for each and every individual member of that nation. Martha and Mary were proved to be right. Jesus showed his friendship for Lazarus by calling him from back from the dead.

Lazarus was "called back" – but from where? It is quite common to find stories in the newspapers or on TV about near-death experiences. You must have heard how some dying people claim to have looked down upon themselves as their souls briefly separated from their bodies. Many people say they seemed to enter a tunnel with a light at the end. Others even relate how Jesus appeared at the end of the tunnel. They tell how they saw their whole life flashing before them, as if it were a kind of film, and how all was understood and forgiven. They describe how friends and family members were waiting to welcome them, but how they had to return to their bodies to carry on living. Did Lazarus go through a similar kind of experience?

When Lazarus came back to life, everything was just the same as it had been before he died. What happened to Lazarus was no Easter, because Easter means new life – the type of life Jesus lived among us. Jesus' life was admired by many, but in the end was considered to be too good, too unreal, and too naive by almost everyone. No wonder Jesus was crucified! Just as the laughter of the risen Lazarus became too much for the people of his village, Jesus' life was eventually too much for those around him. Yet, on that first Easter day, Jesus proved that his life was indestructible and guaranteed by God as the only real and lasting one.

Fulfilled prophecies
A18. Palm/Passion Sunday

Isaiah 50:4-7

Philippians 2:6-11

194

The drama of the Passion stories is so moving that it often hides from us the different ways in which the four gospel authors present the events. They each tell the same story, but they do it in very different ways. This is because each writer has a different intention, or perhaps you could even say a different theology.

One of the striking things about Matthew's version is that it is full of both direct and indirect references to the sacred Hebrew scriptures. Here are just a few instances:

• When no violence is used at the arrest of Jesus, Matthew notes that it is to fulfil the scriptures (26:51-56).

• On the Cross, Jesus is given some vinegar to sip (27:48), drawing parallels with Psalm 69:21.

• Matthew also mentions the price of thirty shekels of silver paid to Judas for betraying Jesus, which is the price of a slave in Exodus 21:32.

• Similarly, when he tells us how Judas throws those silver pieces into the Temple and the priests decide to use it to buy the potter's field, Matthew refers to the prophet Jeremiah. (Here, Matthew makes a mistake, because the reference should be to Zechariah 11:13!)

Matthew is keen on making connections, not only between the life of Jesus and the Law and Prophets, but also between Jesus' Passion and the things Jesus had said during his life. He wants to show how Jesus is the fulfilment not just of the old laws and prophecies, but also of the new attitudes and way of life he himself introduced into the world. For example:

• Jesus had told the disciples: "Offer the wicked man no resistance" (Matthew 5:39), and during the potentially explosive situation of his arrest he says to one of his disciples: "Put your sword back" (26:52).

• He had told them: "Do not swear at all" (5:34), and before the judges at his trial he refuses to take an oath (26:63).

• During his agony in the Garden of Gethsemane (26:39), Jesus prays the prayer he had taught his followers: "Your will be done" (6:10), and in going to the cross he submits to God's will.

In describing the events of Jesus' Passion, Matthew is at great pains to put them firmly in the context of the rest of Jesus' life. The message here is that Christians should view their own lives in the context of the life of Jesus.

In Mark's gospel, Jesus' Passion follows immediately after his prediction of the end of the world. Matthew, however, adds three parables between the two events. The parable of the sensible and the foolish bridesmaids and the parable of the last judgement are told only by

195

Matthew. The third parable, on the use and non-use of the talents, also occurs in Luke's gospel, although in a different context. All three of these parables tell us that between Jesus' first and second comings we should be working at fulfilling the Law, the words of the prophets, and the newness brought by Jesus.

Matthew wants to prevent us from thinking that Jesus' Passion and resurrection are the end of the story. His death and resurrection are the crowning events of his life among us. But the story goes on as we, too, ask for God's grace to live our own lives as the fulfilment of both the old and the new .

Brothers and sisters
A19. Easter Vigil

Matthew 28:1-10

Matthew's story of the resurrection is by far the most dramatic of the four gospels. It tells us how Mary Magdalene goes with another woman called Mary to Jesus' tomb one morning before dawn. Suddenly, all kinds of unexpected things start happening! First, there is a powerful earthquake. Then an angel descends from heaven, rolls away the stone at the tomb's entrance, and sits on it. The angel's face is like lightning and its robe white as snow. The poor guards at the tomb are so frightened that they are "like dead men" – they probably lose consciousness and collapse.

The angel addresses the women, telling them that Jesus has risen. The angel then shows them the empty tomb and instructs the women to tell the disciples about Jesus' resurrection, and to ask them to join Jesus in Galilee. As they are rushing away to tell the disciples, filled with awe and joy, they suddenly see Jesus, who greets them. They fall down before him, clasping his feet, and he says: "Do not be afraid; go and tell my brothers that they must leave for Galilee; they will see me there."

The real drama of this report lies beyond the surface details. One of Matthew's intentions in his gospel is to show how the new life Jesus brings upsets the older, unjust order of things. Matthew depicts Jesus as the herald of true equality for all human beings. This theme runs throughout Matthew's gospel, and is seen clearly in the resurrection story. It is significant that Jesus appears initially to women. Both Jesus and the angel ask the women to be the first witnesses to what has happened, and then to go and tell the men. Remember that in Israel at that time the witness of a woman was not legally admissible – it simply didn't count! So by addressing the women first, Jesus is rejecting that old inequality and restoring their true dignity.

In a way, this is the continuation of what Matthew begins to imply when he tells of how the shepherds, another group of marginalised people, come to visit the infant Jesus (see A6: Jesus the stranger). The truth that Matthew is trying to hammer home is that Jesus came to give all neglected people their rightful place in the world.

When Jesus says he wants the disciples to meet him in Galilee, he calls them "brothers". Of course, this also means that the women he speaks to are "sisters" of himself and the disciples. Some commentators make much of the fact that Jesus is, for the first time, directly referring to people as his "brothers", because from that first Easter onwards we all form one family – the family of God, in which all are equal.

The "brothers" and "sisters" must meet Jesus in Galilee. In Matthew 4:15, Galilee is described as the "Galilee of the nations". The new family will not be restricted simply to the disciples and the women who were at Jerusalem. Rather, it is to be open to the whole world, to all the nations. From the very outset, this tiny new community is given a massive universal mission of social justice. They can hardly have an inkling about what is going to happen to them, or what the consequences will be. Just fifty days later, at Jesus ascension in Galilee, he commands them to "make disciples of all the nations". What a mission!

They are not allowed to stay at home and celebrate Jesus' victory over death. Instead, they are sent out on a mission to the ends of the Earth. Their role – and ours – is to bring together the whole of humanity and the whole of creation, recognising that we all have the same divine parent and the same destiny, and that we all share the same divine life. Matthew's resurrection story is the beginning of the life of a whole new family!

Risen life

A20. Easter Sunday

Acts 10:34, 37-43

1 Corinthians 5:6-8

John 20:1-9

The new, risen life did not begin with Jesus's crucifixion and resurrection at Easter. It began much earlier, with his birth in Bethlehem. Jesus was crucified because this new life – outlined in his work, teaching, and ministry – was too challenging for those around him. Easter is, however, the final proof that the new life is guaranteed by God.

When Jesus departed this world, he did not leave us a political or social structure to follow, or a philosophy or theology to believe in.

Instead, he left us the Holy Spirit – his risen life within us. This life binds us together as God's family. As we are sprinkled with water during the Easter service, we are reminded of the baptismal formula of Father, Son, and Holy Spirit. We remember that we all have the same Father, that through Jesus we are all God's offspring, and that we have all been given the same Spirit. This is because God loves us all in exactly the same way.

Jesus said that the Holy Spirit will gradually introduce us into the full implication of that truth and help us to make it a reality in our personal lives. It is not such a simple process as it sounds, because the growth of the new, risen life – which is given to every Christian in a lasting and unchangeable way – has to happen within the context of all the social, political, and economic structures of this world. It is God's project that we should change those structures and realise the kingdom of God here on Earth as that life grows within us.

Historically, we have allowed our concept of God to be influenced by the very structures we are meant to change. In the past, when supreme power was invested in kings and queens, or emperors and empresses, God was seen as a fearsome, authoritarian ruler. Today, in the age of the capitalistic entrepreneur, God is portrayed more like the managing director of an industrial concern. In a social-welfare state, God comes across as some sort of celestial welfare officer, whose role is to take care of each one of us and make our lives as comfortable and painless as possible.

When the Church is rooted in the structures of this world, it causes all sorts of problems. It means that we have constantly to tailor our message to suit the changing times. It never works, because the institutional expression of Christianity is always slow to change, and lags behind changes in the secular world.

Rather than trying to follow developments in society, we should become agents of change ourselves by working for the righteousness and justice (*diakosune*) that Jesus introduced into our world. We only have to look around at all the problems in the world to know that we have a long way to go.

If that reality seems a long way off today, just imagine how it seemed to Jesus. That is why he left us not only with the gift of the Holy Spirit and the new, risen life, but also with an urgent mission. He added that we would be able to do more to change this world than he had himself: "I tell you solemnly, whoever believes in me will ... perform greater works, because I am going to the Father," (John 14:12). We have the security of knowing that this awesome mission is underwritten by a tremendous promise.

Fear

A21. Second Sunday of Easter

Acts 2:42-47

1 Peter 1:3-9

John 20:19-31

The disciples are hiding in an upper room. We are not told how many are in the room. Certainly, the group is no longer complete, because Thomas is missing (John 20:24). They are hiding behind closed doors. Although the text does not actually say it, we can guess that the windows and shutters are also probably closed. So the disciples are most likely sitting in the dark, hardly talking, save for the occasional whisper. Perhaps even the cracks between the windows and the walls are filled up with earth to block out the light and keep their presence even more of a secret?

If this all sounds a bit nonsensical, think about their situation for a moment. They are afraid of what the Jewish authorities might do. Jesus has been crucified – will they be next? They are probably equally terrified of Jesus. In Luke's gospel they are "in a state of alarm and fright" (Luke 24:37) when he appears to them. And there is good reason to be scared, because they have betrayed and failed him. The news of Jesus' resurrection is tempered by the knowledge of how they deserted him. How will he react?

It is a situation we all recognise. Most us have betrayed someone at one time or another, even if it was only in a small way. We have left them alone in the hour of their greatest need, refusing to listen, to open our hearts, to offer a word of support or a helping hand. Maybe we acted in this way because we thought that we would not see the person again. However, as today's gospel text clearly shows, people we have wronged in the past have a habit of appearing again out of the blue. One day we suddenly see that person walking down the street. A meeting, perhaps even a confrontation, is inevitable. How will that person react to our betrayal and desertion?

The disciples know that Jesus is alive, and that Mary has even embraced him, but he has not appeared to them in person – could that signify his anger with them? So there they are, shut in that dim room, afraid to move, listening anxiously for any noise. Suddenly Jesus is standing in their midst, saying: "Peace be with you"! That simple phrase is sufficient to let them know that their betrayal and desertion are forgiven, and they are filled with joy.

Their betrayal has not overcome Jesus. His sense of self-worth is great

199

enough not to let his love for them be tempered by their treacherous behaviour. He had told them before – and he repeats it in the gospel of Matthew before he sends them out into the world (Matthew 28:20) – that he always will be with them, even till the end of time. There is nothing that can undo his love. In John 20:21, Jesus says: "As the Father sent me, so I am sending you." In doing so, he passes on to us his self-esteem, spiritual maturity, and love. They become our own. This does not mean that we are as mature and emancipated as he is, but it does mean that, through him, we now have the capacity to develop in that way.

At the end of his gospel, John writes that Jesus came to give us new life, life to the full – his life. Fear is the enemy of this new life, because it eats away at that self-esteem, spiritual maturity, and love Jesus came to restore to people. Too often, fear leads church leaders to treat their congregations as if they are little children, perhaps because they fear challenges to their authority. Equally, there are many of us who prefer to be treated like that, because our poor sense of self-worth makes us fear responsibility. There should be no fear in the new life that Jesus brings!

The hint
A22. Third Sunday of Easter

Acts 2:14, 22-33

1 Peter 1:17-21

Luke 24:13-35

The "Road to Emmaus" story is a very beautiful one. Today's gospel reading is not about penetrating closed doors or windows, as we saw in last Sunday's text. Rather, it is about penetrating closed hearts and minds. It is a story with several puzzling aspects. For example, who are the two people walking along the road? Why is only one name mentioned, that of Cleopas, and who is Cleopas' companion? This question has been keeping commentators guessing since the time of Origenes. Was it Peter, as Rembrandt seemed to think when he painted his famous picture of the scene, or John, or maybe even Cleopas' wife? We will never know.

Even the name of the village is a bit of a mystery. There is a Roman list of village names, dating from AD 66, which shows two places called Ammaous. One village is much too far from Jerusalem – about 26 miles – so it must be discounted. The other Ammaous listed lies about 3.5 miles from Jerusalem. Luke says that the village is 7 miles away – could he be referring to the round trip, there and back?

Another problem is that this second Ammaous is not an actual village, but a Roman barracks, perhaps with houses around it for the people who worked there. This probably means that Cleopas and his companion were servants in the barracks. Hebrew servants to the Roman army – no wonder that they were eager to see Israel liberated from the Roman occupation! As they say in the story: "Our own hope had been that he [Jesus] would be the one to set Israel free" (Luke 24:21). They have heard how Jesus had been received like a king in Jerusalem before the Passover. So they went to Jerusalem, hoping that Jesus would end their misery and free them from Roman rule.

When the story starts, they are returning from Jerusalem. They are disappointed, as their expectations of Jesus have been shattered. Jesus has been arrested, condemned, and crucified – the usual punishment for rebels. They have heard the women's news of his resurrection, and their friends have checked out the story and found it to be true. How strange: they know of the resurrection, and yet they are disappointed!

Working in the Roman barracks, they have probably been hoping for an insurrection, certainly not a resurrection. What is the use of a resurrection? Lazarus had been raised from the dead, but had that changed the world? No. They yearned for the restoration Israel's old national glory and pride.

While they are talking about this, Jesus approaches and walks beside them. He asks what they are talking about. "They stopped short, their faces downcast" (24:17). They cannot believe that he has not heard about the things that have been happening in Jerusalem recently? "What things?", he asks, and they begin to tell him the story – his own story!

Jesus responds and explains the role of the Messiah. He uses their own sacred Hebrew scriptures. He quotes prophets. He points out that the Messiah is about far more than their own national and provincial interests. The Messiah is about all nations, and about the whole world. He widens their outlook. We do not know exactly what he says, but from the events in the rest of the story it seems likely that he describes the events of the Last Supper – how, when the Messiah broke the bread, he was inviting the disciples to recognise who he really was, and understand his true mission.

When they arrive at the village, Jesus implies that he wants to go on, but they ask him to stay and he does. They share their meal with him and, during the meal, Jesus takes their bread and breaks it in the same way he has just described to them. Instantly, they recognise him, but he suddenly disappears from sight. We should remember this each time we take part in the Eucharist, for Jesus still invites each of us to recognise him as the Messiah, and to share in his messianic mission.

Called by name

A23. Fourth Sunday of Easter

Acts 2:14, 36-41

1 Peter 2:20-25

John 10:1-10

All four gospel writers use the metaphor of Jesus as shepherd. God is also described as a shepherd in Hebrew scripture. So John's use of this metaphor is nothing new. What is new is John's description of the relationship between the shepherd and the individual sheep.

John is intent on explaining that the life and work of Jesus demonstrate God's love for every individual. In John's gospel, this is expressed by Jesus in many different ways. One example is how Jesus the shepherd knows the name of each one of his sheep. Knowing someone by name indicates intimacy. The Hebrew scriptures tell us how the name of Israel, the chosen nation, is imprinted on the palm of Yahweh's hand (Isaiah 49:16). John, however, goes much further: God in fact knows the name of each individual, not simply the whole nation, and has a personal love for each one of us.

It was in while I was in Africa that I first began to understand the real power of names. Many Africans are very cautious about telling other people their names. It is felt that if you know the name of a person, you can exercise an influence over them. When you give your name away, you are giving away some essential element of yourself. The more you know about the magic power of names, the more careful you are.

The Irish author and wordsmith James Joyce also had a strong belief in the power of names; so much so, in fact, that in his correspondence with his wife Nora he never mentioned the name of the man with whom he thought she had deceived him. Joyce simply referred to this man as "the other".

Each one of us knows the power our own name has over us. When we hear our Christian name being spoken, it is almost as if a very sensitive emotional string is being tugged within in our heart. It gives us a warm feeling, especially when we are called by someone who is important to us, such as a person we love or respect. We sometimes get a similar feeling when a person we have not seen for many years remembers our name without any prompting.

It is that kind of intimacy John implies when he writes that Jesus calls each one of us by our individual name. When he adds that we will recognise Jesus' voice, he is saying that it is a two-way relationship. Jesus knows us, and we know his voice when he calls us. This kind of love resembles the love the Father has for Jesus. It is a love that binds us at once to the Father, to Jesus, and to each other, as John remarks later on in this chapter (John 10:16):

"And there are other sheep I have that are not of this fold, and these I have to lead as well. They too will listen to my voice, and there will be only one flock, and only one shepherd."

John stresses that, as far as he is concerned, Jesus' individual personal relationships with his sheep take priority over his relationship with the flock as a whole. In today's text, there is only an indirect reference to that flock, or to anything that resembles a church-like community. John wants to explain that there cannot be such a community before the personal bonds with Jesus are established. It is our love for Jesus that expresses itself in our love for others. Everything starts with that one-to-one loving relationship each of has with Jesus.

Dwelling with God
A24. Fifth Sunday of Easter

Acts 6:1-7

1 Peter 2:4-9

John 14:1-12

In today's gospel reading, the English phrase "there are many rooms in my Father's house" (John 14:2) is more of an interpretation than a direct translation of the original Greek. In different versions of the text, the Greek words for "in my Father's house" can also be read as "with my Father". The many "rooms" in that house can also be interpreted as "spaces". The Greek word used for space is *mone*, a word that also means a "stopping place" – a road stop, a station, or something similar. So Jesus' words can also be interpreted as saying that there are many stages on the road to the house of the Father. This remark would have fitted in well with the Gnostic context of John's gospel. Gnostics thought that the soul had to go through all kinds of stages and phases of purification before being totally redeemed from the world.

The most likely translation is, however, that of many "rooms" or "dwelling places" in the house of God. Perhaps "dwelling places" is most appropriate to John's line of thought. The concept of living or remaining with God is a key theme in John's theology and spirituality, as we will note later on in these reflections (see A30: The Spirit that remains). The important thing is to remain with the Father and to dwell with him. John often uses the Greek word menein, meaning "to stay", to express this idea.

Just before Jesus leaves the disciples (John never makes a distinction between apostles and disciples), he tells them that the Father has many "dwelling places" for those who are faithful. The Father will reward their faithfulness by dwelling with them. The disciples know that Jesus is leaving them to go to the Father, and they, too, want to be with the Father. But they do not know the way – how are they going to get to the Father?

Thomas asks this of Jesus in a round-about way: "Lord, we don't know where you are going, so how can we know the way?" Then Philip – an apostle who we only hear speak in John's gospel, asking questions others dare not ask – turns Thomas's question into a direct plea: "Lord, let us see the Father" (14:8).

This is quite a request, and one few people would hardly like to make so directly, even at an advanced age. I remember how, in the Netherlands, the chaplain of a nursing home for senior citizens placed on the altar a cloth embroidered with the text: "The Lord stands at the door and knocks." The text caused an uproar, and the altar cloth had to be removed. No one wanted to see the Lord – maybe in the future, but not just yet!

Philip's question is not well received, either. Jesus reprimands him. He explains that a person who is with Jesus is with the Father. Philip should have realised that. Jesus is the way to the Father, so to be in Jesus' presence is to be in the Father's presence. Jesus' life and activity show that he is with the Father, because he does the Father's work.

This is also the answer to Thomas's question. Thomas, too, will be with the Father when he does the work of Jesus and, consequently, the work of the Father. Doing God's work in our world means that you "dwell" or "stay" with the Father. It is an important answer, not only for Thomas, but also for all Jesus' followers. It helps us to live our lives in the absence of Jesus and without seeing God. Our works will show whether the "God-in-Jesus" dwells within us.

Spiritual adulthood
A25. Sixth Sunday of Easter

Acts 8:5-8, 14-17

1 Peter 3:15-18

John 14:5-21

In today's gospel reading, the last Sunday before Ascension Day, Jesus explains to the disciples the fulfilment of his relationship with them. He reveals that, once he has gone, they will receive his Spirit, and that through his Spirit he will always be with them.

Jesus is speaking about a process of development, about something that is going to happen to them. He is speaking about a "now", a "then", and a "later". It all sounds rather mysterious, unless we make an analogy between what he is saying and the changing relationship between a child and its parents.

The gospels make it clear that Jesus is the centre of the disciples' world: they know that he can do anything, that he knows everything. Sometimes they have difficulties with what he says and does – on occasion, they even disagree with him – but, in general, they just form a kind of fan-club around him. Their attitude is not a particularly mature one. They are under a kind of spell, rather like the attitude of some young teenagers towards their idols and heroes. But for those teenagers, it is at least a step away from being a mere child. Young children are almost totally dependent on their parents. They also learn to obey their parents in order to be introduced into the joys and pains of human life. A child has much to learn.

One day those bonds will have to be broken, and the child will grow into a teenager. Jesus stopped being a child the day he stayed behind in the Temple at the age of 12. It worried Mary. She thought about it for a long time afterwards. But growing out of childhood does not mean we cease to be the son or daughter of our parents. The old relationships remain, if slightly altered.

Teenagers, who are no longer children, begin to relate more to their peer group than their parents. Sensible parents learn to adapt their role to this new situation. They do not simply tell their children what to do or how to behave. Instead, they try to explain the reasons behind what they ask of their children. They talk with their growing offspring. They become friends with their children, almost like members of their peer group.

In time, even this relationship changes. The moment comes when parents have to say: "That decision you have to take for yourself. You know what I think about it, you know the principles I would use, but from now on the decision is up to you." This does not mean that the family ties are broken. Our parents remain our parents, but eventually we, too, become adults. Today's gospel reading (Jesus' last words to the disciples before his crucifixion, resurrection, and departure) also tells of a changing relationship. Jesus is going to leave his disciples – in a way, thank God! They can be themselves in a new, more enlightened way. They know who he is, what his principles are, and the way he would like them to live their lives.

From now on it is up to them – accompanied by his Spirit. Jesus later tells the disciples that they will discover things he is not able to explain to them as yet (16:12). They will discover them for themselves and they will be able to do even greater things than he had done! Again, this does not mean that their former bond with him is broken. On the contrary, their relationship will become even more intimate and personal. It does not mean either that we are no longer "with the Father"; we have Jesus' Spirit within us, so we are closer to him than ever before.

Heaven and Earth are ours
A26. Ascension Day

Acts 1:1-11

Ephesians 1:17-23

Matthew 28:16-20

Jesus' disciples – the ones he calls now his brothers and sisters – gather together in Galilee to see him for one last time. Just before he leaves them, he gives them their final command. It is an awesome mission, involving all power, all peoples, all things, and all times:

"All authority in heaven and on Earth has been given to me. Go, therefore, make disciples of all the nations; baptise them in the name of the Father and of the Son and of the Spirit, and teach them to observe all the commands I gave you. And know that I am with you always; yes, to the end of time" (Matthew 28:18-20).

The word used for "authority" in the original Greek is exousia – one of the key words in Matthew's gospel. It also means "power". It is a word Matthew uses frequently to explain the identity of Jesus – he is the one with authority and power (see A39: Our strength).

The word "power" does not please the modern ear. In Jesus' time, and in a country under Roman occupation, it would have sounded no better. Today, many countries have democratic political systems and other mechanisms built into their societies to try to safeguard against the misuse of authority, and to restrict the actions of the powerful. Even so, we still hear stories from home and abroad about individuals who abuse the power they have – be it political, mystical, medical, financial, physical, artistic, or any other form of power. We hear of governments, the military, and religious or ethnic groups who use their power against others. In so many corners of the world our fellow human beings are oppressed, tortured, imprisoned, and killed.

As we read the gospels, we realise that the source of Jesus' power is God's Spirit within him. His contemporaries witness examples of his power again and again. He calms the storm and the raging sea, he chases away evil spirits, he turns water into wine, and so on. He also speaks with a moral authority never heard before.

More importantly, perhaps, is the way Jesus uses his power to help

206

those who are powerless, despised, or disadvantaged in society. He sits down to eat with sinners. He speaks to strangers and children. He respects women. He heals lepers. He overthrows rules, customs, and regulations. He is afraid of neither political nor spiritual leaders. He looks straight through their posturing and tells people that they should form one loving human family, eating and drinking together. Just imagine what the world would be like if everyone lived like Jesus!

That is the kind of power Jesus passes on to his disciples, and also to us. It is a power that is directed against all exploitation and oppression. It is the power of love to bring people together as one family, into a common sharing in the life of God.

On the mountain before his ascension, Jesus looks for a last time at his disciples. They have been changed by his life and his words, by his friendship and forgiveness. Wonderful ideas that were locked away in the recesses of their minds have been brought out into the light of day. Treasures hidden deep in their hearts have been discovered. Things that had seemed impossible have become possible.

It had all seemed too good to be true, and they had not been surprised when Jesus was arrested and crucified, for they had warned him of the dangers. Yet, even as the risen Jesus stands among them there on the mountain, some still hesitate with doubt (28:17), but Jesus does not seem to mind. He leaves them knowing that the transformation he has brought about in them is lasting, and that it will change the whole world.

Equipped with his power and Spirit, Jesus knows that they – and we – will be able to fulfil his mission; yes, to the end of time.

The world and its unjust structures
A27. Seventh Sunday of Easter

Acts 1:12-14

1 Peter 4:13-16

John 17:1-11

Some things in John's gospel are difficult to explain, and almost offensive to modern ears. Take the way Jesus relates to "the world". In today's gospel text, John shows Jesus deliberately not praying for the world (John 17:9). It is not the only time that John has difficulties with the world. John's first letter states:

"You must not love this passing world or anything that is in the world. The love of the Father cannot be in any man or [woman] who loves the world ..." (1 John 2:15).

From time to time, we get the impression that John is being rather exclusive, or even sectarian. Later on in his first letter, John writes:

"Those rivals of Christ came out of our own number, but they had never really belonged; if they had belonged, they would have stayed with us; but they left us, to prove that not one of them ever belonged to us" (1 John 2:19).

This is the type of language members of a sect or cult might use when talking about some former members. Even Jesus' new commandment to his followers to "love one another" (John 13:34) might be seen as rather exclusive. Where does this leave Jesus' recommendation to "love your enemies" (Matthew 5:44), when he himself does not pray for a hostile world?

Perhaps there was good reason for John's gospel to portray the world like that. By the time of the final version of this gospel had been written, the persecution of Christians had already started in Rome. The world is now an enemy. Is that why we do not read of Jesus praying for the world?

We can also look at this problem in a different way. If the term "the world" represents everything that goes against the kingdom of God, then it is surely good that Jesus does not pray for the continuation of that world. It means that he does not support it in any way– something that cannot be said of many modern church leaders.

It is possible to make a distinction between the people who are caught in the world's unjust structures and the unjust structures themselves. We must reject the structures, but pray for their victims. We can start to put names to the attitudes embodied by these structures: racism, violence, discrimination, exploitation, materialism, greed, lust, and so on. It is easy to agree when such a broad picture is painted, but it is when we try to fill in the details that the difficulties begin. Some consider communism to be an anti-Christian structure, others capitalism. Pope John Paul II condemned both. For some, the multinational companies are like agents of the devil, but for others, such as the American Catholic conservative Michael Novak, those same multinationals are simply misunderstood servants of Yahweh!

When confronted with evil of any kind, the most obvious ways to get rid of it is to chase it away or to destroy it. But are these necessarily the best options? If you chase away evil, it will only go somewhere else. If you destroy evil, you have to resort to violence yourself. Would it not be better to tackle evil in another way, to try to change it into something good?

John is not always consistent in his description of Jesus' relationship with the world. In John 6:51, a text often quoted in creation and ecological theologies, Jesus says that he is willing to give his life for the life of the world. It is difficult to interpret such a text in a modern ecologi-

208

cal context, and certainly John would not have been thinking about "the world" in ecological terms when he wrote his gospel. Nevertheless, it does not change the urgent task not only to spread the Good News and reform anti-human "world" structures, but also to re-evaluate the way we relate to the physical world, and all that lives within it. After all, did not John say that all is created "in him" – in Jesus?

Dynamics
A28. Pentecost

Acts 2:1-11

1 Corinthians 12:3-7, 12-13

John 20:19-23

Pentecost is the most dynamic feast in the Christian calendar. The dynamism of Pentecost is the dynamism of God's Spirit. This dynamism comes into the world at Christmas, is revealed during the life of Jesus, is guaranteed by his death and resurrection, and is caught by thousands of people at Pentecost. A new period in world history is introduced. What has remained in the dark up until this moment, is suddenly announced from the rooftops.

There are different versions of how Jesus' disciples received this dynamism. In the reading from John's gospel we are told how Jesus breathes on them, while the report from the Acts of the Apostles is more dramatic. There is an earthquake, the sound of thunder, a ball of fire, and a riot in the street.

In both stories, the same thing happens to the disciples. It resembles what happens to Jesus at his baptism in the River Jordan. Like Jesus, the disciples suddenly come to themselves: at last they know and feel who they really are. They know that they come from God and are sustained by God's Spirit and life. They find in themselves the same central focus that had made Jesus into an irresistible hero.

A few years ago, I attended a seminar on "Social Change and Humanisation" held by the School of Philosophy at the Catholic University in Washington DC, USA. The delegates had come from all over the world, representing all kinds of religious and non-religious points of view. Among the delegates were Russians whose country had recently undergone massive social changes, and Chinese who had witnessed the failure of similar attempts at reform in their own country.

One of the questions for discussion was, "What was the basis of the dynamism that led to the recent people's movements and revolutions throughout the world?" Before that question could be answered, someone asked what the real nature of these social changes had been. A Russian delegate from Moscow thought that people who had up until then only been objects in human history, had suddenly become the subjects of history.

The delegates discussed how that change had come about. Many cited the importance of the Universal Declaration of Human Rights, while some suggested that the changes resulted from the dynamics of Marxist socialism. Others highlighted the role of the Pope, whose voice was highly influential in Eastern Europe. No single answer satisfied all those present. However, they did agree that the changes had been profound, and that at their root was a type of "spiritual" crisis. They all agreed on that word.

A Chinese delegate, who had been studying for quite some time in the West and who could not return to China after the Tiananmen Square massacre in 1990, intervened in the debate. He said that when we speak about spirituality, we are dealing with something "transcendent" – something that lies beyond what we feel, see, smell, hear, and taste. He explained, almost apologetically, that he had been reading the Bible and studying Christianity. He had been struck by what baptism reveals about human beings – that we come from God and live with God's Spirit.

He added that when we really believe this, the whole world changes for us, as does our own place in that world. Listening to him talk, many of us rediscovered the dynamism that is inherent in the baptismal rite.

This dynamism was first let loose among a group of men and women in that upper room at Pentecost all those years ago. When people become aware of their true identity, their own value, and their rights, social change is inevitable. Pentecost is the end of any "lord"-ship. No state or church can do anything against the dynamism of Pentecost!

Society and the individual
A29. Trinity Sunday

Exodus 34:4-6, 8-9

2 Corinthians 13:11-13

John 3:16-18

At Pentecost humanity discovered its spiritual adulthood. Perhaps this is a misleading statement, because it is not something that happened to humanity en masse, but to individual people. Not everyone was aware of it. It is something that had been growing within Jesus' disciples, and only really dawned upon them (and upon those in the street) at

Pentecost. All this leads to a new issue. How do you organise a society in which each member is aware that he or she is a fully individualised adult personality?

In the Old Testament, it is the same problem Moses faces once he has persuaded his fellow Israelites that they can resist the Egyptians, that they are supported in this by God, and that they will be able to escape from their slave masters. As soon as the Israelites have passed through the Red Sea the difficulties begin. They refuse to accept Moses' leadership – they are now too emancipated for that. The difficulties are so great, that he needs 40 years to get them organised again! Moses himself does not seem to realise the extent of the problem, and this is perhaps the dilemma faced by any emancipator.

Just think of the problems experienced by Mikhail Gorbachev when he was President of the USSR. Once his reforms had given people more freedom and allowed them to be themselves, they turned against him. Similarly, when some teenagers experience the beginnings of adulthood and a growing independence, they rebel against their parents' values.

If we look in the gospels, we find that it is also something that puzzles Jesus' contemporaries. The Pharisees, who are so convinced of a person's individual value that they believe in a personal resurrection, foresee difficulties in Jesus' approach. Just imagine what would happen if the freedom and independence Jesus preaches were to become a reality for every single woman and man, if everyone realised that they could be loved by God in the kind of personal way Jesus suggests!

God's love extends not only to you and me, but also to the homeless people we ignore in the street, to the starving children we see on TV, and to everyone else in the world, no matter what their status in society. We are all loved in exactly the same way by the same divine lover. We are equal. This is wonderful news, but how then should we organise society, taking into account this love and equality? Surely this kind of equality and individuality would undermine the very basis of our social structures?

It is an issue the Pharisees and lawyers raise when they question Jesus about his priorities. Should we love God first and foremost, and then ourselves, or should we love our neighbour first, and then the rest of society? Jesus' answer is clear: "You must love the Lord your God with all your heart, with all your soul, and with all your mind" (Matthew 22:37) and "You must love your neighbour as yourself" (22:39). Following these two precepts, everything else will fall into place. It is a beautiful answer, but is it possible? Is there a model for such a love?

Fortunately, there is such a model: the Trinity. In the Trinity there is no hierarchy. The Father, Son, and Spirit love each other as equals. That is why the triangle is not a good symbol for the Trinity, because it always places someone at the top. When Leonardo Boff suggested some

211

years ago that the Trinity would be the best model for the Church, the hierarchy got nervous. Yet it is precisely in the Trinity that we find the answer to the question of how adult persons should relate to one another. It is the same answer that Jesus gave to the Pharisees. The answer is: with love. That is why the best symbol for the Trinity is a circle.

The Spirit that remains
A30. Second Sunday of the year

Isaiah 49:3, 5-6

1 Corinthians 1:1-3

John 1:29-34

You do not need much experience of life to know that many of the much-heralded changes, revolutions, and reforms that occur in our world do not last for long. We are surrounded by the ruins of initiatives, projects, and programmes that never came to fruition, or which could not last the pace. Filing cabinets and computers around the globe are filled with the details of countless well-intentioned schemes and plans that eventually came to nothing.

Some of the most important initiatives fall away because they depend too much on one person. Take, for example, Mother Teresa's work among the poorest of the poor, from Calcutta, India, to Washington DC, USA. Even her own admirers sometimes wonder what will happen to her work after her death, because it is so bound up with her personality and her charisma.

In today's gospel reading, John the Baptist's disciples are confronted with a similar problem. They have dedicated themselves, heart and soul, to that rough, sympathetic prophet of doom. But now, at the arrival of Jesus, John seems to be nervous about his leadership. He wants to quit, to hand over responsibility. He even directs them to Jesus. What is happening? Have they made a mistake in following John? Besides, if they become followers of Jesus, what guarantees do they have that he, too, will not later tell them to follow someone else? What good would it do them simply to be passed around from one prophet to another?

This is a good time to have a second look at a key word in John's gospel. The word (mentioned before in A24: Dwelling with God) is the Greek *meneini*, meaning "to stay with", "to remain with", or "to rest with". It occurs twice in today's reading. The first occasion is when John the Baptist explains to his followers what happened when he baptised Jesus: "I saw the Spirit coming down on him from heaven like a dove and resting on him" (John 1:33). The second time is when he tells them how he heard a voice saying: "The man on whom you see the Spirit come down and rest is the one who is going to baptise with the Spirit" (1:34). The Spirit not only descends upon Jesus, but also remains, or "rests", with him. It is not simply the inspiration of a fleeting moment. It is something much more lasting.

John uses the word menein forty times in his written work, particularly in the context of the Spirit. He wants to stress that the Spirit is different from anything else in human life. Everything in human life, including human love, is in a constant state of flux. The divine Spirit, however, is a lasting reality that stays with us. In Jesus we meet someone we can trust. He says, "I will be with you always," and he says this irrespective of anything that might happen to us. This is a key theme in John's gospel – the lasting presence of Jesus through the Spirit. It also resembles the main message of Matthew, our evangelist for the year, who begins and ends his gospel with the theme of Emmanuel, "God-with-us".

If we continue reading today's gospel text a little further than our prescribed verses, we find John using that word menein again. Once John the Baptist has told his own disciples that they will find in Jesus everything they are looking for, two of them decide to follow Jesus. When Jesus notices that they are following him, he turns around and asks: "What do you want?" They ask him where he lives. "Come and see," he replies, so they go with him and "stay" with him (1:39).

The big issue
A31. Third Sunday of the year

Isaiah 8:23-9:3

1 Corinthians 1:10-13, 17

Matthew 4:12-23

When Jesus hears that John the Baptist has been arrested, he goes back to Galilee. At first glance, it might seem as though Jesus is trying to hide or escape from a difficult situation – if John has been arrested, will it be Jesus next? But this is not the case. The Herod who arrested John rules over the whole of Galilee, so by settling in Capernaum, Jesus is actually establishing himself in the eye of the storm. So, from the very start of his ministry, Jesus is ready to face head-on all the problems and difficulties in the world around him.

Matthew wants to show us that Jesus did not come to impart some kind of simplistic individualistic piety. Rather, he came to create totally new initiatives and structures that would revolutionise our human society – in short, he came to establish the kingdom of God, the "year" or era of grace, the Jubilee.

Matthew helps us to understand this by putting Jesus' return to Galilee in the context of one of Isaiah's prophecies. If we read the whole of that prophecy in today's Old Testament reading, we find that Isaiah is telling of a time when the yoke oppressing the people will be taken away and the stick of the oppressor broken (Isaiah 9:4). Matthew is implying that when Jesus starts his ministry, the kingdom of God and the liberation of humanity will begin to be realised here on Earth. This is, without a doubt, a grandiose vision.

The second reading tells us what became of that vision in one of the earliest Christian communities, the one begun by Saint Paul in Corinth. Reading Paul's first letter to the Corinthians, you can almost hear them gossiping and quarrelling among themselves. Paul is writing the letter because someone from the household of Chloe has been back-biting about them, telling Paul that the community is a shambles. It has become divided, with various groups and factions trading slogans to show their different allegiances: "I am of Paul", "I am for Apollos", "I am for Cephas", or "I am for Christ" (verse 12). The grandiose vision of the kingdom of God has been reduced to that kind of bickering and squabbling. No wonder Paul is upset! Their spiritual energy is lost in those senseless polarisations between personalities and ideas.

The situation in the Corinth is one that still plagues the Church today, even in our own parishes. As soon as we meet someone we become judgmental (either consciously or unconsciously) about their views on worship, theology, doctrine, mission, and endless other matters. In a short time, we have buttonholed them into certain categories: she is very conservative; that man is a real "Bishop-X" person; he is absolutely 100 per cent pre-Vatican II, and so on.

Such divisive talk makes us forget that these views and opinions are all part of the same broad spectrum, each part of which defines itself in terms of its difference from the others. In other words, they all depend on each other – they need each other to exist.

Perhaps Paul expects too much when he asks the Corinthian Christians to forget their divisions and be totally at one in their thinking and feeling. He is, however, right when he says that there are more important things to bother about – namely, the Gospel. Jesus came to bring about the reorganisation and reconstruction of this world. That is our real programme and agenda. It is not about whether you are pre- or post-Vatican II. That is not the question you will be asked at the end of your life! Even so, many of us get so caught up, like fish in a net, struggling with particular views, opinions, theological stances, and doctrinal debates that we lose sight of the kingdom of God.

While the disciples are busy with their fishing nets, Jesus comes along and tells them to follow him, because there is work to be done. Immediately they leave their nets and follow him.

Time differences
A32. Fourth Sunday of the year

Zephaniah 2:3; 3:12-13

1 Corinthians 1:26-31

Matthew 5:1-12

Jesus climbs the hill, sits down, and begins his Sermon on the Mount, with its eight beatitudes. The hill is an important part of the way Matthew depicts this scene, because he is keen to make his readers see the connection between Jesus and Moses. Moses, for example, gave the Ten Commandments from on top of a mountain; in the same way, Matthew shows Jesus giving the eight beatitudes from a "mountain" (the text reads "hill", because there are no real mountains in that region).

The hill is not the only literary device that Matthew uses in this text. According to many biblical scholars, Jesus did not give the Sermon on the Mount in the way that Matthew presents it here. We usually speak of the eight beatitudes, but there are actually nine in the text. The ninth one (Matthew 5:11) is the odd one out. You notice that even when reading it: "Happy are you when people abuse you and persecute you and speak all kinds of calumny against you on my account." It sounds very different from the others, less poetic and more prosaic. That is why many believe the ninth beatitude to be a later addition, probably by Matthew himself.

The Sermon on the Mount – and the eight beatitudes in particular – tell us new things about our human existence. The Sermon on the Mount gives a colourful description of what is possible for a person when he or she experiences God's love in the way Jesus does. Jesus is not aiming to replace the Ten Commandments, because they remain vital for human life and for its survival. Later in Matthew's gospel, Jesus says explicitly that he has not come to abolish the Ten Commandments ("the Law") but to complete or supplement them (5:17). The people have developed so much in the time between Moses and Jesus that this update is now not only possible but also necessary.

It is good to pay attention to the importance of this time difference: what could not be done in the beginning is now possible. Idealistic

Christians have always lived their lives trying to live up to the standards set by the beatitudes. They are often contradicted by Christians more engaged in the world, who say that it is impossible to do that in this life.

If we look at the beatitudes more closely, we see that Jesus does not place them all within the same time frame. The gentle, the mourners, the hungry, the merciful, the pure in heart, and the peacemakers will be rewarded in the future. But the kingdom of heaven already belongs to the poor in spirit (5:3) and those persecuted in the cause of right (5:10).

The poor in spirit know that none of us has yet reached our fulfilment. They know that we cannot just sit down, because too much remains to be done. While we might have all we need – and often much more – others simply do not have enough. This means that we have to work in the cause of justice and righteousness, breaking through all the structures, barriers, customs, and laws, that hinder that justice.

The poor in spirit are the ones who are interested in that true justice, who are willing to undo the existing situation, and who consequently suffer violence and persecution because they struggle for what is right. Remember the importance of the time difference: what could not be done in the past will one day be possible. Things change with time, so we should not let the present situation become a lasting prison for those who are poor and marginalised in our societies.

The poor in spirit and those persecuted in the cause of right are the reason that all the other beatitudes are going to be fulfilled. They are the reason that all weeping, homelessness, injustice, poverty, and war will one day disappear from the face of the Earth. They are already liberated, and they ask for the liberation of all.

Salt and light
A33. Fifth Sunday of the year

Isaiah 58:7-10

1 Corinthians 2:1-5

Matthew 5:13-16

In today's gospel text, Jesus gives two new titles to those who understand and follow him: "You are the salt of the Earth ... You are the light of the world." He immediately adds two qualifying remarks. He warns us that we run the risk of being obsessed with our "saltiness", to the point where we no longer give taste to the world around us. Similarly, if we do not share our light with others, we may as well hide it under a bucket.

In order to make those two errors, we must first discover that we have that taste-giving power and that light-giving ability. It is a discovery or "conscientisation" (to put it in the language of liberation theology) that is not welcomed by everyone.

In 1978, a 54-year-old American priest named Joseph F. Girzone was advised by his doctor take some rest from his work. He had been working with youth gangs in New York, and with the poor in the mining region of Pennsylvania. He had also chaired a committee for human rights, and mediated in a difficult prison riot and in race conflicts in several schools. It was demanding work, and it had taken its toll.

Girzone decided to take the doctor's advice. While he was recuperating, he started to write books. His first books were not well received by publishers, so Girzone decided to take a risk and publish his book *Joshua* on his own. To his surprise, it sold so well that a local publisher decided to re-publish it. The book was again so successful that a bigger publishing firm bought it. Eventually, it appeared under the imprint of one of the largest publishers in the USA. At present, more than one million copies have been sold. I first heard about *Joshua* at a parish meeting. One of the parishioners told me that it was the only book he had ever finished reading in his life; he then read it four more times!

It is a very simple book – rather naïve, really – about Jesus appearing in a village in Middle America as a woodcutter/carpenter named Joshua. No one recognises him as Jesus. He gets on well with the villagers, so the Jewish and Christian communities give him some work. He first cuts wooden statues of Peter and Moses, and then of other people. His statues cause problems with the religious leaders of both communities because they show how every human being – and not only hierarchical figures like Moses and Peter – carries God's Spirit within them. At the end of the book he goes to Rome to give an account of himself and his work before a jury. Six out of the seven jurors vote to silence him. When his friends seek him out after the verdict, they see only his disappearing shadow as they enter his room. In the room they find his sandals, a medal, and two silver coins – nothing more.

One of Girzone's reviewers exclaimed: "Girzone's *Joshua* is of the same class as Dostoyevsky and Tolstoy". This is an exaggeration, but the story definitely embodies the same theme as Dostoyevsky's *The Great Inquisitor*, which places Jesus in Spain during the time of the Inquisition. Immediately after a number of heretics have been burned at the stake in Seville, the Inquisitor recognises Jesus in the crowd and has him arrested. During the night he visits Jesus and tells him that he is not allowed to tell people how they carry God's Spirit within them – such a thing would be a great folly. Jesus does not answer him, but simply kisses the old man on his bloodless lips. The Inquisitor trembles, opens the prison door, and says to Jesus: "Get out, and never come back again!"

Yet, Jesus is coming back – again and again. The old story is not dead; it has to be told and retold. When we tell it, we become salt and light, giving the world the flavour of the Gospel, and lighting up the darkness with God's love.

Ideal and law
A34. Sixth Sunday of the year

Sirach 15:15-20

1 Corinthians 2:6-10

Matthew 5:17-37

In today's reading from the Sermon on the Mount, Jesus says: "Do not imagine that I have come to abolish the Law or the Prophets, I have not come to abolish but to complete them." What does Jesus mean by this? This text is sometimes wrongly used to set Jesus up against the Jewish people, and the Jewish people against him. That cannot have been Jesus' intention. He tells his Jewish audience that he has not come to do away with their Law. In fact, he says that nothing will ever happen to it. Not one dot, not one little stroke will disappear from it until its purpose is achieved. The old Law, passed down from Moses, does not become invalid as time passes. Who could envisage a humane, functioning society without something like the Ten Commandments as its corner stone?

What Jesus is saying is that we need to reach beyond those commandments – we need to transcend the Law. The Law will always regulate human life and actions, but there is a further ideal to be realised. In the gospels, Jesus makes it clear that we originate from God, who is our true parent. Because of this, he says, we should be like God. We carry God's life within us, so we should be "divine" in relation to ourselves, our neighbours, and the whole of creation. The presence of God's life within us is the real reason the Law commands us not to kill others or to make them an object of our lust, and not to lie about them or steal from them. In other words, we have to love like God loves. That is quite a challenge! It is the challenge presented by the eight beatitudes at the heart of the Sermon on the Mount. The challenge stands before us like a high mountain reaching right up to heaven.

It is here that the Law comes in to help. The framework of discipline and order that the Ten Commandments provides enables us to scale this mountain inch by inch. Without this discipline, it would be difficult – if not impossible – even to start our ascent. The Ten Commandments still govern our lives, but Jesus shows us that the Law has to be tran-

218

scended all the time. Transcending the Law is at the core of the Sermon on the Mount. We are required go beyond what the Law demands. If we dismiss this as just wishful thinking, we only have to look at Jesus's life. He himself fulfils this ideal. His is the kind of life we are called to live.

Sometimes there are those among us who also live up to this ideal. Take, for example, those who helped Jews to escape from the holocaust during the Second World War. They were only a few in number. The great majority thought it more important to protect their own interests than save the lives of the Jews. In their own minds they probably constructed what seemed to be reasonable arguments to justify their inaction. When reason and morality point in different directions, there are bound to be tragic consequences.

In the end, it is of little importance how many live the ideal. Only one is sufficient to prove that it is possible for a human being to take the risk out of loving others. When Jesus says that we should love others and the world as God does, it is not just a question of well-meaning words. In his own life this love is a hard fact, and he refuses to surrender it.

When Neil Armstrong became the first human being to walk on the moon, humanity set foot there with him. What was once an impossibility had suddenly became reality. In the same way, it had seemed impossible for a human being to transcend the Law until Jesus came and did exactly that. We, too, can follow his example.

Inclusivity
A35. Seventh Sunday of the year

Leviticus 19:1-2, 17-18

1 Corinthians 3:16-23

Matthew 5:38-48

In the Sermon on the Mount, Matthew offers us a summary of Jesus' vision. There is one theme, one thread, that runs right through that summary and keeps it all together. It is the notion of inclusivity. This is the same divine logic we discern elsewhere in the gospels, in stories such as those of the good shepherd, the prodigal son, and the good Samaritan. In every case, God and humanity, men and women, parents and children, peoples and nations, human beings and the created world are all kept together in the "wholeness" of God's love. Anything that contradicts this divine wholeness denies the inclusivity of God's love.

There is a story from the life of the Prophet Muhammad about this inclusivity and exclusivity. It is also a story about the discernment of the spirit. When Muhammad, who initially called himself "Prophet of the Poor", hoped to be able to get the Jewish and Christian communities to help in his efforts to emancipate his people, they did not listen to him. Muhammad's conclusion was logical. He concluded that neither the Jews nor the Christians could have been faithful to God for the simple reason that they excluded his people. How could anyone, coming from God, exclude others? God can only be inclusive, and not exclusive. Muhammad felt called to re-establish the umma, the one family of God.

Inclusivity, being the divine logic, is the logic of Jesus. In the Sermon on the Mount, Jesus tells us that God makes the sun rise and the rain fall on all, without making any distinction between the honest and the dishonest (Matthew 5:45). He also offers us a bold, challenging command: "Offer the wicked man no resistance" (5:39). This means that if our wholeness is violated, it must not be further damaged by taking violent revenge on the perpetrators. If we respond to aggression with aggression, we risk creating an endless cycle of violence, in which both parties perish in their isolation one from another. Non-violence is the language of inclusivity.

When Jesus, at the end of Matthew's gospel, says, "And know that I am with you always; yes, to the end of time" (28:20), he is speaking to everyone. It is his promise to do his utmost to keep us together, to preserve that wholeness. However, violence harms our unity, setting one person against another and making co-operation impossible. Unfortunately, aggression is one of our most instinctive reactions to difficult situations. It is not only in the worlds of business and politics that this aggression rears its head – it is also run of the mill in the daily life of our society. Just think, for example, how today's aggressive driving so often leads to outbursts of violent road rage, as the media calls it. In such a society, it there any wonder that people sometimes start to believe that aggression is often the best and easiest way so solve their problems?

Make no mistake about it, violence and aggression are not the answer, because they are exclusive responses that break up unity and destroy the wholeness in which God wants humanity to live. The lives of successful non-violent reformers such as Mahatma Gandhi and Martin Luther King are cast-iron proof of that. Because they did not adopt an exclusive stance, they succeeded in bringing about genuine social and political change that was lasting and meaningful. There is a logic in that! It is the divine logic – it is Jesus' logic.

Mammon

A36. Eighth Sunday of the year

Isaiah 49:14-15

1 Corinthians 4:1-5

Matthew 6:24-34

It is interesting to note that many Bible translations do not bother to translate the Aramaic Greek word *mammon*. It is surprising, because it is so easy: this archaic word simply means "money" or "capital". Perhaps by not translating that word we make it easier for ourselves to overlook the painful truth that Jesus is pointing out here. Jesus does not beat about the bush. There is no middle way. It is either God or the idol mammon. He is not speaking about a mysterious divinity, but about money and the kind of society that is based upon it.

The French political philosopher Jean Jacques Rousseau thought that the whole world changed not at the moment that someone fenced off a piece of land and put up a sign saying "Private property – keep out", but on the first occasion that someone believed the sign and did not dare to climb over the fence. Land that belonged to nobody – and there-fore everybody – suddenly changed its character. It is difficult to judge whether what happened at that moment was for better or for worse.

In his encyclical *Sollicitudo Rei Socialis* (1987), Pope John Paul II recognises the right to and need for private property, but he adds that "The goods of this world are originally meant for all" (39 and 42) and that "Private property is under a social mortgage" (42). These quota-tions seem harsh – so harsh that they do not sound very "Christian".

Not long ago, a group of well-to-do American business people invit-ed a moral theologian to give them a seminar on the social teaching of the Church. He started the meeting with a quiz. Each person was given two lists: one contained sayings by well known personalities, and the other gave the names of the people quoted. The delegates at the semi-nar were asked to match the quotes to the personalities. There were quotations from politicians, philosophers, historical figures, film stars, business people, newsreaders, and church leaders. Among the quotes on the list were the two mentioned above: "The goods of this world are originally meant for all," and, "Private property is under a social mort-gage". Most participants had no difficulty in guessing where those quotes came from – they were obviously both from Karl Marx. No one thought they could have come from John Paul II!

In the light of this ignorance of the Church's social teaching, it is not surprising that CAFOD in England and Wales and SCIAF in Scotland, together with the Center of Concern in the USA, felt it necessary to pub-lish the book *Our Best Kept Secret – The Rich Heritage of Catholic Social Teaching*. It is not simply a case of Catholics not being aware of this social teaching. Even when people are familiar with it, they fre-quently do not practice those biblical truths. We are accustomed to

221

interpreting them in such a way that we make sure that they fit into our own value system and culture, so that we can remain "Christian" without any sacrifice or pain. This enables us to carry on believing in the need for further economic growth, the manufacture of weapons, murderous competition, the exploitation of the environment for profit, and businesses run not only at the expense of the welfare of our own population, but also of people in far-off countries.

There is also another tragic price we pay for our ignorance and complacency. Many people throughout the world are desperately looking for an alternative to the oppressive, unjust systems that have the world in their grip, but they will not find that alternative with us, the followers of Jesus Christ, if we ignore the social responsibilities of our faith. We talk a lot about the problems of our world – the unjust distribution of goods, the growing gap between the rich and the poor, the misery of the so-called Third World, and the poisoning of our environment – but talk alone does not make the kingdom of God a reality, or put God's justice on the centre stage of people's lives.

Firm foundations

A37. Ninth Sunday of the year

Deuteronomy 11:18, 26-28, 32

Romans 3:21-25, 28

Matthew 7:21-27

"It is not those who say to me, 'Lord, Lord', who will enter the kingdom of heaven, but the person who does the will of the Father in heaven," begins this Sunday's gospel reading. Jesus is telling us that it is not a question of words, but of deeds. It is not sufficient just to shout "Father, Father"; you also have to take your hands out of your pockets and do some work! Jesus then names several activities – prophesying, chasing away evil spirits, working miracles – and makes it clear that, no matter how awesome they may be, they will not of themselves help anyone enter the kingdom of God.

If such incredible feats are of no use, we might be tempted to wonder what hope there is. Such thinking would be to miss the point, and to fail to understand the real issue here. The question we have to ask is what exactly is the true nature of the work Jesus wants us to do? This Sunday's gospel text does not actually answer that question. It does not need to, because we already know the answer. From the beginning of his gospel – as we noted in our reflections on Jesus' baptism (see A11: Justice and righteousness) – Matthew makes it plain that the main issue is to work for justice (*dikaiosune*).

222

Later in Matthew's gospel (19:16-22), a rich young man comes to ask Jesus the same question: "What should I do?" Jesus does not ask him to go out and preach or work miracles; rather, he asks the young man to sell what he possesses, to divide the proceeds among the poor, and to come and follow Jesus. It is the same thread of divine logic that runs throughout Matthew's gospel.

Working for God's righteousness and justice is not something that Jesus is going to force upon us. We know that we should be working for this justice, but in our human frailty we do not always do what is right. Pope John Paul II has written much about justice. Like Jesus, he does not try to impose on us his feelings about it. In one of his encyclicals (*Sollicitudo Rei Socialis*) he suggests – in line with what Jesus asks of the rich young man – that the Church should sell its unnecessary treasures in order to help the poor. One wonders how far this has ever happened. From this, we can conclude either that he never meant it in the first place or, more likely, that he has not been able to persuade church officials to act upon his suggestion.

Promoting justice is vital. It is not simply a precondition for entering the kingdom of God when we die. It is also a precondition for ensuring that our human existence is pleasing to God, and for establishing the kingdom of God here on Earth. In the depth of our hearts, we all know that this is true. Jesus reminds us of it when he tells his story about a house built on sand (verse 27). It looked fine from the outside and seemed quite safe – that is, until it was battered by a storm. In no time at all it fell apart and floated away, because it was built on nothing but loose sand.

To be able to keep our "human homestead" together, we have to build our house on foundations of God-willed *dikaiosune* – the righteousness Jesus came to restore among us. Without that restoration, we can keep busy being religious – and we might even be able to work miracles and chase the away evil spirits – but the kingdom of God will escape us. One day we, too, will find that our house is built on loose sand.

Exodus and worship

A38. Tenth Sunday of the year

Hosea 6:1, 3-6

Romans 4:8-25

Matthew 9:9-13

In today's gospel reading, Jesus encounters a tax collector, one of the most hated representatives of the Roman occupation. Matthew is sitting by the customs house, where he probably collects not only the obligatory tax, but also anything else he can extort from people. When Jesus sees him he says, "Follow me," and Matthew immediately gets up and follows Jesus.

Until this point, Matthew has not been a free man. Like his country, he has been "colonised" by the Romans. He has made himself completely dependent on the oppressors of his own people. He has constantly to show his loyalty to them, dancing to the tune of their music. As far as most people are concerned, Matthew is traitor, a collaborator.

Matthew has also lost his freedom at an even deeper level – he is a sinner. He is caught up in his love for money and for his money-making career. Now he is trapped in a corrupt system. He has lost control over himself, his priorities, and his life. In other words, he resembles almost every one of us! This is the reason that his story is so important.

Then Jesus enters his life. At first it seems that he is just passing by, but then he stops, looks at Matthew, and invites him to break away from all the things that have imprisoned him. Note that Jesus does not force him, he simply says, in effect: "Come, follow me. Start again. Live the life you would like to live!" It is an offer too good to refuse. Matthew follows Jesus and, in doing so, he liberates himself from the Romans and from his all-consuming interest in money.

So, you see, it is an "exodus" story. Matthew walks away from his old life and begins a new one – the life of Jesus. Jesus himself waits until the Passover to finalise his own exodus from this world, an exodus that leads us out of sin and into new life.

The Passover is the Jewish festival commemorating the Israelites' exodus from Egypt, and how Yahweh helped Moses lead them out of slavery to a new freedom and a new future. The most important ceremony is the seder, a meal in which some of the food has special meaning. There is horseradish to remind people of the bitter taste of slavery; salt water to symbolise tears; an egg to symbolise new life; and a roasted lamb bone as a reminder of the eve of the exodus, when Yahweh told the Israelites to daub the blood of sheep or goats on their doorposts as a signal to the angel of death to pass over them (Exodus 12:1-14).

On the night of the Passover, Jesus's shares his last meal with the disciples before his resurrection (the Last Supper), and institutes the Eucharist. This is Jesus' own exodus feast. It is not his intention that we simply commemorate it as a religious rite in our worship. It is an invitation to participate in the life of Jesus.

The West Indian psychiatrist Franz Fanon once described how colonised peoples often celebrate their religious rites. He wrote how people come together at a fixed hour and at a fixed place to make the fixed dance movements prescribed by the rites, shaking their heads, arching their backs, and rhythmically moving their bodies. He explains how these are "exodus" rites, intended to deliver the participants from their frustrations, anger, and aggression. He adds that, in reality, their dance is not very much more than a sedative, a deception, an opiate.

We, too, often celebrate our liturgy in such a way. We stand, sit, kneel, bow our heads, share the bread, take the wine, raise our eyes, and so on. This is not really the type of "exodus" worship Jesus desires of us. His life, death, and resurrection are an invitation to us, saying, "Follow me." Jesus wants us to get up and step out of our old lives – our own Egypt – and take up the new life he offers, following him the way Matthew did.

Our strength
A39. Eleventh Sunday of the year

Exodus 19:2-6

Romans 5:6-11

Matthew 9:36-10:8

From its beginning to its end, Matthew's gospel is about the kingdom of God being established in this world – that is, the Good News appearing to us in the person of Jesus Christ. We are invited to follow Jesus, just as Matthew was invited to follow him in last Sunday's gospel reading. If we accept this invitation, the kingdom of God will become present within us and we will share in a power that comes straight from Jesus.

Matthew is thinking of this same power when he writes: "He summoned his twelve disciples, and gave them authority over unclean spirits with power to cast them out and to cure all kinds of diseases and sickness" (Matthew 10:1). The Greek word Matthew uses to describe that power is *exousia* (see A26: Heaven and Earth are ours). In this context, it means that Jesus' disciples receive his authority, his power, and his influence.

This is the "God-with-us" power that Jesus gives to every one of us. We each carry with us the guiding principle of the kingdom of God. If we are true to this principle we, too, will be able to chase away evil spirits, to heal the world, and to practice righteousness (*dikaiosune*). The kingdom of God is like a seed. If we allow it to, it will grow within us, not because the end of the world is near or anything like that, but simply because we are "with God".

Whenever we come together as a Christian community, studying the words and deeds of Jesus Christ and reflecting on the state of the world, our task and mission become clear. If we listen to what moves our hearts and begin to act accordingly, we will become what Matthew calls "the just" or "the virtuous" (*dikaioi* in the Greek). Jesus tells us that the just will shine like the sun in the kingdom of the Father (Matthew 13:43). They will also shine here on Earth, because they are the "light of the world" (5:14). Their mission is to transform the world and heal it, to chase away whatever harms it, and to encourage whatever is good and wholesome. Those who find the "treasure" of the kingdom of heaven will make it the centre of their lives and leave everything else behind (13:44-46). By doing this, they will change the whole world

Once, long ago, I was invited to speak at a youth festival on today's gospel text. When I arrived, the liturgical committee asked me not to read the text straight out of the Bible, because they felt that the young people would have heard it read so often that they simply would not listen. Instead, they asked me to put on a fisherman's cap, wear a jacket over my liturgical clothes, and tell the story from Matthew's point of view, saying: "My name is Matthew. I would like to tell you something about one of my friends – in fact, about my best friend. His name is Jesus and this is what he did ...."

When we dramatise the gospel stories and parables like this we rediscover just how electrifying they can really be. We often treat the gospel stories as myths. Myths are stories that stabilise, support, or bolster the existing order. They are explanations, defences, and apologies for the way things are. The antidote to myth is satire, which uses humour to attack the existing status quo.

The stories about Jesus and his parables are of a different nature. Instead of supporting or attacking the existing order, their spiritual and moral authority undermine and overthrow it. The kingdom of God in us is a power (the "God-with-us" power) that subverts the economic, political, social, psychological, and religious systems created by the current world order. This power creates a new world, a civilisation of love. It is with this task in their hearts and minds that the disciples are sent out, first among the lost sheep of Israel, and then among all the nations and peoples of the Earth.

Do not be afraid

A40. Twelfth Sunday of the year

Jeremiah 20:10-13

Romans 5:12-15

Matthew 10:26-33

Today's gospel reading is preceded by Jesus' commission to the disciples to go out in his name and proclaim that God's kingdom is close at hand. But the reading is a bit mysterious. It is about things that are hidden now being revealed tomorrow, about light and dark, and about whispers and proclamations. Above all, it is about not being afraid of people who might abuse, arrest, torture, or even execute us when we preach the Good News, because they cannot kill our souls – only God has the power to do that.

Jesus promises that he will declare himself for us in the presence of the Father, if we declare ourselves for him in the presence of other people. But what does it mean to declare ourselves for Jesus? Some think that it involves going to Mass every Sunday, making the sign of the cross, and saying grace before each meal. Others feel that it requires them to give vast amounts towards the building of new churches in honour of Jesus, or telling as many people as possible that Jesus is their personal saviour.

However, the question remains, are these really the kind of witnesses and "declarations" that Jesus asks for? Did Jesus come into this world to ask us to build grand churches? Probably not, because he told the Samaritan woman at the well that there would come an end to worshipping God in temples (and, by implication, churches) and on mountain tops, and instead God would be worshipped in spirit and truth (John 4:23).

Does Jesus demand that we fill our lives with religious ritual? The answer to that must be no, because he condemns the Pharisees for their hollow, ostentatious religious practices (Matthew 23:1-36). So is it simply about proclaiming our faith to others? Undoubtedly this is an integral part of the witness he requires of us, but we know that he demands actions to back up our words. Remember how Jesus told the disciples that just to shout "Lord, Lord!" would not be sufficient to enter the kingdom of God (Matthew 7:21)? The missing element of declaring ourselves for Jesus is doing the will of God – working justice (*dikaiosune*) in this world.

Jesus does not intend that we should go about this on our own. When Jesus taught us how to pray, he told us to address God as Abba, which means "Daddy". He said this to explain that we will not be able to reach God (and hence do God's will) unless we are ready to acknowledge that we are all related to each other. We have the same divine parent, being brothers and sisters in the same family with equal rights and duties. It is from this collective standpoint that we embark upon doing God's will.

Jesus also left us the Eucharist as a unifying act to remind us that we are all part of his body and blood, and that we all share one common origin. The witness Jesus asks for is summed up by the breaking of bread and the drinking of wine in his memory. Whenever we do this, we share in the sacrifice he made so that God's kingdom might be realised here on Earth, and we commit ourselves to working for justice and righteousness. We should celebrate the Eucharist singing: "Alleluia, alleluia, amen, amen. We are saved by him!"

So, if we meet any opposition when we proclaim the Good News of God's love for all people, and the justice and righteousness that the kingdom of God will bring, we have nothing to fear. For we know that we are under the loving protection of a God who cares for every sparrow that falls from the sky, and knows exactly how many hairs there are on each of our heads (Matthew 10:28-31). If we witness fearlessly to Jesus like this, who will be able to resist believing what we say?

Baptised, but still waiting
A41. Thirteenth Sunday of the year

2 Kings 4:8-11, 14-16

Romans 6:3-4, 8-11

Matthew 10:37-42

In today's text from Paul's letter to the church in Rome, Paul writes about life – the new life of people who have been baptised in Christ. These men and women have discovered in their lives a new possibility, a new dimension, and a new perspective. Paul dramatises this change by treating baptism as a journey through death and the tomb, before being raised from the dead into immortality.

For those of us accustomed to infant baptism, it is difficult to see something as innocent and fresh as the baptism of a child in such dramatic terms. We can all envisage the scene: a rather nervous mother and (perhaps) a proud father standing by the font with their beautifully washed and dressed child. They are accompanied by the godparents-to-be, while nearby the grandparents and other family members offer support and encouragement. The water is warmed to just the right temperature – we would never hear the end of it if the priest were responsible for the child catching a cold! Later, a candle will be lit. After the ceremony, there will be a tea party or some cheese and wine for the family and friends.

In other parts of the world, baptism can be much more dynamic than that. I had the privilege of witnessing a river baptism in a small Christian community in East Africa. The pastor and the godparents kept the heads of the adults being baptised underwater for so long that they started struggling, desperate for air! When released, they came to the surface gasping, taking in great gulps of fresh oxygen, but with huge smiles on their faces. The baptisers told me that all the candidates asked for this kind of baptism. They wanted to feel that their old selves had died, and that they were passing through death to a new start and a new life.

They wanted to be delivered from their sins, because sins obstruct lives, spoil relationships, and make people self-centred. However, they also wanted a new life to live, a new name to be called by, a new world to live in. They wanted to belong to a new community, in which they could truly be themselves, celebrating together their common origin, breaking bread, sharing wine, dancing and singing. This enormous family is the family of God.

This is the life that really counts. However, it is a life neither they nor we can live to the full as yet. We are too compromised and restricted by the structures, systems, and cultures of this world. Even when we try to be genuinely radical in the way we live our Christian lives, we usually end up acting in an over-prudent and over-hesitant way. Reading today's gospel text, we realise that this is something Jesus cannot stand: "Anyone who does not take his cross and follow in my footsteps is not worthy of me" (Matthew 10:38).

Yet Jesus is patient, just as God is patient. Those people who were baptised in Africa are also patient, waiting to form with us the new family of God. Perhaps we sometimes feel let down or cheated in some way – after all, who would have guessed that we would have had to wait so long for the realisation of the new brother-and-sisterhood? If the "new life" has already begun, why do we still have to wait to enjoy the fullness of God's family? From time to time, the waiting becomes too much, just like it did some years ago for the people of Eastern Europe, who ran into the streets demanding freedom.

Unfortunately, waiting is sometimes the only thing we are able to do. Waiting in a slow, hesitant Church, in a stifling, restrictive world, and with wavering hearts and sometimes doubting minds. However long it may take, we must be reassured that everything will be accomplished in the fullness of time. While we are waiting, we can at least respect God's prophets, and support those who are carrying his cross through the world.

Our yoke
A42. Fourteenth Sunday of the year

Zechariah 9:9-10

Romans 8:9, 11-13

Matthew 11:25-30

In the text from Matthew's gospel, Jesus says that he is going to reveal things that until now have remained hidden. He says that it will be easier for children to understand and accept these things than for the learned and the clever. Jesus is speaking of the awareness or the consciousness of the kingdom of God. The issue is whether we are willing to receive it, and to be open to the challenge it presents to us. Jesus tells us that if we are willing to shoulder the yoke of this knowledge, our burden will be light. If this seems a little contradictory, let me explain further.

We can all try to escape from something we know about by mentally suppressing it, so that we hide it from ourselves and others and live in a permanent state of denial. There are many examples of this kind of psychosis. We may know that smoking is bad for us, but we carry on regardless, ignoring the warnings. Perhaps we are aware that a certain relationship is not constructive, but we still try to convince ourselves otherwise. We may know that we drink more than is good for us, but we tell ourselves that we are not alcoholics, and that we can stop drinking whenever we want. Or maybe we realise that there is something wrong with our health and that we should consult a doctor, but delay making the appointment by telling ourselves that we do not have the time.

Our consciousness can push all kinds of things deep down into in our subconscious, where each day they become heavier burdens. We may refuse to take such burdens upon our shoulders and face up to our responsibilities, but the subconscious burdens still remain, often haunting our daydreams and nightmares, where we are chased by the dangers we refuse to name.

It is not just a question of suppressing personal problems. There are many public issues we carefully hide from ourselves in a kind of communal denial. For example, most of us have no qualms about using our cars for journeys we could easily walk, wasting energy in our homes, and producing mountains of rubbish every month, even though we know that such behaviour harms the environment. So much still has to happen economically, politically, socially, and ecologically before the kingdom of God is fully realised. Too often, we are well aware of the issues involved, but we push them to the back of our minds.

The subconscious issues that we refuse to face give us such a heavy and stressful load to carry. Perhaps that is why so many people these days fall victim to drug and alcohol addiction, why so many people have chaotic and disastrous personal relationships, and why so many live in fear or experience a complete feeling of meaninglessness in their lives. Jesus asks us not to treat these burdens as a threat, but to shoulder them as a yoke that can liberate us: "Shoulder my yoke and learn from me ... and you will find rest for your souls. Yes, my yoke is easy and my burden light" (verses 29-30).

Jesus admits that the new consciousness he offers is a burden, but says that it will be easier to carry this burden than to remain hiding, suppressing, and denying it. The cause of nightmares, tensions, depressions and many other kinds of mental misery can become a source of inspiration and creativity once brought into the light of day. Acknowledging that burden can suddenly endow us with power.

We are all capable of denying the kingdom of God, but that does not mean that we can escape from its truth and its challenge. Even the learned and the clever cannot do that. That brings us back to the children Jesus spoke about. They have such a sharp insight into what is good and just that it is often better not to ask their opinion about the "adult" decisions we take. Their answers and reactions might be too hard to accommodate!

Leaving home
A43. Fifteenth Sunday of the year

Isaiah 55:10-11

Romans 8:18-23

Matthew 13:1-23

In today's gospel text we read how Jesus leaves his house and goes to sit by the lakeside. We know from Matthew's gospel that Jesus faced some problems with his home and family life, and with his acquaintances. Perhaps he is sitting there at the waterside just to escape from it all for a while – to "recharge his batteries", as the saying goes. Jesus is to crowds what a magnet is to iron filings, and sure enough it is not long before he has attracted quite a gathering again. Realising that they have come to hear him speak, he gets into a boat and, using the lake as a sounding board, he begins to tell them the parable of the sower.

Later in the same chapter, we read how Jesus returns to his house (*elthen eis ten oikian*, Matthew 13:36). The theme of a departure followed by a home-coming is unique to Matthew's gospel, where we find it used six times. Jesus is portrayed as someone who leaves his home – even the home of his heavenly Father – to make a new home with us. This constant uprooting and starting afresh elsewhere is something that many Christians seem led to do as they follow the promptings of the Holy Spirit in their lives. There is something dynamic about it.

Why should this be? Is there anything wrong with having a permanent home? Of course not, but the dynamism of moving on has to do with the nature of houses and homes. In a house we feel comfortable, secure, and protected from the outside world. Homes are cosy and intimate, and give us a sense of belonging. These things are good, and we all need them, but if we do not take care they can become restricting and oppressive, limiting our horizons.

Matthew's gospel shows Jesus as a person constantly on the move, right from his earliest years, when Mary and Joseph flee with him to Egypt to escape Herod's wrath. When they return to Israel, they settle in Nazareth, where Jesus spends his youth. As Jesus becomes aware of the incredible mission before him, Nazareth and his family home become too small and restrictive. So Jesus leaves Nazareth, is baptised by John the Baptist, and settles in Capernaum. As his ministry progresses, his circle of influence gets wider and wider. Any house or home will always be too small for him. All borders and boundaries are too limiting. Again and again he leaves what has only recently become a new home to go and settle elsewhere.

Biblical experts are pretty sure that Matthew is writing his gospel for a group of Christian refugees from Jerusalem who settled somewhere in the Middle East (Troas, perhaps?) – before the destruction of their home city in AD 70. They probably yearn for a home-coming, but Matthew is at pains to point out the positive aspects of leaving and putting down new roots elsewhere.

Our own Church would do well to listen to this message. Time and time again we run the risk of getting bogged down with the familiar structures, habits, traditions, and customs that make us feel at home but at the same time hinder us from bringing anything new to the world. For this reason, Christians throughout history have often thrown off traditional church structures to start dynamic new "faith-households", where familiarity, cosiness, and security do not restrict the growth of the new life within them, or cloud the message of the Good News. Innumerable lay and religious associations, congregations, and societies have organised themselves like that in the past, and many groups are doing the same today, including the Small Christian Communities in Africa, and the Basic Christian Communities in Latin America.

We are warned about letting our spiritual lives grow stagnant. Moving on is the supreme antidote to that.

Wheat and weeds
A44. Sixteenth Sunday of the year

Wisdom 12:13, 16-19

Romans 8:26-27

Matthew 13:24-43

We are waging war all the time, not just guerrilla wars and full-scale

232

military conflicts, but we also have trade wars and myriad other "wars" against terrorism, abortion, crime, drugs, cancer, and all kinds of things. War is definitely a deep-rooted idea, and it has strong links in our imagination with the old notion of the Apocalypse.

One of the most dangerous aspects of Ronald Reagan's presidency of the USA was his belief that Armageddon, the mythical last battle between good and evil, was just around the corner. A dangerous belief for a man with his finger on the nuclear button! According to that myth, a war will begin in the Middle East, during which the heavens will open and the world's "goodies" will, with heavenly support, overcome the "baddies" once and for all, introducing the reign of God here on Earth. Reagan thought he belonged to the good side, if only because he believed that the Soviet Union was the empire of the devil – the Antichrist. Many others have these apocalyptic visions in which the kingdom of God erupts into this world in power and might.

Jesus, however, thinks differently. To him, the power of the kingdom of God is like the growth potential of a tiny mustard seed, or the transforming qualities of yeast. Jesus views the kingdom not as something that God forces upon the world with a terrifying, vengeful force, but as a tender power that grows from within. The tiny mustard seed sends its roots penetrating deep into the soil and its branches stretching up into the sky. The yeast makes dough ferment, producing thousands of bubbles. When it is baked, those bubbles rise and expand, giving light, airy bread that would otherwise be heavy and indigestible. These tiny seeds and yeast spores have a dynamic potential for change that is out of all proportion to their size.

When change from outside is forced upon us, it seems foreign and alien and is likely to be rejected or resented. With the metaphors of the mustard seed and the yeast, Jesus is showing us that growth and change must come from within. Jesus asks us to trust our inner energies. The kingdom of God begins with the power of the Spirit, which is given to each one of us. It is within us here and now as a tiny seed or spore that will, in time, grow to maturity. This means that we can all be agents of change.

After having told a story about the man sowing the mustard seed, Jesus tells another parable about the woman using yeast to make bread. Note how Jesus places the examples side by side to reinforce the idea that all of us – men and women, young and old – are equally involved in the process of the growth of the kingdom of God. Once again, we see the inclusive nature of Jesus' vision.

The parable of the darnel gives us a different example of inclusivity. When the owner's servants discover so many weeds in the wheat field, the question is not only where they could have come from, but also what should be done about them. To their surprise, the owner tells them not to weed the field but to let the wheat grow. The owner is concerned that by weeding the field they would also pull up a lot of the wheat.

We can apply this parable to our own Christian lives. God's Spirit is in us, but its growth and its positive influence intermingles with many negative aspects of our own personalities. To try, first and foremost, to uproot all the negative things within us might hinder the growth of the Spirit's positive influence. It is better to give priority to that growth. That is what counts in the end. When the field is harvested at the end of the season, the wheat will be stored in the barn and the weeds burned.

New stories
A45. Seventeenth Sunday of the year

1 Kings 3:5, 7-12

Romans 8:28-30

Matthew 13:44-52

"The story tellers rule the world", wrote a Navajo author introducing a series of native American tales. The stories she had collected came from her own trampled and marginalised culture – from what the ruling elite would call the underside of American society. Such stories are rarely promoted by the media, because they differ greatly from the ones middle-class Americans usually tell about their country. The "safe" stories of conventional American society simply reinforce the experience of the "average" (ie comfortably-off) American, and rarely offer any new insights. Because of this, they tend to legitimise the established order, affirming and supporting the status quo.

This is not only true of the USA, but also of every country and nation. It even applies to science and theology – witness the often vitriolic reaction to new ideas and theories. In short, it is something of which we are all guilty. Just listen to the stories we tell each other at home and in the pub, pay attention to the fairy tales parents tell their children, and study the sermons that preachers make from the pulpit. What are we telling each other? Do our stories simply bolster the current situation, or do they offer dynamic new insights and descriptions that challenge our preconceptions?

Jesus scandalises his contemporaries by mixing with prostitutes, tax collectors, poor fishermen, and others considered to be of a dubious character by any "decent citizen" of his time. Is he trying to draw attention to the stories they have to tell, to the view from the underside of society? Are they the people most open to change? Is the hunger and thirst for justice and holiness greatest among them?

At the end of his series of parables in Matthew's gospel, Jesus asks the disciples whether they have understood what he has told them. They say that they have. (It is interesting that Matthew frequently notes how the disciples understand what Jesus means by the parables; Mark, in contrast, often points out that the disciples do not grasp what Jesus is saying.) Having heard their answer, Jesus tells them one last parable:

"Well then, every scribe who becomes a disciple of the kingdom of heaven is like a householder who brings out from his storeroom things both new and old," (Matthew 13:52).

Jesus describes each of his disciples as a householder (*oikodespotes* in Greek). Back in verse 27 of the same chapter, Jesus uses the same Greek term to refer to himself. He tells how the servants come to let the owner/householder know that they have found weeds in the field. From this, it is clear that we, the followers of Jesus, are called to be "householders" just like him – the storeroom is our responsibility, too. We must produce both the new and the old from the storeroom. We cannot do this simply by telling the same old stories; we have to go beyond our own familiar circle.

The greatest challenge for the Church today comes from the Christians in Africa, Latin America, and Asia, from our dialogue with people from other religions, from minority groups, and from the world of feminist theology. There we will find the dynamic new store of stories that we have to listen to and pass on in order to progress further.

The temptation to repeat the same old stories is great. When theologians, preachers, and faithful refuse to listen to new ideas they are mistaken, just as journalists, politicians, and business people would be wrong to ignore new events and trends. Good "householders" in God's family are always producing new things from out of the storeroom.

God's love
A46. Eighteenth Sunday of the year

Isaiah 55:1-3
Romans 8:35, 37-39
Matthew 14:13-21

In the reading from Paul's letter to the Romans, Paul speaks about his personal experience and knowledge of God's love. It is the type of thing we rarely talk about in our reserved western culture, except on special occasions. That is a pity, particularly because on those special occasions we mostly use "special" forms of language. The result is that we are unaccustomed to expressing in everyday language our experience of God's presence with us.

When we go to funerals, marriages, baptisms, or other religious ceremonies, the words used are often old-fashioned and the language lifeless, so that they communicate little or nothing to us. In such solemn, ceremonial contexts, we sometimes fail to be inspired by scriptural readings because we do not grasp their meaning. How often, for example, have you heard today's text from Romans read in such a way that it truly fires up both the reader and the listeners? Language, presentation, and circumstance can sometimes hinder our understanding of God's word.

Not so long ago, Bishop Dom Helder Camara – the Emeritus Archbishop of Recife, Brazil, who was often in dispute with the authorities in Rome – was giving a talk in Australia before a hall packed with eager listeners. Unfortunately, Camara's accent made his speech practically incomprehensible to his Australian audience. If that was not bad enough, he also got the notes from which he was reading mixed up.

At the end of his faltering, stammering address, the archbishop put both his hands in the air and said: "God loves us. God loves each one of us. I am sure of that. Jesus died for us." At that moment something truly amazing happened to the whole of the hall. It was as if everyone suddenly realised the truth of what he had said, and as if the warmth of that knowledge suddenly made everyone glow. All those present, both young and old, stood up, and began to applaud, to embrace each other, and to sing. They had all been touched to their the depths of their hearts by Camara's simple, heartfelt reminder of God's love for them.

That is the kind of love Paul is writing about. When he writes about his love for Jesus Christ, he is really writing about Jesus' love for him, which is the foundation of Paul's life. It is the same love that is evident in today's Old Testament reading from Isaiah. At first, the text reads a bit like the cry of a street seller in a Middle-Eastern town, saying: "Come and drink fresh, clear, cooled water. The finest wine, the freshest milk, the tastiest bread." But this is not the cry of someone looking for business, because it is all being offered for free – there is no charge! These are the words of someone who is in love.

It is the same invitation we find in the reading from Matthew's gospel. Matthew tells us that Jesus provides enough free food for 5,000 hungry men. (Matthew does not count how many women and children there are; fortunately, Jesus does count them, for we read at the end of the story that everyone is satisfied – men, women, and children.) Matthew also gives Jesus' reason for organising this enormous picnic: he has pity on the crowd, sitting there by the shore with their empty stomachs at the end of an unbelievable day. He has pity on them because he loves them, and he shows this love in a practical way by feeding them.

236

Throughout the story of the feeding of the 5,000 you can hear the voice of the street vendor – or, better still, of the lover – saying: "Eat and drink for free!" It is a story that makes us understand who, ultimately, provides all our life, drink, and food for free. It also makes us realise that this is done out of endless and boundless love.

Jesus' Authority
A47. Nineteenth Sunday of the year

1 Kings 19.9, 11-13

Romans 9:1-5

Matthew 14:22-33

Fear is our enemy. Some time ago, a group of priests organised a meeting at which they aimed to learn how best to integrate the Gospel into their lives. They decided to do some "conscientisation", and a sister was invited to help them in the process. She spoke about sexism in the Church, explaining how the Church as an institution discriminates against women, and how priests do the same in their language, in the liturgy, and by excluding women from leadership functions. She made it clear that this was not right, and that they should study Jesus' attitude towards women. When she had finished talking, one of the priests was outraged, and exploded with anger, exclaiming: "God is male! He is our Father, he is the Son, that is what has been revealed about him!"

Why was that priest so furious? Was it really because he believed that God can only be seen as male, or was it because he was afraid that allowing women to participate in leadership would undermine his clerical position in the Church? From time to time, each of us allows fear to hamper our spiritual growth.

We sometimes use the German term angst for this sort of fear. Angst affects not only individuals, but also whole communities and even nations. Take, for example, the mutual fear between the USA and the USSR, which triggered off a nuclear arms race that lasted decades. Fear is also a murderer. Thousands of Rwandans were killed during 1994 because of the mutual fear between the Hutu and Tutsi peoples of that country. Our fear needs to be dealt with before it harms ourselves or other people.

In today's gospel reading, we find Peter in the boat with the disciples, battling with rough weather. Peter is terrified – not of the storm around him, but of Jesus, who is going to change his life. When the disciples see Jesus walking towards them over the water, they start to shout in fear. Then they hear his voice amid the terrible noise of the storm: "Courage! It is I! Do not be afraid!"

Peter decides to deal with his fear. He shouts, "Lord, if it is you, tell me to come to you across the water!" Jesus answers, "Come!" and Peter steps out of the boat and walks over the water towards Jesus. Just when Peter thinks his fear is gone, he feels the force of the wind and his fear returns. Panicking, he shouts to Jesus, "Lord, save me!" Jesus holds him and they both climb aboard the boat as the wind and waves (and the disciples!) calm down. The disciples bow down in front of Jesus, in recognition of his authority and his power to master not just the storm, but also their fears. They confess: "Truly, you are the Son of God."

At the end of Matthew's gospel, Jesus bequeaths this power to his disciples, saying: "All authority in heaven and on Earth has been given to me. Go, therefore, make disciples of all the nations; baptise them in the name of the Father and of the Son and of the Holy Spirit, and teach them to observe all the commands I gave you ..." (28:18-20).

The Greek word that Matthew uses for Jesus' authority is *exousia*, a word we have already encountered (see A26: Heaven and Earth are ours). This authority embodies the power to overcome fear, to master the elements, and to realise the kingdom of God. It is a power given to everyone. Christian communities should equally share the charisma and authority of Jesus. However, our communities do not always live up to this ideal, and what was at first given to all eventually becomes the privilege of a few. The priest at the beginning of this reflection was afraid that he was going to lose his *exousia*. In the end, his outburst, based upon fear, led him to lose authority in the eyes of others.

Jesus and fascism
A48. Twentieth Sunday of the year

Isaiah 56:1, 6-7

Romans 11:11-13, 29-32

Matthew 15:21-28

Everyone has heard of fascism, but not everyone knows that the word derives from the Latin term *fascis*, which means "a bundle". It was the name given to the bundle of sticks or arrows carried in front of a military commander in ancient Rome. The number of sticks or arrows in the bundle indicated how many soldiers he commanded. In a way, the fascis had a similar functioned to the stars and the pips on the shoulders and sleeves of military personnel today.

Fascism was the authoritarian nationalistic movement led by Benito Mussolini in Italy (1922-1943). Today, the word is generally used to refer to the separatist attitude by which a group of people – perhaps even a whole society – deems itself to be superior to others. Fascism is at the root of many of the world's troubles, including racial and sexual discrimination, political and religious persecution, nepotism, tyranny, apartheid, and economic and cultural isolationism. Jesus is confronted with it in today's gospel text.

Jesus has left Galilee and is in the pagan region around the townships of Tyre and Sidon. A Canaanite women, who has an uncontrollable teenage daughter at home, recognises him. She starts to follow him, shouting, "Sir!" and then adding derisively, "Son of David!" From the mouths of Jesus' co-patriots, that would have been an honourable form of address. But from the mouth of a foreigner, it must have sounded like, "Oi, Jew!" None of us wants to be abused as we walk down the street, but the abuse is made so much worse when it derisively picks up on our skin-colour, religion, or cultural background, pointing out how "different" we are (and, by implication, inferior) to those hurling the abuse.

Jesus does what many of us would do under the same circumstances – he simply ignores her shouts and walks on. However, the woman is not willing to give up so easily and she follows him, shouting all the time. The disciples are anxious about all the attention they are drawing, so they plead with Jesus: "Give her what she wants, because she is shouting after us." Jesus replies, "I was sent only to the lost sheep of the House of Israel." He seems to be going along with her discriminatory stance and saying, in effect, "If she derisively calls me a Jew, why should I bother speaking to a non-Jew?" Yet he stops, and the woman kneels at his feet.

It is then that Jesus says something that you would not expect from him: "It is not fair to take the children's food and throw it to the house-dogs." The harsh term "dogs" is slightly softened in the Greek text, as Jesus actually uses the diminutive "doggies". Jesus probably refers to the pagans in this way to react to the derisive taunt of "Son of David". The woman addresses Jesus not as an individual, but as a member of a particular group, so he, in return, does the same to her. Was he doing this to let her feel how unpleasant and wrong it is to be addressed like that?

The woman instinctively knows that she has done something wrong, so she says, "Ah yes sir; but even house-dogs can eat the scraps that fall from their master's table." In other words, she is saying: "Are both Jews and pagans not fed by the same God?" As soon as Jesus hears the woman speaking in such unprejudiced terms, talking about the whole of humanity as the one family of God, he declares, "Woman, you have great faith. Let your wish be granted." The evil spirit leaves her daughter the moment she stops discriminating against others.

There is no room for separatist attitudes in the kingdom of God, because we are all equal members of the same divine family.

The mind of the Lord

A49. Twenty-first Sunday of the year

Isaiah 22:19-23

Romans 11:33-36

Matthew 16:13-20

Paul asks in his letter to the Romans: "Who could ever know the mind of the Lord?" It is a rhetorical question, and Paul does not expect the readers to answer it. In today's gospel reading, Jesus says to the disciples: "Who do people say the Son of Man is?" This, however, is not a rhetorical question – Jesus does expect an answer. When the disciples reply, it is clear that they do not really grasp what Jesus is getting at, so he makes the question more direct: "But you, who do you say I am?" In a way, this question is very similar to the one Paul asks the Romans.

Simon is the only one who answers the question: "You are the Christ, the Son of the living God." Jesus congratulates him on his reply, and tells Simon that what he understands about Jesus has been revealed to him by the Father. Simon has at last became conscious of what is happening – he knows the mind of the Lord! That knowledge is like a rock that cannot be overthrown, not even by the devilish powers of the underworld, and all faith and authority are based upon it. Jesus gives Simon a new name to acknowledge this: "You are Peter and on this rock I will build my Church. And the gates of the underworld can never hold out against it."

Anyone who shares in this understanding and faith has access to reality as it really is. We are not simply talking about becoming aware of what is right and wrong from an ethical or moral perspective. It is something far deeper than that. It is about understanding the fundamental nature and purpose of God's creation. People with this awareness are vital to realising the kingdom of God here on Earth. It is a kingdom in which God is central, yet it only begins to function in our world the moment human beings share in God's insight – the moment they begin to understand the mind of the Lord.

Simon Peter is the first one to see what it is all about, and who Jesus really is. He is the primus inter pares, the first among equals, and he remains so even after Jesus' death, resurrection, and ascension. The other disciples are aware of this, which is why they send out Peter (Acts 8:14) and call him to give account of himself when necessary (Acts 11:1-18). It is worth pointing out that the foundation "rock" about which Jesus talks is not Peter's personality, but his insight and his faith. This insight was not revealed to him by any human being (by "flesh or blood", Matthew 16:17) but by God.

Wherever you find that insight and that faith in Jesus, you find "church". The word for "church" used by Matthew in the original Greek text is *ecclesia*. This is a translation of the word *qahal* used in the sacred Hebrew scriptures, a term that means "those-who-are-called-together" or "the-people-of God".

Why do we need to know this? Well, it is a useful term, because it emphasises togetherness and equality, with no mention of or reference to organisation, institution, hierarchy, liturgy, worship, or even role of Peter. In its widest sense, it has to do with what Jesus said earlier in Matthew's gospel:

"... Everyone who listens to these words of mine and acts on them will be like a sensible man who built his house on rock. Rain came down, floods rose, gales blew and hurled themselves against that house, and it did not fall: it was founded on rock" (7:24-25, cf. Luke 6:47-48).

No one can contest that Peter has a special place in the story of the Gospel. However, all of us are supposed to be as he is: centred on the rock that is our faith in Jesus Christ, and joint key-holders to God's kingdom here on Earth.

Life given away
A50. Twenty-second Sunday of the year

Jeremiah 20:7-9

Romans 12:1-2

Matthew 16:21-27

When Florence Nightingale decided to devote her life to helping wounded soldiers, her family and friends told her to reconsider and think of herself. The Flemish priest Damien de Veuster, who spent his life caring for the lepers on the Hawaiian island of Molokai (and whose statue stands in the Hall of National Heroes it the Capitol building, Washington DC, USA) was given the same advice.

Jesus was put under the same sort of pressure by his own family and friends. We have already seen (see A9: Mary, mother of God) how Jesus' family try to get him to come home, thinking that he is going too far, that what he is doing will end in disaster, and even that he has lost his mind. They want Jesus to think of himself. They are mistaken to think that Jesus has not considered the consequences of his words and deeds, because he has. The story of his temptations in the desert shows how he has already been tempted by Satan to think only of himself.

When Jesus explains to the disciples how his mission has destined him to go to Jerusalem and suffer at the hands of the authorities, Peter's protestations renew that temptation. Considering that Peter is the "first among equals", the others are probably doing the same. Peter exclaims: "Heaven preserve you, Lord, this must not happen to you!" (Matthew 16:22). The disciples cannot see how giving away one's life out of love for another can do any good at all. They do not comprehend, even though Jesus tries to explain how, if we were to live and die in that way, we would discover our real selves: "For anyone who wants to save his life will lose it; but anyone who loses his life for my sake will find it" (16:25).

When Dietrich Bonhoeffer's executioners came to take him from his cell to be hanged, Bonhoeffer turned to his fellow prisoners, saying: "This is the end, and for me the beginning of my life." He understood. Those who think that it is useless to give one's life away for the life of the world – which is what Bonhoeffer did – simply do not understand.

In T.S. Eliot's play *The Cocktail Party*, the friends and acquaintances of Celia Coplestone are very sad when they hear how she has been tortured and murdered during a revolt, while nursing dying people in a far-off country. The guests at the party consider Celia's death to be a useless waste. Her physician, Sir Henry Harcourt Reilly, tells them that they feel guilty because they have not made the sacrifices that Celia did. Refusing to acknowledge their guilt, they convince themselves that Celia's death was pointless; however, Sir Henry adds: "It was a triumph."

The gospel reading presents us with a similar situation. Peter's protest is motivated partly by his concern for Jesus, but more so by his awareness that he, too, should act like Jesus – sacrificing his body and blood for our human dignity, freedom, and life. Peter is not yet ready for this, and neither are the others. Peter is not willing to sacrifice his life, and that is why he tries to convince Jesus of the futility of such an act.

Jesus, who only a few verses before called Peter his "rock", now calls Peter "Satan"! The American Bible commentator John Mackenzie once suggested that it might be a good idea to mint both words on the Vatican coins: "Rock" on one side and "Satan" on the other! Jesus' reproach to Peter could equally apply to us, because Peter is the first among equals – that is, among us. Which of us has Jesus' integrity? Who genuinely would be willing to give his or her life in the way that Jesus did? Do we not all secretly consider this an unnecessary or exaggerated gesture, even if we profess otherwise in our liturgies and creed?

Households of faith

A51. Twenty-third Sunday of the year

Ezekiel 33:7-9

Romans 13:8-10
Matthew 18:15-20

Karl Barth's commentary on this part of Matthew's gospel is called "The Order of the Community". It is a very apt title, because Matthew is talking about how to behave in community. Matthew is writing for the early Church, which was made up of small groups of Christians living in "faith-households". When we hear the term household, most of us immediately think of a patriarchal family set-up.

On his first visit to Kenya, Pope John Paul II explained that every family is an *ecclesiola*, a small church community. The national director of the Kenyan Catholic Lay Organisation interpreted the Pope's words as supporting the old patriarchal system of Kenyan family life. He declared on TV that he was glad the Pope had said what he did, because it would mean the restoration of the old Gikuyu pattern of family life, in which the father is not only lord and master, but also the plays the role of priest, connecting the family to God.

About a century ago, biblical scholars began to say that it was not correct to think of the early faith-households as patriarchal. In 1876, the German religious thinker called Georg Heinrici declared that these groups of Christians were probably organised as associations or societies, without a patriarchal hierarchy. Later, another theologian, the Belgian Edward Schillebeeckx, stated that he thought these communities were a kind of brother-and-sisterhood, within which all were considered equal. This equality was theologically based upon the baptism in the Holy Spirit, and sociologically structured as a free association. This interpretation fits well in with what we read in Matthew's gospel, where Jesus encourages people to leave their parents and to follow him freely (Matthew 8:21; 10:37). He also prohibits us to call anyone here on Earth "father", because we have only one Father in heaven (23:9).

Jesus speaks 13 times in Matthew's gospel about "your Father" while addressing his disciples. We, too, should address God as "our Father" (6:9). Matthew uses the term "Father" a total of 45 times when speaking about God. As the commentator Joachim Jeremias notes, when Middle Eastern people of Jesus' time used the term "Father" to refer to God, it also implied the idea of "Mother". In other words, it represents a single, loving, divine parent.

All this has its implications and repercussions for the relationships between the members of the "faith-household". There is one God who is our Father and Mother, and consequently we are all sisters and brothers (*adelphai* and *adelphoi*) of Jesus and of each other. In Matthew's gospel, Jesus does not call his followers "apostles" or even "disciples", but brothers and sisters.

In today's gospel text there is another indication of the lack of a patriarchal structure of these "faith-households". If a problem arises between two members that they cannot solve amicably themselves, two others should mediate between them. If that approach does not work, then the whole of the community should get involved. The final authority rests with the community.

The organisation of the Church today seems to be a long way from Jesus' recommendations and ideals. Jesus promised to be in our midst whenever two or three of us come together in his name. The French-Hebrew visionary Simone Weil once said there should be two or three, but no more! That is an exaggeration, yet it should be possible for us to achieve something of the equality and spirit of those small, non-patriarchal faith-households in the Church today. Only when there is true equality in our midst will we be able to live Jesus' life fully.

The living and the dead
A52. Twenty-fourth Sunday of the year

Sirach 27:30-28:7

Romans 14:7-9

Matthew 18:21-35

The last story in James Joyce's book *Dubliners* is entitled "The Dead", and it concerns a group of friends and acquaintances who meet on New Year's Eve in Dublin. While they eat, drink, and sing along to the piano, they are constantly reminiscing about their dead friends and relations. Their recollections are so vivid that when one reads the story one is almost in doubt as to which characters are alive, and which are dead.

When the evening is over, Gretta Conroy and her husband Gabriel go to their hotel. As she begins to undress, he makes an advance, but she rebuffs him. He asks her what is on her mind. She answers that she is thinking of a song called "The Lass of Aughrim". She starts to weep, so Gabriel asks her why the song makes her cry. "I am thinking about a person long ago who used to sing that song," she says. Gabriel quizzes her as to whether it was someone she was once in love with. She replies: "It was a young boy I used to know named Michael Furey." She tells Gabriel that he is dead, that she loved him very much when she was a young girl, and that he died for her.

It was winter. Michael was sick and Gretta was not allowed to visit him. She wrote to him saying that she had to go away to Dublin to a convent school, and that she hoped he would be better when she returned for the holidays. The evening before she left, she heard some gravel being thrown against her window. She could see nothing through the rain on the glass so she ran downstairs into the back garden, where she caught sight of Michael standing under a tree, shivering. She told him to go home, because the cold and the rain might kill him. He told her that he did not want to live any longer. A week later she heard that he had died and had been buried in Oughterard, where his family came from.

She is shaking as she tells Gabriel this. He leaves her alone, and she falls asleep weeping. He, too, get tears in his eyes as he lies there in bed. It is as if he can see the boy standing under the dripping tree. Gabriel realises that Michael is not alone: his soul is now in the place where the enormous numbers of the dead dwell in their strange and flickering existence. He hears some noise, some light pats upon the window pane – it has begun to snow again. The newspaper forecasts were right: snow is falling all over Ireland, including over the cemetery where Michael Furey lies buried, over the crooked crosses and headstones, on the spears of the little gate, on the barren bushes – upon all the living and the dead.

Like the image of the tree that gave shelter in that Irish garden, Jesus uses the metaphor of a tree grown from a mustard seed to describe the kingdom of God (Matthew 13:31-32). We belong together like the branches, trunk, flowers, and leaves of a tree – the one tree of life. It is the tree that carries God's promise of eternal life. When the leaves of a tree are alive, they give life to the tree; when they die, they enrich the soil from which the tree takes its nutrients. The theme of Joyce's story – that the dead remain alive through their lasting influence on the living – echoes the words of Saint Paul in today's text from his letter to the Roman Christians:

"The death and life of each of us has its influence on others; if we live, we live for the Lord; and if we die, we die for the Lord, so that alive or dead we belong to the Lord. This explains why Christ both died and came to life, it was so that he might be Lord both of the dead and of the living."

The first and the last
A53. Twenty-fifth Sunday of the year

Isaiah 55:6-9

Philippians 1:20-24, 27

Matthew 20:1-16

Jesus tells the story about the vineyard labourers in order to teach us something about God's kingdom. It also teaches us something about ourselves and the society we live in. God's kingdom puts no store by social status – in fact, it turns all our social norms upside down. The key phrases are verse 30 of chapter 19 ("Many who are first will be last, and the last, first") and chapter 20 verse 16 ("Thus the last will be first and the first, last"). The fact that Jesus repeats the same message either side of the parable shows us how important he considers it. What Jesus is saying is that, in the final and last instance, everything is a generous gift from God. The reaction of some of the labourers in the parable shows us that generosity does not always go down well with everyone.

When I was a studying in Rome in the 1950s, I went with some fellow students one very chilly evening to the home of an extremely poor immigrant family. They lived in a shelter made out of cardboard boxes and flattened petrol cans in the Valle del' Inferno (the Valley of Hell) by the walls of the Vatican City. Into those surroundings had been born a little baby that very afternoon. We had come to give a blanket to the mother and child. The neighbours saw what we did, and immediately began to complain we were being unfair because we had not brought blankets for them as well. We tried to explain that giving one blanket to a needy family with a frail child did not automatically create a right for everybody to have one. It was no use. They were angry because we had shown kindness to others.

God hears many complaints like that:

• "Why are others healthy, while I am sick and in pain?"

• "Why do others seem to be so happy, while I am so miserable?"

• "Why did she have to die so young and not live into old age, like most people?"

• "Why do other people seem to be so much more gifted than I am?"

These are often bitter cries that no social welfare system can quieten. The parable in today's gospel reading addresses this problem: everything is a gift from God and no-one has an *a priori* right to anything – even to be called into existence. We should be thankful for what we have got, and not complain about what we have not been given.

The other side of the coin is that we too readily look down upon those who are less fortunate or who are simply different from us, trying to convince ourselves that we are better than they are. The owner of a Mercedes Benz may think he or she has a right to quicker service than the person in a Ford Fiesta. Not so very long ago, left-handed people were forced to use their right hands instead, because they were considered abnormal. Similarly, people with disabilities are often despised and treated as second- or third-class citizens. We find non-smokers looking down upon smokers, vegetarians looking down upon meat-eaters, and so on, *ad infinitum*.

There is an endless list of criteria by which those who consider themselves to be among the "first" in our society judge themselves to be better than those who are "last" – from people's wealth, physique, looks, health, skin colour, age, sex, religion, diet, race, and culture, down to which region or city they come from, and even which side of the street they live on.

When Jesus says that "the last will be first, and the first, last", he is not so much turning that order around as abolishing it. He does not intend to set up a new queuing system for God's gifts, with a different group of people heading the queue. He is saying that, in God's eyes, the "first" and the "last" are brothers and sisters who stand before God as friends and equals.

Practising God's will
A54. Twenty-sixth Sunday of the year

Ezekiel 18:25-28
Philippians 2:1-11
Matthew 21:28-32

The parable of the two sons is only found in Matthew's gospel. It is a typical Matthew story, as it tackles another problem relating to families, households, and communities. It is not about what the members say, but what they actually do. It is about practising God's will, which we now know is summed up by the word dikaiosune, meaning "righteousness" or "justice". Commentators and biblical scholars who have studied this term have come to the conclusion that Matthew did not find it in his written sources or in the oral tradition he used when writing his gospel. It is a word he introduces himself. For Matthew, it means that we must put God's equal love for all people into practice every day of our lives, and with everyone we meet.

Practising justice is not a question of words, but of deeds. Whether we resemble the first son, who said "No" to his father but then decided to obey him, or the second son, who said "Yes" but then did nothing, we should always regret the times when we either do nothing or initially hesitate by saying no to God. We should concentrate on practising justice, saying yes to whatever God asks of us and always backing up that response with concrete action. The inequality and injustice in the world are too great for us to do otherwise.

The goods of the Earth are given by God for the benefit of all. But they have been unequally divided, and today some have far too much while others have virtually nothing at all. Here is one extreme but shocking example that illustrates the point very well: some time ago, the

New York Times ran an advertisement by a wine merchant offering for sale three bottles of 1865 Lafite-Rothschild wine. The price for a single bottle was US$15,000, and US$50,000 for the set of three. The lead article on the front page of that same issue of the *New York Times* concerned a famine where 2.5 million people were starving.

Such differences in wealth and access to the Earth's resources make our world an unjust, inhuman, and godless place. They ridicule God's love for humanity, and make a mockery of God's creation. We cannot take a backseat: if we do not try to do something about inequality, then we are co-responsible for all the suffering it causes. In Matthew's gospel, the heart of Jesus' spirituality is to restore the original equality of all human beings in God's eye's. As Jesus says when he is baptised by John: "it is fitting that we should ... do all that righteousness demands" (Matthew 3:15).

Matthew's Jesus speaks about the traditional ways in which we can respond to God's love. We can give alms, we can pray, and we can fast. Note that prayer and fasting alone are not enough to restructure the world. There is more to it than that – there is practical help, such as alms-giving. The Vatican often has problems coming to terms with theologians and church movements that actually try to practise this restructuring. Nevertheless, Pope John Paul II has shown in his encyclicals on the human person, social justice, and ecology, that he ultimately is in favour of such changes. Many political analysts agree that his visits to Poland were at the root of the revolutionary changes that happened throughout Eastern Europe. Once we have been touched by the Spirit of God, we have to be politically involved in this world. There is no other option!

God's ballad
A55. Twenty-seventh Sunday of the year

Isaiah 5:1-7

Philippians 4:6-9

Matthew 21:33-43

In today's Old Testament text, Isaiah sings us a song from God: the song of the vineyard. The prophet becomes a minstrel and he sings a ballad. In a way, it is rather like a love song, with a bitter lover (the vineyard owner) describing how he was jilted by his true love (the vines).

The song's tone is initially light and joyful, celebrating the establishment of the vineyard. However, the mood changes when the vines – planted in choice, fertile soil and lavished with tender loving care –

produce nothing but sour grapes. The singer reveals himself to be the vineyard owner (rather than his "friend", as he first states). He explains that he has done his best for his vineyard, but he has been let down. We, the listeners, are asked to judge between the vineyard and the owner. Suddenly we realise that the song is about the vineyard of Yahweh, and that we are the vines producing those miserable grapes!

The song ends with a harsh, bleak statement: "He expected justice, but found bloodshed; integrity, but only a cry of distress." The sour grapes that so disappoint God are more the fruits of our collective and communal acts of injustice, rather than those of our personal and individual sins. No-one is saying that personal sins should be overlooked, but the unethical decisions we each take as individuals do not explain all the misery we see around us today. We have organised our worldly affairs in such a way that they institutionalise injustice. Many of the structures at the core of our society and civilisation are fundamentally "sinful", because they perpetuate a system that prevents God's justice and righteousness being realised in this world.

We have become accustomed to seeing sin as something purely individual and personal. We are familiar with sermons that stress personal conversion, atonement, and peace, and we are used to personally confessing our own individual sins in confidence and in private. But if this is all we do, we will never tackle the structural sinfulness of society.

Structural sin was the theme of the famous Kairos document produced by an ecumenical group of South African Christians during the time of apartheid. The document analysed some of the different theologies that existed in the country: the racist state theology, the theology of the churches (including the Catholic church), and the theology of the Basic Christian Communities. The state theology was, obviously, deemed to be fundamentally unjust. The theology of the churches was also found wanting. Although they officially protested against apartheid, their theology did not go deep enough, because they only preached personal conversion and reconciliation. They did not tackle the structures of the apartheid system itself. The Basic Christian Communities, however, had taken up the gauntlet and were fighting against those structures through their work of solidarity with the oppressed.

It would be foolish to deny the contribution of personal sin to the injustice that plagues our world. However, we should take note of the way Isaiah prophesies in the name of God. Isaiah speaks primarily about social injustice and structural sinfulness. These are so rampant in our world today that we tolerate as acceptable a situation in which we routinely we speak of a "first", a "second", and a "third" world. Perhaps the growing underclass of people in our western civilisation even constitutes a "fourth" world?

We strengthen these unjust, sinful structures whenever we drink coffee, tea, chocolate, and orange juice from regions where the producers of those goods are practically starving; whenever we dress ourselves in blouses and shirts that are stitched together by children and exploited women in third-world sweat shops; and whenever we spend luxurious holidays in "exotic" countries in the developing world, being waited on hand and foot by impoverished people.

Isaiah is singing God's ballad for us. We should listen carefully and take it to heart, before God decides to "lay waste" to the vineyard.

The suspicious guest
A56. Twenty-eighth Sunday of the year

Isaiah 25:6-10

Philippians 4:12-14, 19-20

Matthew 22:1-14

At long last, the hall is full and the wedding feast can start. It has not been an easy job, because the guests who were originally invited have not come. For all kinds of different reasons, they have sent in their apologies. Though we might not like to admit it to ourselves, most of us have our worries about getting too close to God. Like those invited to the wedding feast, there are countless worries and excuses that we use to justify our hesitation:

• "Would I have to work among the poor, like Mother Teresa?"

• "I wouldn't want to go to church every blessed Sunday."

• "I get the shivers just thinking about the possibility of having mystical or religious experiences!"

• "Would I have to give up everything I enjoy for God?"

• "My family and friends would make me a laughing stock."

• "I don't trust God sufficiently to do something like that – after all, you can't be absolutely certain of God's existence, can you?"

• "I am not willing to surrender my independence to anyone, including God. I don't want to lose control of my life."

• "I am afraid it would change me too much."

• "I'm not ready yet, perhaps later in life."

Talking so negatively, we will never be able to appreciate God's open invitation to us. The difficulty is our hesitation. As in so many other areas of life, we think only of the worst possible scenario.

The American Quaker Thomas R. Kelly (1893–1941) wrote that we feel often unhappy, ill at ease, tense, sad and superficial, because at the horizon of our existence there always is that whispered word, that humble invitation, that suspicion of a richer and a more fulfilling life.

When we do become aware of that invitation to experience God, we often react as the gardener did in the fairy tale called *The Last Unicorn*. The gardener is digging the soil when a magnificent unicorn passes by. He stops working, looks at it, and says: "Oh, how wonderful! You are even more beautiful than I ever imagined you would be," adding, against his better knowledge, "What a magnificent mare, what a beautiful horse!" He knows that it is not a horse, but he does not want to admit it. He is afraid of the consequences of what he has seen.

We often react to God in a similar way. Most of us are more pious than we would like to admit, having seen or experienced things that we would not want to discuss in public. Perhaps we have seen rays of light, heard unearthly music, had a mystical experience, or witnessed an act of such goodness from a fellow human being that it seemed to come straight from heaven. Many will have felt that they have been in the company of people who in other times would have been called angels. Despite all this, we usually act as if nothing has happened.

In the book *The Color Purple*, the African-American author Alice Walker writes how this behaviour makes God feel "pissed-off"! God decorates the whole world, fills it with flowers and fruits, peoples it with the cutest children, and yet nobody seems to notice. God creates endless fields of magnificent purple lavender with an enchanting fragrance, and yet no-one appreciates seeing it or smelling it. God is irritated by that total indifference. "What does God do in such a case?" asks a character in her book. "Oh, God tries something else," is the reply.

Trying something else is exactly what the king does in today's gospel story of the "wedding-feast-without-guests". When the first plan falls through, a second one is concocted. At all crossroads and byways new guests are invited – rich and poor, good and bad alike. The hall fills up with eager guests, but there is one who has come without bothering to put on his best clothes, because he is still hesitant and suspicious about the whole affair. The sad guest is removed, and the feast begins without him.

World mission

A57. Twenty-ninth Sunday of the year

Isaiah 45:1, 4-6

1 Thessalonians 1:1-5

Matthew 22:15-21

Full of pride, joy, and missionary zeal, Paul writes to his friends in Thessalonika, "when we brought the Good News to you, it came to you not only as words, but as power and as the Holy Spirit and as utter conviction." Mission was a popular issue throughout the Church at the beginning of this century. The whole Catholic population was involved in it. Almost everyone knew someone in either their family or parish community who was on missionary service. All kinds of things were collected to raise money for the mission, including the metal foil from around chocolate bars, the lead strips from tea chests, and used stamps.

Today, the number of missionaries is falling the world over. Many of those who do heed the missionary call live their mission-ideal in a new way. The majority of missionaries now find their inspiration in their option for the poor. This does not mean that they are merely dedicating themselves to charity work, assisting others in their hunger, thirst, or lack of medical care and educational possibilities. Taking up the option for the poor immediately engages them in the struggle for justice.

Matthew stresses again and again that we are all equal. He urges us to practise and realise that equality, forming here on Earth the one family of God. It is a family that will find its fulfilment at the end of time, when we all gather together into the kingdom of God for ever and ever. The Good News that God loves us all and that we are all chosen by God is the core and heart of Jesus' message. This message needs to be announced throughout the whole world, from the valleys and mountains of Africa and Asia, to the poor slums and rich suburbs of Europe, Australia, and the Americas – in short, everywhere. At the end of Matthew's gospel, Jesus gives the disciples their great commission: to go out and make disciples of all the nations, baptising them in the name of the Father, Son, and Holy Spirit (28:19).

This message and mission may not be such good news for those with a vested interest in the status quo, because it means that we have to fundamentally rethink and reorganise our world. With so many people wanting for the bare essentials in life, those who are wealthy must be prepared to give to others. Likewise, the knowledge of our equality before God means that those with authority should consider sharing it with others. Not everyone will like the challenge of the Good News!

Missionaries are well aware of this dilemma. Sometimes they can only find the money to finance their work on condition that they concentrate on practical help and do not get involved with contentious issues such as educating people about the causes of world poverty. Even though this work is vital to realising God's justice and righteousness, it often brings them accusations that they are getting "political" and acting beyond their remit. Let us get this straight once and for all: the Good News has to be realised in the social, political, and economic life of the world, just as it does in our own individual lives. Part and parcel of this is that human rights must be respected throughout the whole world.

It is a fact that we are all children of God. It is true that Jesus lived, died, and rose among us to show God's love for us all. The Good News is that each one of us is loved by the mysterious power that hides behind and shines through the whole of creation. It is a fantastic message! We should not be surprised if not everyone appreciates what the Good News really means, but it is our Christian duty to tell it again and again, until the end of human history.

Self-love
A58. Thirtieth Sunday of the year

Exodus 22:20-26

1 Thessalonians 1:5-10

Matthew 22:34-40

In today's reading from Matthew's gospel, the Pharisees come to ask Jesus a tricky question in order to catch him out. But there is more to it than that. They are also intrigued by his behaviour. Some biblical commentators think that Jesus himself might have been a Pharisee, or at least under the influence of the pharisaic school of thinking. One of the developments in that school of thought was the "personalisation" of morality. The Pharisees were the first in that society to consider God's laws as given not only to the Jewish people as a whole, but also to each individual person. This approach led them to consider seriously the possibility of a personal life after death and a personal resurrection.

The question they ask Jesus is an important one: "Master, which is the greatest commandment of the Law?" It is a question that preoccupied the Pharisees and caused much debate among them. In this instance, it is given even more significance because they have been monitoring Jesus' teaching and his attitude towards the people around him. Jesus' life and words show that the individual is the focal point of God's love. When it comes down to it, a human being is more important in God's eyes than any law. The Law is given to make human life possible, not to thwart it. Jesus demonstrates this truth every time he heals someone on the Sabbath, putting the needs of people before any slavish adherence to the minutiae of the Law.

Jesus' tendency to stress our personal relationship with God perhaps explains his suggestion to call God not only Father, but also Abba. The word Abba is rather like our word "Daddy", but it implies at the same time a motherly love as well. The Pharisees have no difficulty in calling God "Father", but Abba is much too familiar, and perhaps even irreverent, for them. After all, how could society function healthily if every person related to God in such a familiar, cosy way? Would this not produce a set of self-obsessed individuals, so independent from one another that living together would become an impossibility? Would this kind of individuality not mean the end of society, community, family, and nationhood? The Pharisees were curious as to how Jesus would solve this problem.

There are many modern parallels to the problem the Pharisees present to Jesus. Western societies are becoming more and more fragmented as their citizens are turned into individual, private "consumers", encouraged by advertising and the media to think of themselves and their own needs above all else. Without a stake in the community, many people find themselves overwhelmed by a sense of isolation and lack of belonging. Some see this as a threat to the very fabric of society.

How should we respond to such an unhealthy trend, which seems to confirm the Pharisees' worst fears. Jesus shows us how to establish our priorities when faced with such a situation. In answer to the Pharisees' question about which is the greatest commandment, he says:

"You must love the Lord your God with all your heart, with all your soul, and with all your mind. This is the greatest and the first commandment. The second resembles it: you must love your neighbour as yourself. On these two commandments hang the whole Law, and the Prophets also."

To counteract the individualisation of our society, we must love others as we love ourselves. If we are honest in this, then we will never do anything to others that we would not like others to do to us. Self-love is important, because it is based on our relationship with God. Jesus' life and work show that God loves each one of us; in response, we are commanded to love God with all our heart, mind, and soul. To know that God values our love should give us a tremendous feeling of self-esteem. Respecting both our own self-esteem and the self-esteem of others is a sound foundation for a healthy society.

New age
A59. Thirty-first Sunday of the year

Malachi 1:14 – 2:2, 8-10

1 Thessalonians 2:7-9, 13

Matthew 23:1-12

Matthew is the only gospel author who uses the Greek word *paliggenesia*. He does that in chapter 19, verse 28, when he talks about the time when "all is made new". The word *paliggenesia* is made up of two other Greek words: *palin* meaning "new", and the easily recognisable *genesis*, meaning "creation". This new creation involves the renewal of all things – it is a new beginning, a new world, and a new age.

Matthew uses this word to indicate that the old order, with all its hierarchies and structures, is to be done away with. He wants the new Christian communities to avoid adopting the old hierarchies, which place some in positions of greater importance than others. This contradicts what Jesus says in today's gospel text:

"You, however, must not allow yourselves to be called Rabbi, since you have only one Master, and you are all brothers [and sisters]. You must call no one on Earth your father, since you have only one Father, and he is in heaven. Nor must you allow yourselves to be called teachers, for you have only one Teacher, the Christ" (Matthew 23:8-11).

At the start of today's text, Jesus criticises the overbearing religious leaders of his time. In his words, we hear an echo of the Old Testament reading from the tough-talking prophet Malachi. This is a stinging rebuke to those priests who offer poor-quality meat in sacrifices to Yahweh. Malachi goes on to take the priests to task for their unjust and haughty treatment of women, widows, orphans, immigrants, and aliens (3:5). Exasperated, he exclaims: "Have we not all one Father? Did not one God create us? Why, then, do we break faith with one another ...?" (2:10).

Malachi is not trying to undermine the authority of the priesthood, or indeed any other sort of authority. No prophet would suggest a thing like that, for if all authority were wrong no-one would listen to the prophet either. The prophet speaks in the name of God. Malachi – who is part of the old order of things – knows that he has a message from God, and that he has to tell people that message, whatever the dangers. A prophet wants to be heard.

Jesus – in the new age that is dawning – also wants to be heard. He presents himself as a teacher who has come so that we might listen to God. We are all addressed in the same way, making it clear that all are under the same obligation to be listeners to God's message. We create problems for ourselves whenever we overlook or forget this. Too often, those in positions of authority make pronouncements on moral and ethical issues that overlook the conscience, moral insight, and the common sense of ordinary people. Over a prolonged period of time, this can lead to the sort of mentality that assumes those in authority have an innate right to rule people's lives because "they know best". Eventually, those at the bottom of the ladder of power even start to mistrust their own judgement.

Authority only works when it respects the fact that all of us can – and should – listen to God. We have to do this listening together, regardless of our supposed status in society. When we listen to God, we are all equal – there are no "firsts" and no "lasts" in God's family. All have the gift of the Holy Spirit, and all are able to tune-in to that Spirit. This new equality and communion is the characteristic of the "new age" that Jesus initiated among us.

Millennium
A60. Thirty-second Sunday of the year

Wisdom 6:12-16

1 Thessalonians 4:13-18

Matthew 25:1-13

We are not only approaching the end of the liturgical year, but also the end of the calendar year and end of the century. These last years before the new millennium are a thrilling time. All over the world people are looking forward to celebrating this momentous occasion. Right from his very first encyclical, Pope John Paul II has been preparing himself – and us – for the new millennium, calling these last years a time of New Advent. At the same time, prophecies about the end of the world abound. Chapters 24 and 25 of Matthew's gospel concentrate on the idea of being prepared for an approaching end to things, a time of great change, and a new beginning. This theme seems to preoccupy Jesus, just as many people today are obsessed with the idea we are living out the last chapters of human history.

At the end of the last millennium, many people were convinced that the world would end at the year 1000. Pope Sylvester II celebrated a midnight Mass on the last day of the year 999. Many who attended that Mass had given away their property to the poor, in anticipation of what was to come. The congregation wore sackcloth and ashes, and lay flat on the church floor with their arms stretched out in the form of a cross. When midnight came, some quite literally died of fear! But, as the first minutes of the first day of the new millennium went by, the ground was not torn apart by earthquakes, and fire did not fall from heaven. Gradually, everyone came to their senses, as if waking from a nightmare. Weeping and laughing, they embraced each other, while the bells of Rome rang out.

The current millennium hysteria is not yet as bad as that, but the interest in "prophets of doom" such as Nostradamus, who wrote down his prophecies in France about 450 years ago, has been growing over the last few decades. Some "experts" in these matters maintain that

Nostradamus predicted the French Revolution, Napoleon, Hitler, Hiroshima, the murder of the Kennedys, Ayatollah Khomeini, and Abu Nidal. Some also say that Nostradamus foretold how the world as we know it will come to an end in 1999.

Few of us can resist thinking about such gloomy forecasts of impending doom. As the story of that Mass 1,000 years ago shows, this is nothing new. Such an apocalyptic mentality seems to be part of our human nature – something that is ingrained into our collective psyche. Today, our nuclear weapons, our relentless pollution of the environment, and our unthinking exploitation of the world's resources make "the-end-of-the-world-as-we know-it" an even more believable proposition.

Is Jesus thinking about such an apocalypse when he tells his story about the five sensible and the five foolish bridesmaids? It is certainly a parable about being awake and being prepared, about waiting for the end, and about what will happen when the end comes. But it also has positive side to it. The wedding – a fulfilment and a new beginning for the wise bridesmaids – represents the beginning of God's kingdom on Earth.

According to the Bible commentator Joachim Jeremias, this text can be read in two ways. It can be seen as a warning to the faith-households of Matthew's time, who are being told to prepare themselves for the imminent coming of Christ. However, it can also interpreted as being directed at Jesus' disciples, who are listening to the parable. They are being told that they should be prepared to receive Jesus right then and there. In the first instance, the message concerns something that will happen to us at the end of our days, while in the second, it is about the "here and now" of our daily lives. It is one of those ambiguities we often find in Matthew's gospel. It is not a question of either one thing or the other – both are equally valid and worthy of consideration.

Application
A61. Thirty-third Sunday of the year

Proverbs 31:10-13, 19-20, 30-31

1 Thessalonians 5:1-6

Matthew 25:14-30

In the text of last Sunday's reading from Matthew's gospel, Jesus speaks of the end of this world and the coming of the kingdom of God. He warns that we should be vigilant, awake, and alert, keeping our lamps burning. In today's text, he uses another parable to qualify this vigilance with the command that we should also be busy. We have to apply ourselves actively to realising here on Earth what Jesus calls the kingdom of God.

The story Jesus uses in today's gospel reading is simple. It fits neatly in with his observations about the "last days", which he makes while journeying towards his own apocalypse – his crucifixion – in Jerusalem. The story is about submitting your final account, and about making as much money as possible. The story concerns the gifts and talents we were given by God when we entered this world (although the "talents" mentioned in the text are actually silver coins). We are expected to make the most of them – even to double them!

Another theme is woven throughout the whole story. It is that of zealous application to a particular task. Jesus often expresses his amazement about the way in which people are willing to apply themselves to amassing money and goods, sacrificing anything to obtain them. Things are no different in our modern world. While some of us are forced to endure long-term unemployment, those of us who earn a decent wage often work excessively long hours in search of greater wealth.

This obsession with money makes us disregard the needs of our bodies by skipping meals and forgoing sleep, because our overbooked agendas do not allow time for such trivial things. Similarly, we disregard the needs of others by lying, cheating, and deceiving others in order to earn more, and by keeping as much of our earnings as we can for ourselves. Everything – life and health, ethics and morality, honour and integrity, culture and religion – is sacrificed in the cause of greater profit. Jesus calls such people "children of darkness", because it is impossible to combine that overriding interest in Mammon with a concern for God's kingdom.

Hundreds of years ago, the theologian Bartolomé de las Casas described the Spanish conquistadores' thirst for gold in Central and South America:

"I don't mean to say that they are just out to murder and kill. I do mean to say that they want to be rich. They want to swim in money using the labour and sweat of the tortured and exploited natives who live in utter misery. They use them as common tools. The unavoidable consequence is that they are all dying."

To Bartolomé de las Casas, these people were not particularly wicked or evil. They simply wanted to get rich, and that is why everything went wrong. Thousands and thousands of indigenous people died because gold was the only thing that mattered to the conquistadores. We still find that materialistic zeal all around us, and it often produces similarly tragic consequences. Jesus despises this mentality, but is amazed by the application it inspires. Just imagine, however, how things could be changed if people directed such zealous effort into working for justice rather than satisfying their greed! If only we "children of the light", as

258

Paul calls us in his letter to the Thessalonians (5:5), would apply ourselves with the same energy to establishing of the kingdom of God.

We must apply our talents to the realisation of our true humanity with all the efficiency and know-how of the business world. If we were to do this, it would transform and bring justice to issues such as health, education, food production and distribution, housing, and environmental care. All through his life, Jesus dreamt of that possibility!

Living like royalty
A62. Thirty-fourth and last Sunday of the year

Ezekiel 34:11-12, 15-17

1 Corinthians 15:20-26, 28

Matthew 25:31-46

The time of kings and queens seems to be over. Monarchies throughout the world have largely been replaced by republics, where kings, queens, princes, and princesses feature only in fairy tales. In the few countries where monarchies do survive, they rarely wield political power any more. In a republic such as the United States, people sometimes have difficulty relating to the idea of the kingdom of God. To make it more accessible to their audience, some preachers ingeniously replace the term "kingdom" with "kindom", which encompasses the more egalitarian idea of "kith and kin".

Most of us have difficulties with the idea of a royal elite entrusted with unchecked authority and power. Like Jesus and Matthew, we cannot tolerate the idea that some should be first and others last. Matthew's Jesus keeps repeating that there are no fathers, no superiors, no masters, and no teachers among us any more. We are all equal.

The same idea crops up in the Hebrew scriptures. The older prophets in particular warn that there should be no kings. According to them, kings mean trouble! The people look up to them and lose their self-respect, dignity, sense of responsibility, and even their conscience. There is no need for kings, because everyone is "royal" in God's eyes. In addition, people have very high expectations of any king or queen – expectations that they rarely live up to. Those expectations are expressed clearly in Psalm 72, which prays for the king, but also describes his ideal role:

"God, give your own justice to the king, your own righteousness to the royal son, so that he may rule your people rightly and your poor with justice. ... He will free the poor man who calls to him, and those who need help, he will have pity on the poor and feeble, and save the lives of those in need; he will redeem their lives from exploitation and outrage, their lives will be precious in his sight" (verses 1-2, 12-14).

At the beginning of Jesus' ministry, he goes into the synagogue at Narareth and reads the following extract from the scroll of the prophet Isaiah:

"The spirit of the Lord has been given to me, for he has anointed me. He has sent me to bring the good news to the poor, to proclaim liberty to captives and to the blind new sight, to set the downtrodden free, to proclaim the Lord's year of favour" (Luke 4:18-19).

When he has finished reading, Jesus says to those in the synagogue: "This text is being fulfilled today even as you listen." In effect, he is saying: "I am that king!"

Jesus is not only describing himself, but also how he expects us – his disciples, his brothers and sisters, his friends – to act. In Matthew's account of the Last Judgement, the nations are not gathered together before Jesus to pass judgement on whether he has been a good king or not. On that day, the question will be whether we have lived like good queens and kings, in the way foreseen in Psalm 72. Jesus will ask each of us whether we helped those in need, visited the sick, freed those in captivity, fed the hungry, and dressed the naked? Jesus identifies with these people and their sufferings, so our attitude to them also sums up our true attitude to Jesus.

We should pray that we may live lives that give liberating and redeeming hope to others. We must open our hearts, minds, and spirits to all who are in need. We are supposed to establish God's righteousness and justice (remember that word dikaiosune?) throughout the world, making it roll over the hills, down the valleys, and across the plains. At the Last Judgement, we will be reminded of our baptism, when we were anointed like kings and queens. The question will be whether we lived, or at least tried to live, as royally as he did.

Other Millennium Resources from CAFOD

The Coming of the Third Millennium
£2.95
A simplified and illustrated version of Pope John Paul II's Apostolic Letter, *Tertio Millennio Adveniente*. In the Old Testament we learn about the tradition of Jubilee. The Jubilee years were times of liberation and grace. When Jesus came he announced a Jubilee for the poor. It is in this spirit that the Pope has called on Christians to prepare for the Great Jubilee of the year 2000 in his Apostolic Letter.

published with Columban Missionary Society/SCIAF/Trócaire

Tertio Millennio Adveniente
£2.50
The full text of the Apostolic Letter of Pope John Paul II on preparation for the Jubilee of the year 2000.

published with Catholic Truth Society

The Millennium Jubilee
£2.95
Reflections from Brian Davis, Mary Grey, Ed O'Connell, Jim O'Keefe, Aloys Opiyo, Jon Sobrino and David Williamson placing our preparations for the millennium in the context of biblical teaching and concern for social justice.

The Church and the Millennium
£1.00
This is the text of CAFOD's Pope Paul VI Lecture, delivered in 1996 by Cardinal Roger Etchegaray, President of the Pontifical Council for Justice and Peace.

The Jubilee Challenge of Jesus
£9.95
A fifteen minute video, with Resource Booklet, which brings alive the Jubilee theme of *Tertio Millennio Adveniente*.
'I am delighted that the Columban Missionary Society and Catholic Aid Agencies have collaborated to produce this popular video which explains the Jubilee vision and suggests avenues which adult and youth groups can explore to work towards constructing a more just world.' **Cardinal Basil Hume**

To order these, or any other CAFOD publications, contact CAFOD Sales and Distribution, Romero Close, Stockwell Road, London SW9 9TY. Tel: 0171 733 7900.